The Tabloid Terrorist

The Predicative Construction of New Terrorism in the Media

Alexander Spencer

palgrave
macmillan

First published 2010 by
PALGRAVE MACMILLAN

Palgrave Macmillan in the UK is an imprint of Macmillan Publishers Limited, registered in England, company number 785998, of Houndmills, Basingstoke, Hampshire RG21 6XS.

Palgrave Macmillan in the US is a division of St Martin's Press LLC, 175 Fifth Avenue, New York, NY 10010.

Palgrave Macmillan is the global academic imprint of the above companies and has companies and representatives throughout the world.

Palgrave® and Macmillan® are registered trademarks in the United States, the United Kingdom, Europe and other countries

ISBN 978-1349-36569-2   ISBN 978-0-230-28130-1 (eBook)
DOI 10.1007/978-0-230-28130-1

A catalogue record for this book is available from the British Library.

A catalogue record for this book is available from the Library of Congress.

10   9   8   7   6   5   4   3   2   1
19 18 17 16 15 14 13 12 11 10

To Bob

Contents

List of Tables and Figures

Tables

Figures

Acknowledgements

This book would not have been written without the support and help of a number of very important people. Above all I want to thank my parents, Monika and Mike Spencer for their encouragement and continuous support in all kinds of ways. Without their help this book would never have materialised. I must also deeply thank Judith Renner for her love and support and for her critical comments and suggestions. I am also extremely grateful to Stefan Beeck who had to live with me and put up with all my confused rambling throughout the writing of the book.

This book is the result of my Dr. phil. dissertation at the Ludwig-Maximilians-University Munich. I would like to thank those who read, commented on and helped me with this project: Christopher Daase, Stefan Engert, Wilhelm Hofmann, Rainer Hülsse, Marina Karbowski, Alexander Kocks, Andreas Kruck, Renate Strassner and Bernhard Zangl as well as all the participants of the research colloquium at the Geschwister-Scholl-Institute for Political Science. I must also thank Alexandra Webster and Renée Taken at Palgrave Macmillan for their support, assistance and patience in seeing this project through.

Material especially from Chapter 4 and 5 has previously been published as 'Metaphor of Terror: Terrorism Studies and the Constructivist Turn', *Security Dialogue*, Vol. 39, No. 6 (2008), 571–592 and is reprinted by permission Sage Publications Ltd. A shorter version of Chapter 1 has appeared as 'The "new" Terrorism of Al Qaeda is not so new', in Stuart Gottlieb (ed.) *Debating Terrorism and Counterterrorism* (Washington: CQ Press, 2009) and some parts of Chapter 3 have been published as 'The Problems of Evaluating Counter-Terrorism', *UNISCI Discussion Papers*, No. 12 (2006), 179–201.

Finally I would also like to thank my friends Andi Sieme and Elizabeth Chambers as well as my dog Charly who constantly reminded me that walks, food and his stuffed toy rabbit Roger are far more important than work. This book is dedicated to Bob Spencer who sadly did not see the day of its publication. Of course all mistakes, omissions and opinions expressed in this book are solely my own.

Alexander Spencer

List of Abbreviations

AAA	Alianza Anticommunista Argentina
ANC	African National Congress
ATCSA	Anti-terrorism, Crime and Security Act 2001
BBK	Bundesamt für Bevölkerungsschutz und Katastrophenhilfe
CDA	Critical Discourse Analysis
EOKA	Ethniki Organosis Kyprion Agoniston
ETA	Euskadi Ta Askatasuna
ETA-PM	Euskadi Ta Askatasuna Politico Militar
deNIS	deutsche Notfallvorsorge-Informationssystem
FLN	Front de Libération Nationale
FLNC	Fronte di Liberazione Naziunale Corsu
GAL	Grupos Antiterroristas de Liberación
GMLZ	Gemeinsames Melde- und Lagezentrum
GSG9	Grenzschutzgruppe 9
GTD	Global Terrorism Database
IR	International Relations
IRA	Irish Republican Army
ISAF	International Security Assistance Force
JRA	Japanese Red Army
KSK	Kommando Specialkräfte
LTTE	Liberation Tigers of Tamil Eelam
MIPT	Memorial Institute for the Prevention of Terrorism
NIS	National Identity Scheme
NOCS	Nucleo Operativo Centrale di Sicurezza
PFLP	Popular Front for the Liberation of Palestine
PIRA	Provisional Irish Republican Army
PLO	Palestine Liberation Organisation
PKK	Partiya Karkerên Kurdistan
RAF	Red Army Faction
SAS	Special Air Service
SBS	Special Boat Service
THW	Technisches Hilfswerk
UKBA	UK Border Agency

Introduction   The 'Terrorist': Words, Labels and Definitions

'[W]hat one calls things matters. There are few neutral terms in politics, because political language affects the perceptions of protagonists and audiences, and such effect acquires a greater urgency in the drama of terrorism' (Crenshaw 1995)

Struggling with words and definitions has tradition in terrorism research. If people know anything about the field of Terrorism Studies it is most probably that it has failed to find a definition of its own subject. All interested in the issue of terrorism are fully aware of the age old definitional problems and the debate about what terrorism 'really' is and whether or not a definition is something worth worrying about. So, 'terrorism' is a one of the many essentially contested concepts (Gallie 1956) and some may ask: So what? We are all pretty much aware of what constituted terrorism, even if we are unable to phrase a suitable three-line dictionary style definition. In general most would agree on many of the central aspects of what terrorism is. Similar to pornography, you know it when you see it (Der Derian 2005: 25; Richardson 2006: 19). So, some may argue that it does not really matter what we call it. They are only words. This book would disagree. Although striving for exact definitions may be overrated, language and words do matter as they are the only way of making sense of the world and assigning meaning to it. Words do not only describe reality, but they actively take part in the construction of the world as we see, talk, hear, imagine and ultimately react to it. It is the phenomenon of reality construction and it is our reaction to such constructions this book is interested in. It hopes to make two contributions. Firstly and more generally it wants to outline the importance of language in the study of terrorists and indicate a con-structivist theoretical understanding of terrorism research. Secondly, and

1

more particularly, it wants to do so by examining how certain constructions of 'the terrorist' in discourse make certain counter-terrorism policies possible, logical and seemingly appropriate. Thereby it wants to demonstrate that constructivist (terrorism) studies can be policy relevant and that such research can breakout of what has been called the 'discursive echo chamber where discourses constitute other discourses that in turn constitute other discourses' (Stokes 2009: 89). The book is therefore not only of interest to Terrorism Research but also to International Relations (IR) more generally, as it provides an example of empirical constructivist research of international political phenomena.

Terrorism research and its fascination with definitions

Terrorism research used to be a fairly small operation with only a handful of academics around the world. However, since 9/11 the amount of literature on terrorism has exploded as there are thousands of books and articles written on the subject every year. In fact, they say that one book on terrorism is published every six hours (Silke 2008) and the subject area of terrorism research is one of the 'fastest expanding areas of research in the English-speaking academic world' (Jackson 2008a: 377). It has its own dedicated peer-reviewed journals,[1] its own conferences, university courses,[2] research centres[3] and academics[4] (Jackson 2009: 66). And many now consider terrorism research to be its own 'stand-alone subject entering a golden age of research' (Shepherd 2007; Attwood 2007). Although terrorism research may have become Terrorism Research and despite this large increase in the literature, the subject has consistently suffered, among other things, from a concrete lack of theory. While few would refute that terrorism is a subject of international politics, international political theory does not seem interested in the subject nor does terrorism research seem particularly bothered about IR theory (Ranstorp 2009). As David Leheny (2002: 58) points out: 'The literature on terrorism has largely developed independent of international relations theory'. Some even go as far as claiming the existence of a 'theoretical vacuum' at the very heart of terrorism research (Wight 2009: 100). This is particularly apparent when considering the non-realist theoretical perspectives. As one of the early constructivist in IR, Nicholas Onuf, has only recently pointed out, IR theory in general has paid little attention to the field of terrorism and in particular 'constructivists are notably missing from discussions of terrorism' (Onuf 2009: 54).[5]

This is really quite surprising considering that words have always played a huge role in the debate about terrorism. For one, this is visible in the difficulty of finding the right words to accurately describe the 'reality' of terrorism. This definitional problem has been at the center stage of terrorism studies from the very start and even prior to 9/11 there was disagreement about almost all elements which may or may not constitute terrorism. While most definition attempts by academics as well as governments included the notion of force or violence and the idea of terrorism being something political, there were vast disagreements over the means and goals of the violence, the nature of the targets and the status of the victims and the perpetrators. While some stressed that terrorism could only be perpetrated by sub-state groups and that this was vital for terrorism, others believed that the state could also be a terrorist. Similarly, there was disagreement whether the victims of terrorism had to be civilian and whether attacks on the police or the military should also be considered a terrorist act. Parallel, there was no agreement on whether targets of terrorism were carefully chosen due to their symbolic character or whether in fact there were elements of indiscriminate random-like violence which was supposed to be the basis of creating widespread fear and terror. At the same time nobody was sure whether the intent of provoking an overreaction, the seeking of publicity or the idea of a communication strategy should be included into a definition.

This argument about what terrorism is resulted in three kinds of perspectives on the definitional debate (Daase and Spencer 2010). The first kind of scholars became exceedingly bored with the topic and believed that the definitional problem could not be solved and that the issue was beyond any solution (Malik 2001). For example, one of the leading terrorism researchers Walter Laqueur (1977: 5) believes that 'a comprehensive definition of terrorism [...] does not exist nor will it be found in the foreseeable future'. Although they have seemingly surrendered their quest for the holy grail known as 'The Definition of Terrorism', they nevertheless have a specific understanding of what terrorism is which implicitly finds its way back into their work. For example, despite Walter Laqueur's earlier relaxed attitude towards a definition, his later work does not get by without defining the all so illusive term (c.f. Laqueur 1987, 1998). In contrast to the first batch of scholars the second type simply continued counting definitions and was content with discussing the strengths and weaknesses of different wordings. For example Jeffrey Simon (1994: 29) in the early 1990s claimed that there were at least 212 different definitions of terrorism in use throughout the world, with 90 of them used by governments and other institutions. Finally, a third type struggled on in the hope of finding a truly universally accepted definition of terrorism. Most notably among these were Alex Schmid and Albert Jongman who in 1988 gathered 109 different definitions, identified 22 key elements within these definitions and combined them into the following consensus definition:

> Terrorism is an anxiety-inspired method of repeated violent action, employed by (semi-)clandestine individuals, groups, or state actors, for idiosyncratic, criminal, or political reasons, whereby – in contrast to assassination – the direct targets of violence are not the main targets. The immediate human victims of violence are generally chosen randomly (targets of opportunity) or selectively (representative or symbolic targets) from a target population, and serve as message generators. Threat- and violence-based communication processes between terrorist (organization), (imperilled) victims, and the main targets are used to manipulate the main target (audience(s)), turning it into a target of terror, a target of demands, or a target of attention, depending on whether intimidation, coercion, or propaganda is primarily sought (Schmid and Jongman 1988: 28).

So while this academic exchange flourished in the 1970s and 80s between a handful of scholars about what the true characteristics of terrorism were and how to neatly combine them into a short but concise definition, the debate at the end of the Cold War seems to have collapsed into an exhausted heap of indifference. Yet, following 9/11 the debate reignited as once again the search for a universally accepted definition began anew (Ganor 2002; Schmid 2004; Weinberg et al. 2004).

The 'terrorist' label and the role of the media

So one part of the definitional problem is finding the 'correct' words to accurately describe the reality of terrorism and differentiate it from other things such as guerrilla warfare, crime or mad serial killers. There is, however, a second maybe more important aspect to the difficulty of establishing what terrorism is, namely the notion of legitimacy. Ultimately the idea of legitimacy has been at the centre of the debate of what makes terrorism terrorism from the very beginning. Here the well-known phrase 'one man's terrorist is another man's freedom fighter', is often used to highlight the problem of implying a moral judgement when classifying the term 'terrorism'. If one identifies with the victim of the attack, then it is considered terrorism, but if one can identify with the perpetrator it is not. No matter how hideous and revolting a 'terrorist' act may be there will always be some who will not share this interpretation of the act as something terroristic. And although this well-worn statement seems hackneyed and dated, it holds within it an essence which seems to have been forgotten and which will be vital for the rest of this book. To qualify as terrorism a certain act has to be recognised, interpreted and ultimately named as such. The label 'terrorism' does not reflect reality but rather our interpretations of reality. In other words, 'the terrorist' is a social construction rather than natural fact. So the early understanding inherent in the age old statement 'one man's terrorist is another man's freedom fighter' may indicate that terrorism research was one of the first branches in political science to unwittingly realise the social construction of political phenomena.

Apart from words the use of language and discourse has also played a fairly substantial role in the study of terrorism when we consider the relationship between terrorism and the media (Paletz and Schmid 1992; Weimann and Winn 1994; Nacos 1994). Traditionally terrorism research considered the media to be vital for a terrorist group as they provide the means of attracting attention and spreading the message of the group. Considering terrorism as a communications strategy, the media have often been considered the terrorist's 'accomplices' (Schmid 1989: 540) or even their 'best friend' (Hoffman 2006: 183) as it appears to provide the 'oxygen of publicity' (Thatcher cited in Wilkinson 2000: 175). As one of the leading terrorism scholars Bruce Hoffman points out:

> The modern news media, as the principal conduit of information about such acts, thus play a vital part in the terrorists' calculus. Indeed, without the media's coverage the act's impact is arguably wasted, remaining narrowly confined to the immediate victim(s) of the attack rather than reaching the wider "target audience" at whom the terrorists' violence is actually aimed. Only by spreading the terror and outrage to a much larger audience can the terrorists gain the maximum potential leverage that they need to effect fundamental political change (Hoffman 2006: 174).

At the same time it has been noted that terrorists provide the media with emotional, exciting and bloody news which helps them sell their product (Ganor 2005: 231). Therefore there are mutual benefits for both and the relationship could be described as 'symbiotic' (Schmid 1989). So while terrorism research predominantly focused on this relationship and its effects and implications for counter-terrorism, there was unfortunately very little interest in the perception of terrorism and the role of language and discourse in the construction of 'the terrorist'. Although others, especially in media and communication studies, have been interested in the medias influence of public opinion with regards to terrorism (Woods 2007; Herron and Jenkins-Smith 2006) or the role of media framing theory on public perceptions (Norris et al. 2003; Craft and Wanta 2004; Papacharissi and de Fatima Oliveira 2008), the theoretical notion of a constructivist terrorism research has until very recently been nonexistent.

The structure of the book

Unfortunately, despite this early potential and its interested in words, definitions and the media, terrorism studies has not become a bastion of constructivist theoretical thought. This book wants to reflect on this situation and illustrate how constructivist terrorism research could look like. It thereby stresses the importance of language and the role of discourse in the perception of terrorism and it ultimately hopes to show that this constitution greatly influences the practical reaction to 'the terrorist'. In pursuit of this, Chapter 2 will investigate the notion of 'new terrorism'. Thereby it will illustrate what many terrorism scholars and politicians consider as 'new' characteristics of terrorism and contrast this to traditional or 'old' terrorism. In a second step the chapter will critique many of the established characteristics of 'new terrorism' as fundamentally new and thereby openly question the predication of 'newness'. Ultimately the aim of this chapter is not to establish a true or correct understanding of current terrorism but to question the dominant interpretations and thereby show the inherently contested nature of the 'new terrorism' discourse. Chapter 3 will follow this style of critique and examine what kind of anti-terrorism measures are considered sensible to counter the threat or 'new terrorism'. This includes a critique of military and judicial responses to terrorism and investigates the seemingly absurd notion engagement and negotiation with 'new terrorists'. Chapter 4 will bring together the first two chapters by asking how one can assess the effectiveness of these counter-measures against 'new terrorism'. This question serves to illustrate some of the difficulties materialist terrorism studies has when investigating its research subject. Chapter 5 hopes to offer an alternative to the materialist understanding of terrorism by outlining what constructivist terrorism studies may look like. This section of the book will emphasise the socially constructed nature of 'new terrorism', highlight the vital role of discourse and thereby question the fundamental importance of 'primary sources' considered vital to 'traditional' and even more 'critical' terrorism research. The chapter will here outline the discourse analytical methodology of metaphor analysis as a means of gaining insight into the construction of terrorism in language. Chapter 6 will apply this constructivist theoretical and methodological framework and analyse the predication of 'new terrorism' in the media in Germany and the United Kingdom through metaphors. It will therefore focus on the tabloid newspapers the *Bild* and *The Sun* and examine how the terrorist and his act of terrorism are constructed in discourse by illustrating the metaphorical expressions found in the text. The expressions found indicate a total of five conceptual metaphors which underlie the construction of 'new terrorism' and constitute the act as a war; a crime; something natural; something uncivilised and evil and as a disease. Chapter 7 will then investigate what these five conceptual metaphors do and how they make certain counter-terrorism policies in Germany and the United Kingdom possible, while at the same time excluding other counter-measures from the options considered appropriate as they do not fit the constructed understanding of what this 'new terrorism' is like. The policy option considered will include military and judicial responses, disaster management and immigration policies and ultimately the constructed impossibility of dialogue and negotiation with 'new terrorists'. Finally the Conclusion will summarise the main arguments of the book and outline areas of potential future research which naturally arise out of the constructivist approach to terrorism research presented in this book.

1
The 'New Terrorism' Discourse

'What we do know is that the terrorist threat today differs greatly, from that of a quarter century ago' (Jenkins 1999)

Even after the excessive wrangling over definitions words continued to play a vital role in the study of terrorism as many scholars, government analysts and politicians claimed that since the mid-1990s terrorism has changed into an inherently new form with new characteristics. Terrorism was said to involve different actors, motivations, aims, tactics and actions, compared to terrorism experienced before. In order to capture these supposed developments they articulated new concepts and predications of terrorism. For example, Laqueur (1996) articulated a notion of 'postmodern' terrorism, Ashton B. Carter, John Deutch and Philip Zelikow (1999) predicated it as 'catastrophic' terrorism and Yonah Alexander and Milton Hoenig (2001) simply called it 'super' terrorism. However, the most dominant discursive label to encompass the characteristics of this kind of terrorism was the idea of 'new terrorism' (Laqueur 1999; Lesser et al. 1999; Aubrey 2004). Although this predication of 'newness' does not say anything about the characteristics of this kind of terrorism other than that it is new, it offers a natural binary opposition to 'old' or 'traditional' terrorism.

This predicative construction 'new terrorism' seems to have slipped past the exhausting definitional controversies in a time where people were tired of conceptual quarrelling. And since 9/11 the concept of 'new terrorism' has firmly established itself in both political and academic discourse as it seemed to provide a means of understanding the attacks in New York and Washington. This chapter, however, wants to question the concept of 'new terrorism' by challenging the predication of 'newness'. By using historical examples and arguments in the existing literature on terrorism it hopes to highlight some of the contradictions in the supposedly almost dichotomous relationship between 'new' and 'old' terrorism. It is, however, very important to stress that the aim of the chapter is not to establish the 'true' nature of current terrorism but to rather offer what Richard Jackson (2009: 68) has referred to as a first order or immanent critique which wants to 'destabilise dominant interpretations and demonstrate the inherently contested and hence political nature of the discourse'. In other words, it does not want to establish whether 'new terrorism' is *really* new or not, but it does want to indicate that knowledge is not as firmly established as it may seem.

Illustrating the discursive construction of 'new terrorism' is therefore not simply an academic exercise. The chapter wants to stress the continued importance of words in terrorism research and give a first indication that language does matter as the use of particular predicates has a huge influence on the way people conceive, construct and ultimately react to terrorism. In pursuit of this goal the first two parts will establish some of the characteristics of what is considered 'old' and 'new' terrorism. The third part will then investigate some of these aspects in more detail and put forward arguments and examples which will question the concept of 'new terrorism' along the lines of their motives, tactics and organisation. The final section summarises the main findings and sets the stage for Chapter 2 which will indicate how the concept of 'new terrorism' automatically makes certain counter-terrorism options appear more appropriate and logical than others.

Old terrorism

Despite the impression one may get in the media, academia does not consider terrorism a new phenomenon. One of the earliest groups to use such political violence cited in the literature are the Sicarii, who were a Zealot religious sect fighting against the Roman rule in Palestine between AD 66–73 (Chaliand and Blin 2007; Waldmann 1998: 99–103). It has been pointed out that during the Middle Ages a religious sect of Ismailis and Nizari called 'Assassins' struggled against the empire of Saladin and in the 16th century small 'terrorist' groups in Albania and other regions resisted the armies of the Ottoman Empire. The term 'terror' was first used around 1794 as a policy to protect the fragile government of the French Republic from counter-revolutionaries.[1] And it is widely acknowledged that from around the mid-19th century to the First World War revolutionaries and anarchists used bombings and assassinations as frequent weapons in their struggle against autocracy and that terrorism became an important part of the anti-colonial struggles after the Second World War (Duyvesteyn 2007). As Paul Wilkinson (1992: 230) points out, this has an important significance as it was 'the only clear instances in modern history where sub-state organizations using terror as their major weapon were able to achieve their long-term political goals, i.e., the withdrawal of the colonial power and establishment of a form of government favoured by the insurgents'. Following this many scholars have argued that the period between the late 1960s and the late 1980s is marked by 'traditional' or so called 'old terrorism', which can be roughly divided into different types of terrorism such as left and right-wing as well as ethno-national separatist terrorism. Although many of these 'old terrorist' groups can be considered a combination of these different types with specific features, it is argued that they all had some general characteristics concerning their motives, tactics and organisation (Enders and Sandler 2000: 310).

For one, 'traditional' terrorists are classed to have predominantly secular motivations and a rational political reason for their acts of terrorism (Ramakrishna and Tan 2002: 6). For example, it is believed that left-wing terrorist groups used violence to politicise the working class masses and get them to rise up against the capitalist system. While ethno-nationalist terrorist wanted either independence for their ethnic group, in the form of a separation of their territory from another country, the creation of their own sovereign nation state, or the merger with another state. Therefore, their specific demands were often considered rationally negotiable, for example when they wanted the release of certain jailed comrades or payment in exchange for the freeing of hostages in a hijacking. Even where demands were difficult to meet, such as the reunification of a divided country, the creation of an ethno-national homeland or the abolishment of the existing capitalist system, authors such as Andrew Guelke (1998: 52–70) pointed out that in many circumstances there appeared to be room for dialogue or negotiation.

Connected to this, it is believed that the tactical use of violence by 'old terrorists' in general was 'targeted and proportionate in scope and intensity to the practical political objectives being pursued' (Simon and Benjamin 2000: 65). It is thought that 'old terrorists' did not want to use excessive indiscriminate violence themselves as this would reduce their claim of legitimacy and alienate them from supporters, therefore reducing their access to new recruits and funding. Thus, by keeping the level of casualties low 'old terrorists' 'preserved their eligibility for a place at the bargaining table and, ultimately, a role in successor governments' (Simon and Benjamin 2000: 66). 'Old terrorism' was seen to be discriminate, with terrorist groups selecting their targets very carefully. Precision attacks were seen to be usually directed at well-defined highly symbolic targets of the authority they opposed. The idea was to target leading politicians, government officials, members of the aristocracy, military or banking sector or other symbolic targets such as government buildings. Many in terrorism research viewed their actions as a means of propaganda to increase their popular support. As Walter Laqueur (2003: 9) wrote: 'It was, more often than not, "propaganda by deed"'. In their view 'old terrorists' wanted maximum publicity for their acts, playing for an audience and spreading their ideological message. In this regard Brian Jenkins (1975: 16) famously pointed out that 'terrorism is theatre' and that terrorist attacks were often choreographed for the media. An attack was nearly always followed by a communiqué taking credit for the act, laying out demands, or explaining why it was carried out against that particular target. In this interpretation of 'old terrorism' the targeted violence was generally perpetrated with conventional tactics such as hand-held guns, machine guns, as well as bombs. They showed little interest in new tactics and nonconventional weapons such as weapons of mass destruction (Hirschmann 2002: 39). In general they tried not to cause innocent casualties as this would alienate the population and go against their aim of inciting a popular uprising. In some cases they even expressed sorrow for the accidental death of someone in the attack (Horchem 1986).

A further widely accepted characteristic of 'old terrorism' is its association with state sponsorship or support (Kidder 1986). Although authors can present little evidence, 'old terrorism' was considered a cheap method of attacking and damaging another country without initiating a full-scale war. Within the Cold War framework, terrorists were often seen as proxies for both superpowers and middle powers (Sterling 1981; Combs 2000: 66–86).

Finally, supporters of this 'old terrorism' idea highlight a clear hierarchical organisation with fairly well-defined command and control structures as a central characteristic of this kind of terrorism. Although it is impossible to clearly demarcate the different layers, James Fraser argues that 'old terrorism' is organised like a pyramid, with the leadership, who decide on the overall policy and plans, at the top. This is followed by a larger layer of active terrorists who carry out the attacks and are often specialised in certain activities such as bomb-making, assassination, or surveillance. On the next level there are the active supporters who supply intelligence, weapons, supplies, communications, transportation and safe houses. At the bottom you have the passive supporters who agree with the goals of the terrorist organisation and spread their ideas and express their emotional support (Fraser cited in Henderson 2001: 17).

New terrorism

Although it is difficult to say where and when 'new terrorism' exactly started (Laqueur 2003: 143), many point to the mid-1990s, and the bombing of the World Trade Center in New York in 1993 as well as the sarin gas attack in the Tokyo underground by the Aum Shinrikyo cult in 1995. It is said, that this terrorism has a different set of new characteristics in comparison to the traditional or 'old terrorism' mentioned above, visible in different motives, tactics and organisation (Simon and Benjamin 2000: 59).

Many supporters of the concept 'new terrorism' believe that this kind of terrorism has global motives and aims (Kegley 2003; Guelke 2006). So in contrast to the 'old terrorist's' national or regional political grievances 'new terrorism' strives for a global revolution and a complete alteration of the status quo (Benjamin and Simon 2002: 220). Here one encounters the prominence of religion which is considered one of the main characteristics of 'new terrorism' (Cilluffo and Tomarchio 1998; Juergensmeyer 2000). Whereas 'old terrorism' was primarily seen as secular in its orientation and inspiration, terrorism linked to religious fanaticism is thought to be on the increase. According to Nadine Gurr and Benjamin Cole (2000: 28–29) only two out of 64 international terrorist organisations in 1980 could be classified as religious. And according to them this figure has risen sharply to 25 out of 58 by 1995. 'New terrorism' is often portrayed as a terrorism, which rejects all other ways and promotes an uncompromising view of the world in accordance with the belief of the religion. In contrast to 'old terrorism' 'new terrorism' is said to lack a political agenda or precise political demands (Simon and Benjamin 2001–2002; Schröm 2005: 111). Bruce Hoffman (1998: 94) believes that this religious motivation is the defining characteristic of terrorism today: A new terrorism which has radically different value system, different mechanisms of legitimisation and justification and ultimately different concepts of morality and an alternate world view.

As a consequence of this religious motivation '"new terrorists" are much less rational in their approach to violence than their "traditional" predecessors' (Field 2009: 199). A large number of 'new terrorism' scholars point out that one of the main features of 'new terrorism' is the increasing willingness to use excessive and indiscriminate violent tactics. Laqueur (1999: 81) argues that 'the new terrorism is different in character, aiming not at clearly defined political demands but at the destruction of society and the elimination of large sections of the population'. Hoffman (1995) highlights that these groups have caused 60 per cent of all fatalities while only being responsible for a quarter of the terrorist actions. It has been argued that '[f]or the religious terrorist, violence is first and foremost a sacramental act or divine duty executed in direct response to some theological demand or imperative' which is ultimately justified by scripture (Hoffman 1998: 94). In their view 'new terrorists' represent a 'potentially far more lethal threat then the more familiar "traditional" terrorist groups' (Hoffman 1998: 200). As Audrey Cronin (2002/2003: 41) points out, religious terrorists see their struggle as good against evil, therefore dehumanising their victims and considering non-members of their group to be infidels or apostates. As a result, indiscriminate violence may not be only morally acceptable, but amount to a righteous and necessary advancement of their religious cause. While 'old terrorists' were thought to strike only selected targets, 'new terrorism' is seen as increasingly indiscriminate and is thought to try and produce as many casualties as possible. As religious terrorists are deemed to be their own constituency it is believed that they are not concerned about alienating their supporters with their acts of destruction as they hold themselves only accountable to God (Ranstorp 1996: 54; Hoffman 1995: 273). For these similar reasons 'new terrorists' are judged to not always claim and sometimes even deny responsibility for their actions. From this angle, the 'new terrorist' sees the action itself as important and not the claim to it (Whine 2002: 4). At the same time 'new terrorists' are considered to not be interested in any sort of negotiation. 'Today's terrorists don't want a seat at the table, they want to destroy the table and everyone sitting at it' (Morgan 2004: 30–31). Moreover, Walter Enders and Todd Sandler (2000: 311) point out that 'new terrorists' are a lot more willing to engage in risky and more complex acts. Whereas most actions by 'old terrorists' involved an escape plan, 'new terrorists' seem more willing to give their own life while orchestrating a terrorist act. They believe that 'new terrorists' are more prepared to die because martyrdom is seen as a way of reaching heaven.

The threat of mass destruction by terrorists is a fundamental part of the concept of 'new terrorism'. As Jessica Stern (2003a: 65) points out: 'Religious terrorist groups are more violent than their secular counterparts and are probably more likely to use weapons of mass destruction'. So many authors believe that due to their motivation to use extreme violence, 'new terrorists' are more likely to not only obtain and use biological, chemical and radiological weapons but they see a threatening potential for the use of nuclear WMDs by 'new terrorists' (Stern 2003b). Hoffman (1998: 197) warns that 'many of the constraints (both self-imposed and technical) which previously inhibited terrorist use of WMD are eroding'. With the collapse of the Soviet Union acquiring material which could be used for WMDs or even a complete WMD has become easier and does not need the cooperation of a state sponsor as much as before.[2] Another of the characteristics of 'new terrorism' in the literature is precisely this direct influence of state backers. Some believe that the willingness to use extreme violence shows that 'new terrorists' do not have an organisation or state sponsor to protect, so they see no reason to limit their violence as they do not fear a backlash (Tucker 2001). Therefore, in their opinion the financing of 'new terrorism' is not based on money received from state sponsors, but on other illegal sources such as drug trafficking, video piracy and credit card fraud, as well as legal business investments, donations from wealthy individuals, charities and Diaspora (Raphaeli 2003).

In addition to this lack of state sponsorship 'new terrorists' are seen to be predominantly amateurs that operate on a part time basis and have not dropped out of society totally. The new amateur terrorists are thought to only come together to conduct their action and then disband. They do not receive training or logistical support from state sponsors but rely on the network of supporters and information on the internet (Tsfati and Weimann 2002). Furthermore, a number of scholars believe that the increasing use of information and communication technologies enables the 'new terrorists' to communicate covertly and to bridge distances more easily. Although 'new terrorists' might be part time amateurs they show a higher degree of technological and operational competence. They use a vast range of communication equipment including mobile and satellite phones as well as email and web-sites to plan their next terrorist acts, communicate with other terrorist groups and spread their message around the world (O'Brien 2003). 'New terrorism' exploits the increase in intercontinental flight connections and the poor customs and immigration control in many countries to move around the world (Wilkinson 1992: 232). 'New terrorists' have 'extended their reach by building globe-circling infrastructure' (Pillar 2001b: 34–35). In other words they do not only have global aims but also a global reach (Takeyh and Gvosdev 2002; Sageman 2004: 61).

Finally, one of the most emphasised aspects of 'new terrorism' is its loose networked and less hierarchical organisational structure (Raufer

1999; Crenshaw 2000; Wilkinson 2003; Münkler 2004). Some authors believe that the amateur terrorist is a manifestation of a new network structure that is facilitated by the emergence of new advanced telecommunications technology. Each group within this network becomes relatively autonomous but is still linked by advanced communication and their common purpose. They thereby become a lot more flexible and can adapt and react more easily to different situations. Although members do communicate with their leadership, groups can, to a certain extent, operate self-sufficiently (Hoffman 1997a; Gunaratna 2003a). Simon and Benjamin (2000: 70) refer to this as a combination of 'a "hub and spoke" structure (where nodes communicate with the centre) with a "wheel" structure (where nodes in the network communicate with each other without reference to the centre)'. John Arquilla, David Ronfeldt and Michele Zanini (1999: 51) note that terrorist leadership is derived from a 'set of principles [that] can set boundaries and provide guidelines for decisions and actions so that members do not have to resort to a hierarchy – "they know what they have to do"'. The authors describe the organisational designs that may 'sometimes appear acephalous (headless), and at the other times polycephalous (Hydra-headed)' (ibid). They consider that this type of integrated structure is a lot more difficult to identify and penetrate than a more traditional hierarchical structure. It is thought to be far more resilient because each cell can still operate even if they lose the leadership of the organisation.

To summarise, the proponents of 'new terrorism' believe that there is something inherently new about the terrorism of today. This includes a fanatical religious motivation, excessive indiscriminate violence together with the possible use of WMDs, an increasing independence from state sponsors as well as a new global network structure helped by communications technology and new amateur terrorists who only come together in ad hoc groupings.

The deconstruction of newness

A number of authors have made comparisons between recent terrorist events and antecedents in history. For example John Gray (2002) notes the similarities between today's terrorism perpetrated by al-Qaeda and Russian anarchist terrorists in the late 19th century.[3] Niall Ferguson (2001) also observes some of the resemblance of the two, including the political religion of their ideologies, the trans-national nature of both sets of terrorists who often lived and planned attacks abroad, as well as the similarity of political economic situation in the world at the end of the 19th and 20th century. In connection with fundamentalist Islamic terrorism often associated with 'new terrorism', he even draws comparisons between the Sudanese revolt of the Mahdi against the British Empire in the 1880s and Osama bin Laden's fight against the United States. Paul Kennedy (2001: 56) also sees parallels and comments on the similarity between the hatred of London as the financial centre of world capitalism at the end of the 19th century and the hatred of the Washington and the United States by 'new terrorists' today.

As a result scholars such as David Tucker (2001), Thomas Copeland (2001), Isabelle Duyvesteyn (2004), Martha Crenshaw (2007) and most recently Antony Field (2009) have explicitly criticised what some of them have referred to as the 'new terrorism' school. The following sections want to summarise some of the criticisms and offer a critique of the established understanding of 'new terrorism' by using historical examples and arguments found in the existing literature to question its predication as new. It thereby does not want to establish the 'true' or 'real' nature of terrorism today but hopes to indicate the contested nature of what is often considered to be established knowledge on terrorism. It will thereby focus on the motives, the tactics and the organisation of 'new terrorism'.

Motives

As mentioned above, proponents of the 'new terrorism' concept argue that the motivations of terrorists are changing and point to the growth of religious fundamentalism. Bruce Hoffman (1998: 87) asserts that 'the religious imperative for terrorism is the most important defining characteristic of terrorist activity today'. Yet, even Hoffman himself believes that historically, religious terrorism is by no means a new phenomenon. David Rapoport (1984) points out that religiously motivated terrorism aimed at killing non-believers has existed for thousands of years. From the 1st century zealots to the 13th century assassins and even up to the 19th century and the emergence of political motives such as national, anarchism and Marxism, 'religion provided the only acceptable justification for terror' (Rapoport 1984: 659). Therefore, religion could be considered not so much a new characteristic but maybe more a cyclic return to earlier and maybe forgotten motivations for terrorism. Cronin (2002/2003: 38) suggests that 'the forces of history seem to be driving international terrorism back to a much earlier time, with echoes of the behavior of 'sacred' terrorists such as the Zealots-Sicarii clearly apparent in the terrorist activities of organizations such as al-Qaeda and its associated groups'. In addition to this point, one should note that many 'old terrorist' organisations are thought to have had close links with and were partly motivated by religion. The most prominent examples being the IRA with a predominantly Catholic membership, the Protestant Ulster Freedom Fighters or Ulster Volunteer Force, the mainly Muslim FLN in Algeria, the Jewish terrorist group Irgun and the EOKA in Cyprus which was influenced partly by the Greek Orthodox Church (Hoffman 1998/99).

In connection to this it is important to recognise that although the actions of Islamist terrorist groups may be viewed as religiously motivated, a number of authors do point to a certain political agenda. According to them, this becomes apparent when examining the demands and goals of al-Qaeda's or other 'new terrorists' associated with them as many of them represent clear regional political targets rather than global religious aims. For example, the spread of political Islam, the withdrawal of foreign influence from the holy lands, the overthrow of the existing governments in Saudi Arabia and Egypt, the creation of a worldwide pan-Islamic Caliphate and the elimination of Israel (Jacquard 2001; Kepel and Milelli 2006). At the same time, one may argue that the 'global aims' of 'new terrorism' are also visible in 'old terrorism'. For example, the Red Army Faction (RAF) could be judged as not only striving for a revolution within Germany but openly propagating their opposition to imperialism, colonialism and capitalism throughout the world. Similar things could be said about the IRA and the PLO. As Martha Crenshaw (2003: 49) points out 'believing in the impossible is not unusual for radial movements'.

Overall one may argue that it is extremely hard if not impossible to distinguish between religious and political motivations. Are Hamas' demands for an independent Islamic state down to religious or political motivations? 'Were the Jewish terrorists in British Palestine fighting for religion or against colonialism? Do the Tamil Tigers want their own homeland because they are Hindus in a Muslim nation or because they are Tamils in a Sinhalese country' (Quillen 2002: 288)? The participation and defeat of the Aum Shinrikyo in the parliamentary elections in Japan in 1989 seems to indicate that even this stereotypical example of 'new terrorism' had political motives and aspirations (Richardson 2006: 85). Furthermore, Chris Quillen (2002: 287) points out that assigning religious motivations to individual terrorist attacks is highly subjective and open to interpretation. He cites the example of the Oklahoma City bombing which one might interpret as an act motivated by Timothy McVeigh's devotion to the Christian Identity movement or as a reaction of a political terrorist against gun control measures and the bloody federal raids at Ruby Ridge and Waco.

Tactics

Supporters of the 'new terrorism' concept have argued that terrorists have become more lethal and willing to use unlimited force to cause large numbers of casualties indiscriminately. In their view, 'traditional' terrorist were more restrained in their use of violence and the number of dead they aimed to produce (Laqueur 2001b). However, one could argue, that indiscriminate mass-casualty attacks have long been a characteristic of terrorism. Examples of 'old terrorists' causing many fatalities include the simultaneous truck bombings of US and French barracks in Lebanon in 1983, which is said to have killed a total of 367 people, the downing of Pan Am Flight 103 over Lockerbie, which took the life of 270, and the bombing of an Air India flight in 1985 by Sikh terrorists with 329 fatalities (Pettiford and Harding 2003). It is easy to forget that one of the most violent incidents of terrorism prior to 9/11 according to Hoffman (1997a) was the attack on an Abadan movie theatre in Iran in 1979 which killed between 400–500 people. As Rapoport (1984) points out, evidence seems to indicate that the Thugs were by far the longest-lasting (400 years) and most murderous of all terrorist organisations killing around half a million people. Even if we consider the indiscriminate targeting of innocent people, such as children in the attack on a school in Beslan in 2004, as a characteristic of 'new terrorism' one could find examples when 'old terrorists' did the same. For example, members of the Democratic Front for the Liberation of Palestine machine-gunned children in an Israeli school in 1974 killing 27 and injuring 70 (Anderson and Sloan 1995: 90). Even if we disregard the numbers and argue that the violence of 'new terrorism', such as the beheading of Daniel Pearl is more excessive than before, one could find examples where 'old terrorists' were just as ruthless. Martin Miller (1995: 45) describes how '[i]n 1884, for example, a Viennese banker and his eleven-year-old son were hacked to death with an axe in front of his other son by anarchists'.

One can argue that none of these can compare to the casualties caused by the 9/11 attacks. However, many of the other attacks by al-Qaeda, the archetype of 'new terrorism', such as the bombings in Madrid and London which killed 191 and 52 people do not really stick out in comparison to Lockerbie or the bombing of the Air India flight (Crenshaw 2003). Therefore, one may question the validity of the concept 'new terrorism' if one of its main characteristics is based on the casualty figures of 9/11. Marie Breen Smyth (2007: 260) points our, 'the scale of atrocity at the World Trade Centre was unprecedented in the practice of modern terror; however, the emphasis on the scale of

Table 1.1   Top ten deadliest terrorist attacks prior to 9/11

Incident	Year of deaths	Number
1. Arson attack at a Abdan Movie theatre in Iran	1979	400+
2. Bombing of an Air India jet from Canada	1985	329
3. Bombing of Pan Am flight 103 over Lockerbie	1988	270
4. Bombing of US Marine barracks in Lebanon	1983	241
5. Bombing of French UTA flight	1989	171
6. Bombing of the Edward P. Murrah building in Oklahoma City	1995	168
7. Bombing of a crowded cathedral in Sofia, Bulgaria	1925	128
8. Bombing of Colombian Avianca aircraft	1989	107
9. Bombing at the Bologna railway station	1980	84
10. Bomb placed inside a telecommunications centre in Teheran	1974	82

Data taken from Hoffman (1997a: 11–12)

the attack has tended to negate the value of previous scholarship and experience of "terrorism". When examining the data on international terrorism incidences, one finds that although the number of terrorist incidences has generally declined from the mid-1980s, the number of fatalities per incident has increased since the 1980s. Considering that 'new terrorism' supposed to have started in the 1990s, this increase of fatalities might not be directly linked to the phenomenon of 'new terrorism' (Duyvesteyn 2004). Even if we consider the coordinated nature of terrorism today to be something new one can stumble across historical precedents which refute such an argument: for example the simultaneous hijacking of three planes by the Popular Front for the Liberation of Palestine in 1970 which clearly has similarities to the events of 9/11 (Crenshaw 2007: 23).

One might be able to argue that the increase of casualties is partly due to better technology. Explosives, timing and remote control devices have been substantially improved and must have an effect on the numbers of casualties (Enders and Sandler 2000: 311). Furthermore, it is important to point out that governments have continuously adapted to terrorist techniques such as kidnapping, hostage taking, hijacking, assassinations and sabotage by providing security at airports, securing embassies, guarding likely kidnap targets, training specialist commando troops and sharing intelligence with other states. In response to this, terrorists may have adjusted their methods since the 1980s by placing more emphasis on coordinated bombing and other hit and run tactics.

Figure 1.1   Fatalities in international terrorist incidences

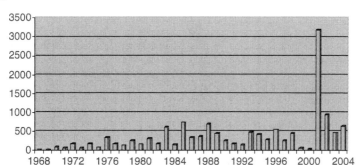

Data taken from MIPT Terrorism Knowledge Base[1]

---

[1]The MIPT Terrorism Knowledge Base ceased operation in 2008. Part of the data can now be found at the Global Terrorism Database (GTD) of the National Consortium for the Study of Terrorism and Responses to Terrorism at the University of Maryland, available at: http://www.start.umd.edu/gtd/, [accessed 09.07.09].

While it is becoming increasingly difficult for terrorists to get close to their traditional targets they may have to find other ways of capturing the media's attention. Using more spectacular coordinated violent tactics is one way of gaining greater media coverage (Wilkinson 2000: 174–186). According to Brigitte Nacos (2006: 213) al-Qaeda training manuals advised members to attack 'sentimental landmarks' as their destruction would 'generate intense publicity'. Although many 'new terrorist' groups may not publish a communiqué following an attack claiming responsibilities and stating the reasons for the attack, 'new terrorists' are thought to be still interested in getting attention and acknowledgement of their cause. Some writers such as Thomas Copeland (2001: 101) claim that they 'do not need to make public statements taking credit for an attack because their constituency is already aware of the actors and their cause'. Although they may be targeted at an internal audience, many of the video and tape recordings of Osama bin Laden seem to indicate his interest in remaining in the public eye. The statement by Brian Jenkins (1975: 16) that 'terrorism is theatre', regarded by many proposing the concept of 'new terrorism' as outdated, perhaps still applies to some extent. It is hard to think of a more symbolic and dramatically theatrical attack than the attacks of 9/11. Targeting the World Trade Center, considered the symbol of western capitalism, the Pentagon, heart of US defence, as well as probably the White House seems too much even for a Hollywood film. 'New terrorists' appear to still want many people watching, and one could argue that the larger, more coordinated and dramatic the attack, the larger the audience is going to be. Therefore, the increasing level of fatalities could be seen as an ongoing process, which does not necessarily represent a unique feature qualifying the concept of 'new terrorism'.

Writers such as Ray Takeyh (2001) argue that public opinion does also still play a vital role in 'new terrorism'. One example here for is the Egyptian group Al-Jama Al-Islamiyya who attacked the Temple of Hatshepsut in Luxor and killed 58 tourists and four Egyptians in 1997. The attack was widely condemned not only by western governments but also by many radical Islamists, who saw the attack as damaging their cause. The author points out that the support for Al-Jama Al-Islamiyya fell dramatically in Egypt as a result of the attack. The group remained active but their attack had alienated the people they most wanted to draw and over time this gravely hindered their efforts. Other scholars point out that public opinion is still rather important when one considers the terrorists' political agenda mentioned above. These political goals, such as the establishment of an Islamic state, may restrain terrorists as they have to take into consideration that they need public support for the establishment of a new state. One can therefore argue that they have to be careful not to alienate their supporters and sympathisers by using excessive violence. Although they see their violence as legitimised by God they are still thought to be dependent on some public support for recruitment and finance (Tucker 2001: 6).

Many have also argued that the proliferation of technology as well as the accessibility to information useful to terrorists on the Internet are dangerous new trends which have contributed to the emergence of a different kind of terrorism (Hoffman 1997b). Others however point out that the availability of information is arguably nothing new. Advice on bomb-making and terrorist tactics has been available in newsletters and handbooks since at least the turn of the century (Grob-Fitzgibbon 2004). An early example of this were pamphlets published by the anarchist Johann Most at the end of the 19th century with information on how to carry out terrorist acts and 'details on "revolutionary chemistry", which included instructions on explosive devices, flammable liquid compounds, poison bullets and daggers, as well as on the best places to hide and use them' (Miller 1995: 45). Here one could also mention one of the most famous DIY bomb-making guides, the Anarchist Cookbook published in the 1960s (Gearson 2002: 15).

Furthermore, the possible use of WMDs as a characteristic of new terrorism is debatable. The example of the sarin gas attack on the underground in Tokyo by Aum Shinirikyo in 1995 is frequently used to make the connection between 'new terrorism' and WMDs. However, various researchers point to evidence that there have been plans and attempts by terrorists to use WMDs for several decades (Tucker 2000). For example, in 1972 members of a right-wing group called 'Order of the Rising Sun' were arrested and found to be in the possession of 30 to 40 kilograms of epidemic typhus pathogens, with which they wanted to poison the water supply of Chicago, St. Louis and other cities in the Mid West in order to create a new master race. Furthermore, former members of the Bhagwan Shree Rajneesh's group contaminated salad bars with Salmonella typhi and poisoned 750 people in Oregon in 1984. Another example in Europe includes the discovery of botulinal toxin and considerable quantities of organophosphorous compounds, used to make nerve gas, in safe houses in France and Germany belonging to the Red Army Faction in the 1980s (Barnaby 2002: 58–59). In addition, the PKK and the Tamil Tigers, both examples of 'old terrorists', are supposed to have used chemical weapons. In 1992 the PKK poisoned water tanks of the Turkish air force near Istanbul with a lethal dose of cyanide, and in 1990 the Tamil Tigers attacked a Sri Lankan military camp with chlorine gas (Schmid 1999: 114; Parachini 2003). 'The LTTE and PKK attacks are significant because they clearly disprove the idea that all "traditional" terrorist groups would avoid using nuclear, chemical or biological weapons under any circumstances' (Cameron 2004: 81). Hoffman (1998: 198), while referring to the RAND – St. Andrew's University Chronology of International Terrorism, notes that since 1968, 60 terrorist incidences involved plans or attempts to use WMDs.[4]

Apart from biological and chemical WMDs, the threat of nuclear terrorism has also been linked to the concept of 'new terrorism'. So far there have been no attacks with nuclear weapons by terrorists and the most devastating terrorist attacks have employed bombs, conventional explosives and most famously box cutters. Authors such as David Claridge (1999) argue that authorities have significantly inflated the threat of terrorists using WMDs to a hysterical level wasting huge amounts of resources. At the same time it should also be noted that although not the same as exploding a purpose-built nuclear bomb, some point out that there have been numerous attacks on nuclear power stations in the 1970s and 1980s. According to Laqueur (1999: 72) one of the first occurred in 1973 when a commando from a left-wing Argentinean group entered the construction site of the Atucha atomic power station north of Buenos Aires. In 1976, bombs were thrown at an atomic power plant in Britanny, France, but the nuclear reactor was not damaged.

During the following years ETA conducted several attacks against the Lemoniz nuclear power station near Bilbao in Spain. Other attacks were directed against plants near San Sebastian, Pamplona, Tafalla, Beriz and other sites in northern Spain. In 1982, the terrorist wing of the ANC sabotaged two South African nuclear power plants. Both their reactors were substantially damaged, but as they were not in operation at the time there was no release of radiation (Ferguson and Potter 2005: 196). Although it was not proven whether these groups aimed at causing a nuclear explosion or contamination, these incidents indicate that even 'old terrorists' were possibly willing to cross the nuclear line.

A similar argument can be made about the suicide tactics often included in the description of the fanatical nature of 'new terrorism' and frequently associated with Islamic fundamentalism. However, one could point out that suicide bombing has been used extensively by Hindu Tamil Tigers in Sri Lanka from 1983 onwards. While Robert Pape (2003: 343) points out that the Tamil Tigers have engaged in 75 out of 186 suicide terrorist attacks between 1980 and 2000, Yoram Schweitzer (2000) argues that the LTTE has conducted more terrorist suicide attacks than all other terrorist organisations together (168 out of 270 from 1980 to 2000). Even prior to this, the use of daggers at close range by the Assassins during the Middle Ages, showed 'a willingness to die in pursuit of their mission' (Gearson 2002: 14). So one may consider suicide terrorism not so much a new phenomenon as it 'existed among Moslem Hashishiyun in the eleventh century and various groups in Asia during the eighteenth century' (Kimhi and Even 2004: 816).[5]

Organisation

One of the other arguments mentioned above is that 'new terrorists' have become independent non-state actors. Some argue that due to the opportunities of globalisation terrorists today have simply diversified their incomes (Copeland 2001: 99). Others believe that the example of al-Qaeda obtaining bases, training camps and sanctuary in Afghanistan shows that state connections are still relevant (Freedman 2002: 38). Following the fall of the Taliban in Afghanistan, evidence of state sponsorship of terrorism is more difficult to find. However, apart from the famous 'axis of evil' identified by President Bush, some analysts remain convinced that there are clandestine links or acquaintances between terrorism and some states such as Saudi Arabia and Pakistan (Stohl 2003: 89). So far, 'proving' or 'disproving' these links remains difficult. Furthermore, the question of what constitutes state sponsorship continues unanswered. Assisting terrorists groups in the form of money, weapons, training or bases for operations seems to easily qualify as sponsoring terrorism. What if a state looses control of parts of its territory and does not have the necessary resources or the political strength in its own country to oppose terrorist activity in the region?

The new international or global characteristic of terrorism is also debatable. Although, there are clearly different types of international action and cooperation Albert J. Bergesen and Omar Lizardo (2004: 45) highlight that while 'the contemporary period is known as one of 'international terrorism', there are clear grounds for considering the anarchist period as one that also had international or global aspects in that terrorism appeared in different parts of the world and involved crossing national boundaries for many attacks'. There are a number of examples which illustrate this such as the assassination of the Spanish prime minister by the Italian Angiolillo in 1892, the fatal stabbing of Empress Elizabeth of Austria by the Italian Luigi Luccheni in 1898 and the assassination of the Austrian Archduke Francis Ferdinand by the Bosnian Serb Gavrilo Princip in 1914 (Bergensen and Han 2005: 137). One may argue that 'terrorists' have received support from foreign rulers or wealthy individuals from other countries throughout history (Rapoport 1984).

Other scholars point out that international cooperation existed between many of the 'traditional' or 'old terrorist' organisations such as the RAF, Red Brigades, Action Directe, PLO, PFLP and IRA. Although, this predominantly took the form of joint training or providing a safe-haven abroad, there also seem to be examples of international cooperation in direct terrorist attacks. In 1977 a Palestinian group hijacked an airline, which landed in Somalia and made demands to the German government for the release of RAF comrades from German prison. In the subsequent storming of the plane by the GSG9 Special Forces several of the Palestinian hijackers were killed. Several German terrorists from the Red Army Faction, the Movement 2 June and the Revolutionary Cells took part in major Popular Front for the Liberation of Palestine (PFLP) operations and operations masterminded by Carlos the Jackal (Ilich Ramirez Sanchez) on behalf of the PFLP. These attacks included the seizure of the OPEC headquarter in Vienna in 1975, the attempted bombing of an El-Al flight in Paris and the attempted hijacking of an El Al flight in Nairobi in January 1975, as well as the hijacking of an Air France flight to Uganda in June 1976 (Karmon 1999; Daase 2008). Other examples of 'old terrorists' cooperating in direct actions include the Japanese Red Army (JRA), who in 1973, together with several Palestinians, hijacked a Japan Airlines flight from Amsterdam, and in 1974 blew up a Shell oilrig in Singapore jointly with PFLP members (Kushner 2003: 191). Although one might argue that this type of collaboration is not exactly the same kind of cooperation found in terrorism today, one can question the notion of a new international terrorism, as most literature proposing the term does not differentiate forms of international cooperation.

In connection to this, one of the main differences postulated by the proponents of 'new terrorism' between 'old' and 'new' terrorists is their organisational structure. Whereas traditional terrorism is viewed to be organised along hierarchical lines with as clear command structure, 'new terrorism' is seen as a loose network, more weakly organised and without a strong command structure. However, the network structure seen in 'new terrorism' is again not held to be totally a new phenomenon in terrorism and even Hoffman (2001: 426) admits that the newness of the loose network structure associated with 'new terrorism' is debatable. For example, over a century ago the anarchist movement, responsible for a number of high profile attacks against heads of state and often referred to as Anarchist or Black International, active mainly in Russia and France, pursued a similar strategy of violence carried out by loosely networked, largely unconnected cells of like-minded radicals (Crenshaw 2003). And others point out that different forms of network structures can be seen in traditional terrorist organisations. For example, the Palestine Liberation Organisation (PLO) can be understood as an umbrella group where the dominant faction, Fatah, did not have a monopoly of power. The different factions within the PLO were fairly independent and had different policies and strategies (Cobban 1981: 140). At the same time one could consider Hezbollah as an umbrella organisation of radical Shiite groups, where the relationship among members is unpredictable and does not follow strict lines of control (Ranstorp 1994: 304). Other scholars even point out that network structures also existed in left-wing revolutionary groups such as the RAF where second, third and fourth generation terrorists did not really form a hierarchical organisation but rather a network with similar common goals (Tucker 2001: 4).

In the same fashion as there are network structures in 'old terrorism', one may observe signs of hierarchical command structures in 'new terrorist' organisations such as Aum Shinrikyo or al-Qaeda. They are considered to possess a clear leadership, operative units conducting the attacks, as well as 'specialized units directly below the top leadership level' who are responsible for issues such as recruitment, finances, procurement and public relations (Mayntz 2004: 11–12). 'Below Bin Laden is the shura majlis or the consultative council. Four committees report to it. A military committee recruits fighters, runs training camps and launches terrorist operations' (Shultz and Vogt 2003a: 10). In other words, terrorist organisations have different types of members including core members or professional terrorists, part-time terrorists or amateurs, who also lead a normal life outside of the organisation, as well as less closely associated supporters. And one can argue that these different types of members exist in both 'old' and 'new terrorism' to a fluctuating degree.

Conclusion

As we have seen, many different characteristics have been attributed to 'new terrorism' including different motives, tactics and organisation. It is said to be motivated by religious fanaticism, use extreme indiscriminate violence and possibly WMDs, be increasingly independent from state sponsors and organise itself in a network structure helped by communications technology and new amateur terrorists who only come together in ad hoc groupings. Nevertheless, one can find arguments and examples in the terrorism literature which can question the established predication of newness. One can argue that fanatical religious terrorism has existed for thousands of years and that the distinction between religiously and politically motivated terrorism is difficult to uphold. The willingness of 'new terrorists' to use more indiscriminate violence may be more a continuation of an existing trend than an all-new phenomenon as terrorism can be considered to have always been a violent business and the trend of increasing deaths per attack initiated in the 1980s, might be down to the need of keeping the media and the world's awareness focused on their grievances. Some judge terrorism to still be theatre, maybe on a much bigger stage, where an act has to be big and shocking to keep the audience's short attention from drifting to other scenes. State sponsorship or support is still judged to be part of terrorism today, even though this may be less obvious and not so much due to financial reasons. Terrorists are perceived to still need a place where they can rest, plan, train and recruit members. Finally the equation of 'old terrorism' = hierarchical structure and 'new terrorism' = network structure is also debatable as hierarchical and network organisational structures have been observed in both 'old' and 'new terrorism'.

As mentioned in the introduction, the aim of this chapter was not to establish the true characteristics of current terrorism or settle the debate about whether 'new terrorism' is really new or not. Its main aim was to show that the meanings of words and concepts such as 'new terrorism' are not fixed. 'New terrorism' is not a brute fact but a social construction. Nevertheless, the '"new terrorism" – as dubbed by government and security experts – has seeped into political language and public discourse, intensifying the feeling that we are living in risky times' (Mythen and Walklate 2006: 379). It is important to acknowledge, that the predicate 'new' has helped to construct and maintain a certain understanding of terrorism which automatically makes certain options of dealing with the phenomenon seem logical. Many of the policies can be directly attributed to some of the supposed features of 'new terrorism'. For example the invasion of Iraq, which was considered to have WMDs, can be interpreted as a counter-terrorism measure aimed at preventing 'new terrorists' from obtaining and using WMDs. As Richard Jackson (2007c: 421) highlights, this kind of 'new terrorism' 'discourse normalizes and legitimizes a restricted set of coercive and punitive counter-terrorism strategies, whilst simultaneously making non-violent alternatives such as dialogue, compromise and reform appear inconceivable and nonsensical'.

It is important to consider the influence of language and predicative phrases such as 'new terrorism' on government policies. One should note the connection between many of the characteristics of 'new terrorism' mentioned above and the current counter-terrorism measures implemented and planned since 9/11. For example, the predicative construction of 'new terrorism' already indicates the need for new counter-terrorism. If we are facing a 'new' kind of terrorism it appears logical that we should also implement new kinds of counter-terrorism measures to deal with this threat effectively. While some argue that this 'new terrorism' clearly requires a set of 'new' counter-terrorism policies to deal with it effectively, other authors such as Ian Lesser et al. (1999: 2) go further and judge that this 'new terrorism' 'renders much previous analysis of terrorism based on established groups obsolete'. So, the acceptance of the term 'new terrorism' appears to have influence on the direction and funding of counter-terrorism measures. As Wyn Rees and Richard J. Aldrich (2005: 913) point out, '[p]oliticians on both sides of the Atlantic have been quick to seize on the rhetoric of "new terrorism" because it mobilized elected assemblies, delivering enhanced budgets and robust packages of security legislation'. Therefore Jessica Wolfendale (2006: 762) warns that the 'historical precedent set by states' counter-terrorism activities makes grim reading and one should therefore be careful about accepting the claim that *this* time the terrorist threat *really* is a different kind of threat requiring different kinds of responses'. The next chapter will examine in more detail some of the counter-terrorism policies which are considered as an option against this idea of 'new terrorism' and some which are not.

2
'New Counter-Terrorism' Possibilities

'Much counterterrorism experience is losing its relevance in light of the "new" terrorism' (Lesser 1999)

What counter-terrorism policies are made possibilities by this 'new terrorism'? This is the central question this chapter wishes to address and again it does not want to establish whether these counter-measures are good or bad but demonstrate the contested nature of the dominant counter-terrorism discourse. And again words play an important role as authors and policy makers in the past distinguished between 'antiterrorism' and 'counter-terrorism'. 'Antiterrorist actions are designed as defensive measures to prevent the occurrence of terrorism as opposed to counterterrorist measures, which are offensive in nature and are designed to respond to a terrorist act' (Celmer 1987: 13). Although the meaning of this distinction seems to have faded in the literature on terrorism (Townshend 2002: 115) a number of other labels and categories of counter-terrorism have established themselves in the discourse on terrorism. Although there may be no agreement which individual counter-terrorism option is most suitable or effective in combating 'new terrorism' there is rough agreement on the range of policies which could make sense. Within this range one comes across a number of mostly binary categories to classify and order the diversity of anti-terror measures.[1] Here one can find categories on different 'levels' such as *national* and *international* measures (Townshend 2002; Bensahel 2006) and in different 'time periods' such as *short-* and *long-term* (Crelinsten and Schmid 1992) or *backward* or *forward-looking* (Heymann 2001/2002) counter-terrorism policies. Graeme Steven and Rohan Gunaratna (2004) expand this into a ternary classification by differentiating *'before'*, *'during'* and *'after'* approaches to dealing with terrorism. However the most prominent means of differentiating between counter-terrorism measures are 'operational' classification. Here one finds for example *active and passive* (Townshend 2002), *offensive and defensive* (Posen 2001/2002; Williams 2004), *site-specific and general* (Powell 2007), *targeted and untargeted* (Heymann 2000) or *discriminate and indiscriminate* (Bueno de Mesquita and Dickson 2007) counter-terrorism policy classifications. Apart from some more unusual classifications such as the one suggested by Bueno de Mesquite (2007) as *observable* and *non-observable*, which makes a distinction as to whether the public are physically able to see the anti-terror policy (new x-ray machines at airports) or not (secret intelligence activity), one of the most common binary categories found in the literature is the distinction between the *military* and a *non-military* (Nacos 2006) or rather the *war model* and the *criminal justice model* of combating terrorism (Crelinsten 1989). The latter sees terrorism as a crime and therefore makes a state's criminal legal system responsible for dealing with it, while the former considers terrorism more along the lines of insurgency or guerrilla warfare and therefore makes the military responsible for addressing the threat posed through the use of things such as air strikes, military intervention and special forces (Chalk 1995).[2]

Classifications serve the purpose of making things easier to comprehend. We all work and think in classifications and this very book is no exception. But it is obvious that classifications are discursive constructs and not socially given entities. They allow only things to make sense if they fit into one or the other classification. In other words classifications pre-select what we consider as an option and therefore inherently hide certain power structures as they limit and set boundaries for what we consider possible. Classifications and categories automatically exclude certain options which do not seem to fit the constructed framework.

The following chapter wants to illustrate some of the counter-terrorism measures which are considered a viable option against 'new terrorism'. The focus will be on the distinction of seeing terrorism as a war or as a crime not only because it is one of the most dominant classifications in the literature, but because it reflects the shift found in the discursive construct of 'new terrorism' and Al-Qaeda in the popular media discourse discussed in Chapter 5. The discussion below is meant to give an insight into the state of the art academic discourse on the military and the criminal justice model responses to terrorism. It is by no means complete or comprehensive. The first part will examine some of the arguments for and against the use of a military response against 'new terrorism', while the second part will examine the arguments for and against a criminal justice response. In the third part the chapter wants to briefly examine some policy options which are considered non-sensical against 'new terrorism' and which are placed outside of the mainstream discourse of counter-terrorism. This will include the idea of a no-policy policy as well as the notion of negotiating with 'new terrorism'. Overall the chapter hopes to indicate to the reader how the characteristics of 'new terrorism' fit into the first two but not into the other options which lie outside of the two established categories. Again it is important to stress that none of the following is supposed to be considered the right or wrong way of conducting counter-terrorism, they are meant to illustrate the contested nature of (counter-)terrorism knowledge by outlining existing arguments for and against such policies.

Military responses: Terrorism as war

A number of scholars believe that '[t]errorism is best understood as a form of warfare' (Silke 1996: 12; Taber 1969; Moss 1972; Clutterbuck 1990) and viewing terrorism as a form of warfare could make sense, especially if one considers the extremely violent nature of 'new terrorism' and its potential for using WMDs (c.f. Wheeler 1991; Merari 1993; Carr 1996/1997). It makes sense to combat a heavily armed, technologically advanced 'new terrorist' who plans and perpetrates sophisticated attacks with military means. And in the literature one encounters a number of arguments for why a defensive and offensive military response can in fact be a viable option for confronting 'new terrorism' both on a national and international level. On the defensive side one can argue that a country's military can be used to tighten internal security for example by patrolling a country's points of entry such as airports and seaports or protecting potential targets and vulnerable infrastructure. As Paul Wilkinson (1996: 6) points out: 'armed forces can contribute the firepower, force projection capability and expertise, such as hostage rescue commandos, sophisticated bomb disposal teams, and specialist marksmen, which the civilian police is unable to provide'. But they could also help civilian actors deal with the aftermath of an attack, for example help take care of casualties, provisionally re-establish necessary infrastructure or deal with contamination.

On the one hand, the military could be used to target those involved in sponsoring or harbouring terrorist groups. Military force could here lead to the destruction of a regime involved in secretly supporting terrorism while at the same time act as a deterrence for others who are considering or continuing to aid terror organisations (Eppright 1997). Military responses both on a small and large scale here are by some considered necessary to uphold the credibility of the threat facing those sponsoring terrorism. They believe that the threat of military strikes and invasion has lead states renowned for harbouring or tolerating terrorist activities within their borders such as Libya and Sudan to join in condemnation of and cease support for 'new terrorism' (Kamp 2002; Collins 2004).

On the other hand a military response could target the terrorist group itself. Here direct military action could limit the power and influence of terrorists and leave them isolated and on the defensive. According to some military forces can be used to find and destroy terrorist infrastructure such as hideouts, bases and training camps and the physical damage can leave the targeted group cut off from its resources and distract them from new acts of terrorism (Shultz and Vogt 2003a). At the same time others point out that a military response can erode their standing by exposing their vulnerability and thereby inflicting a psychologically damaging blow to the groups' leadership, undermining their status and encouraging their removal from power. Not only could a large offensive military operation provide the surveillance that makes it hard for them to plan and organise attacks, but even unsuccessful action, 'which force terrorist units or terrorist cells to stay perpetually on the move to avoid destruction, will help to reduce their capability' (Posen 2001/2002: 47).

Similar to the targeting of sponsors, military strikes could work as a message of deterrence for terrorist groups involved directly as well as other groups who are thinking about or planning an attack. And others believe that military strikes can expose the weakness of terrorist groups to the wider public and thereby draw other states into cooperation against terrorism and stimulate them into enhancing their own counter-terrorism measures (Kosnik 2000). At the same time, renowned scholars such as Paul Wilkinson (2000) add that the mobilisation of the armed forces following a terrorist attack can play an important symbolic role by demonstrating the determination of the state to bring those responsible to justice, thereby upholding the nations moral and answering the public's and media's inevitable demand for a strong response against those responsible.

So while there are a number of arguments for the use of the military against 'new terrorism' there are also scholars which would argue the opposite and heavily criticise the use of military means. For one, some have questioned the use of employing the military as an additional force to enhance internal security. In their opinion one should be aware of the dangers of internally employing the military to deal with 'new terrorist' groups when they are hiding among a certain minority community within a country. Some believe that the internal use of the military may even threaten the very nature of the democratic state. Giving the military excessive powers to deal with a terrorist threat may be like opening Pandora's box and can lead to the dissolution of democracy and the creation of a authoritative military regime where a terrorist becomes a synonym for individuals, groups and communities who disagree with the military leadership. Here winning against terrorism can mean losing democracy. Authors and organisations point to a number of examples such as Chile, Uruguay, Argentina and Brazil (Marchak 1999; Servicio Paz and Justica Uruguay 1992; Wright 2007; Pereira 2005), where the use of the military in the name of 'counter-terrorism' has ultimately led to the retreat or downfall of democracy and the disappearance and death of thousands of civilians (Gearty 1997: 32). As Grant Wardlaw (1989: 69) points out: 'To believe that depriving citizens of their individual rights and suspending the democratic process is necessary to maintain "order" s to put oneself on the same moral plane as the terrorists who believe the "end justifies the means"'.

In contrast to the police the military is considered to lack legitimacy and accountability in the eyes of the general public and are unfamiliar with the local conditions and communities (Wilkinson 2000). It is argued that soldiers are generally not trained for internal security duties where, in contrast to their normal working environment: war zones, it is difficult to identify a clear enemy. As Wilkinson (1996: 5) points out, '[t]here is a constant risk that a repressive overreaction or a minor error of judgement by the military may trigger further civil violence'. In situations where parts of the population are at least supportive and sympathise with the goals of the 'new terrorist' group, simply a heavy military presence could lead to the escalation of violence by polarising the groups involved in the conflict. This is deemed especially problematic, when one thinks of specially trained counter-terrorism commando units. On the one hand these paramilitary squads are said to possess special skills not involved in routine police work and are supposed to have a reactive as well as a preventative function. Not only can they engage as a drastic last option in a security crisis such as a hostage taking but they are also seen as a deterrence for terrorists to not undertake certain types of attack (Combs 2000). On the other hand there is, however, the question of what level of force is considered appropriate and acceptable and how and to what extent these units should be held accountable for their actions in the case of unwarranted violence (Crelinsten and Schmid 1992: 334). Writers point to a number of examples of when counter-terrorist units have overstepped the fine line between warranted and excessive violence including the alleged deliberate killing rather than arresting of PIRA members in Northern Ireland by the SAS in the 1980s, the torture of members of the Red Brigades by Italian NOCS (Nucleo Operativo Centrale di Sicurezza) to force confessions and the deliberate fatal shooting of a wounded RAF terrorist in Germany in 1993 by members of the GSG9 (Chalk 1996: 109). Apart from these occasional excesses other scholars further point to units which were created precisely to fight terrorism with terrorist tactics with the aim of physically eliminating terrorist cells. Examples here include the AAA in Argentina during the Peron government between 1973 and 1976 as well as the GAL in Spain which was created by the socialist democratic government to fight ETA in the 1980s. In both cases the damage caused by these units to public opinion could be considered far greater than the benefit of facing less terrorism (Waldmann 1998: 191).

Considering the use of the military as a means of tightening internal security at borders some note the sheer impossibility of making a national border utterly impervious to 'new terrorists' who are considered to have a global reach. However tight border controls may be 'new terrorists' will find a way to get into the country. Furthermore, it could be argued that increasing the security of one's own national borders only deflects terrorist attacks to other less well-protected regions of the world. So instead of attacking the heart of their enemy's country terrorists may seek to attack their representation and interests abroad such as embassies, businesses or tourists (Lesser 2002). Similarly, even if 'new terrorists' decide to continue attack directly within the country they want to terrorise, they could substitute one type of attack with another if one becomes too difficult to perpetrate. They may shift their attacks from traditional targets which now have become too well defended to new soft targets which lack such protection (Sederberg 2003: 279). This could mean a move away from assaults on military bases such as the ones on US and French barracks in Lebanon in 1984 to attacks on tourist resorts in Bali, public transport in Madrid and London or schools in small towns in North Ossetia. Scholars such as Philip Heymann (2001/2002: 31) therefore point out that it is therefore unclear what targets and resources should be protected. Just as it is impossible to create a 'Maginot Line' at one's border (Bigo 2002a), it is impossible to protect all potential targets, as there are far too many to consider protecting (Sederberg 2003: 274). They argue that if the entire population is considered a valid target then the majority will remain vulnerable and it is easy for 'new terrorists' to find targets (Raymond 2003: 76). Apart from the substitution effect some also highlight the danger of 'terrorist innovation'. So rather than shifting to a different target the implementation of internal security and defence measures may 'invite the terrorists to invent novel circumventions' (Sandler 2003: 795). According to Joao Ricardo Faria (2006) terrorists in the past have proved to be very ingenious in adjusting to and trouncing new security and defence measures (Faria 2006). For example even 'old terrorists' such as the IRA has continuously changed its way of detonating bombs with the help of things such as radar guns or photographic flash equipment in order to circumvent security measures to prevent and jam the detonation remotes (Pillar 2001a: 39). So technologically skilled 'new terrorists' should not have a problem. 'New terrorist' innovations have included the use of aeroplanes as guided missiles, shoe bombs and more recently the attempted use of different liquids which would pass through security undetected to make a bomb on board a plane. Following this line of argument one could go as far as claiming that when traditional methods of terrorism such as conventional bombing cease to work due to the enhanced security and defence measures 'new terrorists' are forced to use unconventional weapons of mass destruction out of desperation (Quillen 2002: 290).

In contrast to the problems of using the military internally to counter-terrorism, the external use of a country's armed forces against 'new terrorism' is said to face a number of further difficulties. Firstly, a number of critics have questioned the usefulness and validity of applying the idea of deterrence to a 'new terrorist' group such as al-Qaeda. The central idea here is that a religiously motivated fanatical terrorist group which is characterised by the extensive use of suicide tactics is beyond deterrence.[3] The willingness to suffer and sacrifice their lives for the cause seems to make deterrence, i.e. the capacity to protect oneself from attack by being able to credibly threaten unacceptable reprisal, pointless. Deterrence in the classical sense does not seem to fit easily into terrorism's central idea of the 'spiral of conflict'.[4] Some point out that instead of deterrence military action against terrorist groups could lead to a counter-retaliation by the group. Here the military (over)reaction by the states is the whole aim of the terrorist attack in the first place (Bowyer-Bell 1978; Rubenstein 1987). In their view the terrorist group's action is meant to lead to repression which leads to consciousness among the oppressed and then more action.

The spiral, would function A1-R/C-A2-R/C-A3 and so on, were A1 represents the initial action undertaken by the terrorist group for example al-Qaeda, which would in turn provoke a repression R on the part of the 'oppressor'. Such repression would then produce an increased awareness or consciousness C on the part of the 'oppressed'. The consequence of this will be further action A2, different from the first in that it would be undertaken by the oppressed themselves. The logic of this schema is that the conflict between oppressor and oppressed will spiral. Each action A1, A2, A3 and so on, will be more extreme that the previous one and thus advance the revolutionary process (Laqueur 1999; Richardson 2006).

According to some, the idea of state repression within the spiral of violence could also lead to a situation in which a more extreme splinter group perpetrates an attack as a result of which the state unknowingly strikes at the main organisation, which then leads to the main group restarting an otherwise dormant campaign of terror. Some terror groups may even mount attacks under the name of a less moderate group in order to get the authorities to crack down rather than negotiate with such a group (Lutz and Lutz 2004: 231).

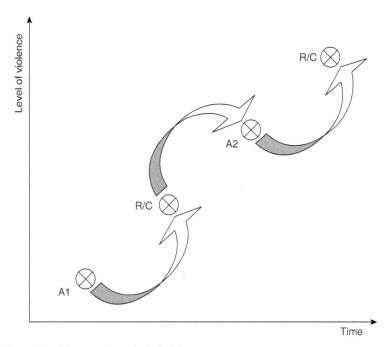

Figure 2.1   The terrorist spiral of violence

There are a number of other practical problems of using military strikes against 'new terrorism'. Critics of a military approach to terrorism have pointed out that 'new terrorists' do not use ordinary or conventional combat methods found in a 'normal' war as they generally do not engage in extensive operations with thousands of combatants which could be prevented by the deployment of a large number of troops (Light 2002). Similarly, one has to note the idea that these kind of terrorist groups do not generally present many or even any targets or infrastructure which a government could strike at. This is considered especially the case concerning high value targets whose destruction would severely damage the organisation. As Paul Pillar (2001a: 103) points out after the US embassy bombings in Africa '[t]he physical impact of the missile strike in Afghanistan was limited by the primitive nature of the facilities that were hit'. One could therefore argue that military retaliation especially in cases such as Afghanistan with million dollar cruise-missiles or laser-guided bombs often does little more than rearrange rocks in a barren landscape in the middle of nowhere.

'New terrorist' groups are believed to rarely have fixed headquarters and scholars point out that the lack of such targets is further compounded by the difficulty of getting good intelligence in order to prove and pinpoint the responsible perpetrators and establish a target quickly enough to mount a strike before the group moves on to somewhere else (Wilkinson 2000). What are considered traditional problems of intelligence such as indirect, fragmentary and ambiguous information are further exacerbated by the 'fact' that gathering intelligence especially tactical intelligence has become more difficult due to looser operational linkages between 'new terrorist' nodes. The smaller the cells of a 'new terrorist' group are and the more the members know each other personally the more difficult it will be to infiltrate such groups. Apart from the problem of getting close to 'new terrorists' and cultivating personal relationships or trying to recruit members as informers, Paul Pillar (2004) believes that there is the problem that those who are in close contact with decision makers, and are therefore more likely to have knowledge of the next terrorist operation, are the most loyal and least likely to betray their group. Something which is believed to be compounded even further by a lack of human intelligence resources, which some say is due to western obsession with technology such as spy satellites or intercepting communication, the over regulation of intelligence agencies or their inability to recruit suitable staff willing to engage in such dangerous activities (Berkowitz 2002).

'The analysis of terrorist intelligence has challenges that parallel the difficulties in collecting it' (Pillar 2001a: 112). According to a number of authors there is simply too much information to analyse everything concerning all the known terrorists groups around the world; those groups who are yet considering the use of violence; and those who have not yet formed or joined a group at all (Lutz and Lutz 2004: 226). Without exactly knowing the 'new terrorists' plans and their where-abouts it is said to be almost impossible to precisely identify targets, and connections between groups who might strike some time in the future as they often only become apparent after an attack has occurred (Hoffman and Morrison-Taw 2000). Focusing on certain specific pro-files such as for example young middle eastern men is considered both under and over-inclusive at the same time. Victor Romero (2003) points out that it is under-inclusive because there are white US or European nationals who may also be terrorist threats. Treating such a large group as suspicious means that government authorities could miss genuine terror-ists who do not fit the profile. At the same time it is over-inclusive because the vast majority of young males from the Middle East have no involvement in terrorism what so ever. Youthfulness, the male gender and a Middle Eastern origin is dangerously inaccurate with probably 99.9 per cent being totally innocent.

Due to the unreliability of intelligence on 'new terrorists', violent mil-itary responses are deemed to involve the possibility of so called 'collateral damage' i.e. causing the tragic, unintended death of innocent civilians (Ross 2006: 204). Some believe that regardless of the increasing sop-histication of modern weaponry, high tech weapons such as cruise missiles, guided-bombs and more recently drones, the problems of accuracy and the mentioned issue of precise intelligence information on the target due to the network structure of 'new terrorism' will con-tinue to cause innocent casualties. This is judged not only problematic from a normative perspective but can be thought of as a practical polit-ical issue in an anti-terror campaign as it may greatly damage one's image and gravely impede the struggle for the heart and minds of the general public around the world (Hoyt 2004; Steven and Gunaratna 2004). This cannot only mean the loss of the moral high ground and the support of international public opinion, but it can strain existing international and regional alliances and lead to the situation where other states may be less willing to cooperate against 'new terrorism' in the future (Wilkinson 2000). It may make the attacking state look no better or even worse than the terrorist group they are fighting against. So it could not only lead to the loss of legitimacy by the state involved in the strike but can also increase the legitimacy of the terrorist group they are fighting (Tucker 1997: 93–94).

According to authors such as Peter Chalk (1996: 97) employing a war like response implicitly acknowledges the political role of the 'new terrorist' group and thereby legitimises their violence or at least portrays it as normal. Such approaches can create 'a symmetry in the perception of the onlooker, permitting the terrorists to portray themselves as soldiers rather than as criminals or terrorists' (Crelinsten and Schmid 1992: 333). In their opinion, military responses can therefore play into the hands of terrorist groups and can represent part of their strategy of provoking repression in order to gain support, recruits and funding from sympathisers to continue their struggle. Striking at terrorist groups with expensive high-tech weaponry increases the groups' publicity and their own self perception. It can reinforce the bad image of western governments and send the message that this evil enemy knows only the language of force (Pillar 2001a).

So a military response to a terrorist attack could not only lead to retaliation by the group but can actively contribute to overall increase in terrorism. While some authors maintain that military strikes do not really have an effect on the long-term level of terrorism (Enders et al. 1990; Brophy-Baermann and Conybeare 1994; Prunckun and Mohr 1996) others believe that especially military intervention in foreign countries does lead to an increase in the overall level of terrorism (Eland 1998). It can provoke a political backlash and has the potential for sparking a wider conflict far outweighing the cost of the original 'new terrorist' attack and with far more serious consequences than envisaged (Barker 2003: 118). There are a number of examples, such as the Israeli invasion of Lebanon or the conflict between India and Pakistan, where the retaliation against the supposed sponsor of terrorism has led to a military confrontation or war.

Judicial responses: Terrorism as crime

A criminal justice model of approaching the problem of 'new terrorism' is generally presented as the dichotomous alternative to the military option. Some of the aspects of 'new terrorism' which appear at odds with a military fit into a judicial response and vice versa. The idea of this response is that 'new terrorism' can be countered with the help of traditional criminal justice tools such as law enforcement, police investigations and special anti-terrorist legislation on a national level as well as international judicial measures such as international conventions and protocols.[5] As Paul Wilkinson (2000: 113, emphasis in original) points out: 'Much anti-terrorism legislation is designed to increase the level of protection of life and property by *providing law enforcement authorities with the powers needed to assist them in the apprehension and conviction of those who commit crimes of terrorism'*. Finding and arresting terrorists using police investigations, prosecuting them in a judicial court and placing them in prison will according to this logic mean that the terrorists are stopped from committing further terrorist acts while in custody. This is deemed to be of even greater importance when one considers the arrest and punishment of high-up members of a terrorist group. The imprisonment of those who are responsible for planning attacks, organising the group, arranging finances and needed resources and giving the group a spiritual and charismatic face so important for recruiting new members, can result in the disruption of the 'new terrorist' network and can suppress and delay further attacks due to the time needed to reorganise. The arrest of members and the existence of strong anti-terrorism laws may also act as a deterrent for certain potential members and other groups which are considering terrorist violence as an option. Supporters and sympathisers are more likely to contemplate the consequences of their actions and possibly reconsider their help in fear of their arrest and punishment. Furthermore, the situation that the 'new terrorists' are wanted by authorities and are being looked for often using wanted posters in public places, television and the internet, together with the promise of a financial reward is thought to hamper their freedom of movement (Pillar 2001a: 81). Again others point out that, although maybe not appropriate for 'new terrorists', laws could also provide positive incentives to abandon the path of terrorist violence. One of the best example here is the *collaboratori di giustizia* or *pentiti* law, which was introduced in Italy in the 1970s to fight terrorism of the Red Brigades. The law substantially reduced sentences for convicted terrorists if they cooperated with authorities and provided information on the organisation of which they had been a member. A number of authors stress the importance of this law for the rapid collapse of the Red Brigades (Jamieson 1990; Della Porta 1995a). 'It was brilliantly successful in providing the police with detailed information which helped them to crack open the Red Brigade cells and columns' (Wilkinson 2000: 98).

Yet again one encounters a number of criticisms of a criminal justice approach to fighting 'new terrorism'. For example, it is considered questionable how far 'new terrorists' would be deterred by new anti-terror law and tough prison or even death sentences. It is assumed that fanatical sections of any 'new terrorist' group will generally disregard the judicial consequences of their terrorist attack due to their motivation and passion for the glorious cause as well as their unacceptance of the legitimacy of the court trying them. Even more apparent is the notion that harsh terrorism laws, long prison sentences or even the death penalty will not deter a 'new terrorist' who is prepared to give his own life in a suicide attack (Heymann 2001/2002: 29). Similarly, '[t]he leaders, who are less likely to be caught, may not care much if the underlings are' (Pillar 2001a: 81).

Scholars more critical of a criminal justice approach also argue that apart from the actual problem of finding the 'new terrorist' responsible for an attack and physically arresting the perpetrator, illustrated by difficulties of infiltration mentioned above, his or her prosecution faces many more difficulties, as it is hard to find concrete evidence of those responsible above those actually carrying out the attack. The role of many senior terrorist leaders and their connection to an attack is judged to be extremely hard to prove. This is considered especially problematic when considering the inherent tension between the prevention of terrorism and the prosecution of terrorists: Intelligence agencies are unwilling to identify sources and use for example their secret agents or informers as prosecution witnesses or present other technical sources or means of gathering information the 'new terrorist' group has been unaware of. Critics believe that such a revelation of their sources would undoubtedly lead to them drying up (Steven and Gunaratna 2004: 106). 'Some of the individuals about whom the strongest criminal cases could be made – because they have significant, known roles in the group – are, for the same reason, among the best sources of intelligence (as either witting informants or as people whose activities and contacts can be secretly monitored)' (Pillar 2001a: 84). In their opinion, therefore it is necessary to consider whether it is worth prosecuting a terrorist or whether it is better to guard one's intelligence sources in order to be able to prevent future attacks. Apart from the problematic collaboration between the judiciary and intelligence agencies, authors such as Martha Crenshaw (2001) believe that cooperation between different agencies in general is problematic due to internal disputes and power struggles.[6] In her view different agencies are often not willing to share information with other departments when the other department then receives the credit for the success. This is generally considered part of the nature of bureau-cracies where the individual agencies have to defend their realm of res-ponsibility as their budget and ultimately their existence and the jobs of its workers depend on their (perceived) value of their contributions. Bureaucracies are therefore often only interested in cooperating when it is in their short-term interest (Crenshaw 2001).

In addition, Tod Sandler (2003) argues that cooperation is made even more difficult by the fact that most attacks on western targets and the necessary planning by the groups' leaders occur abroad. He holds that this situation makes it hard for the perpetrators to be brought to justice quickly as governments have to then arrange for the suspects to be apprehended by their host nation and initiate extradition proceedings. And extraditions are considered to be very difficult even among the closest of allies, for example when the accused faces the possibility of the death sentence (Sandler 2003: 796). Although it is generally accepted that international cooperation is essential in fighting a 'new terrorism' which is global in scope and which makes use of many of the effects of globalisation such as cheap international travel, modern means of international communication and the global financial market, working together is said to be a difficult endeavour (Jenkins 2001; Cordesman 2006). And it is argued that international cooperation in the fight against 'new terrorism' is problematic due to the 'fact' that judicial standards and national legislations regulating a nation's criminal justice system and issues such as the arrest, interrogation and the prosecution of a suspect vary greatly from country to country (Bensahel 2006).

These problems of international cooperation are considered especially acute when it comes to cooperation between different national intelligence agencies as states still place great importance on their sovereignty and especially try to maintain autonomy over national security issues and the inherent sensitivity of intelligence poses a continuous problem (Aldrich 2004). Countries are said to still be concerned that information they share with their cooperation partners may accidentally or intentionally end up in the wrong hands. 'Foreign intelligence services may [...] be penetrated by third parties, who may share intelligence with terrorists and enable them to alter their plans accordingly' (Bensahel 2006: 40). Paul Wilkinson (2000: 196) points out that this is particularly problematic when we consider institutions such as Interpol where some of 'the states engaged in sponsoring terrorism belong to Interpol, and hence other states are reluctant to allow highly sensitive information into the Interpol network'.

International cooperation in other international institutions such as the United Nations is also thought to be difficult. Critics point out that even though the UN has more than thirteen different conventions and protocols relating to terrorism not all countries have signed and ratified them. They stress that there is no central authority which can enforce and guarantee conformity with these rules and regulations (Crelinsten 2000: 174). Sandler (2003) believes that these agreements had to be written in a vague manner in order to be globally accepted; they had to include loop holes to ensure the autonomy of every member. The central problem is considered to be that countries around the world perceive the threat of terrorism very differently. Some such as the United States, Great Britain or Germany are more concerned about a terrorist attack than others such as Jamaica, Lichtenstein or Vanuatu. This, together with the fear of attracting revenge attacks by terrorist organisations through international cooperation, indicates that they seemingly have less of an incentive to cooperate internationally especially if the cooperation involves costs for that country or is at odds with certain economic interests such as a booming financial sector due to favourable banking regulations. Therefore authors such as Heymann (2001/2001: 34) argue that some may therefore only cooperate half-heartedly and ineffectively 'but real enough to be indistinguishable from sanctionable incompetence'.

One prime example for international cooperation with regard to law and regulations has been the attempt to globally prevent the financing of terrorism.[7] The fight against 'new terrorism' has consistently been framed around the need to stop the financing of terrorism. This has generally taken the form suggested by the Financial Action Task Force and has included measures such as criminalising the financing of terrorism, freezing of suspected bank accounts, reporting suspicious transactions related to terrorism, promoting international cooperation among states regarding the financing of terrorism, as well as implementing a number of new banking regulations in order to track and identify the flow of money around the world.[8] One simple reason for this presented in the literature is the idea that terrorists need money to operate. Stopping or at least limiting their financial resources is thought to have a complicating effect on their ability to operate, organise and perpetrate terrorist attacks. Furthermore, authors such as Thomas Biersteker (2002) argue that by tracking the flow of such sources it should be possible to locate the true masterminds and possible state and non-state sponsors of 'new terrorism'. It is assumed that this, together with the general criminalisation of the financial support of terrorist groups can act as a deterrence for potential support (Levitt 2003: 63). Furthermore, once accounts have been frozen they could also be used to encourage support and collaboration of those who own the account in return for their money.[9]

Again the seemingly logical idea of fighting terrorist financing can be questioned. For example, one of the problems with combating the financing of 'new terrorism' is thought to be the difficulty of tracing the money for a number of reasons. Most importantly one has to note that the amounts involved are considered absolutely miniscule in relation to the trillions which flow through the international financial system every day (Navias 2002). Acts of terrorism are said to be very cheap. It is estimated that the truck bombing of the World Trade Center in 1993 cost only 400 dollars and 9/11, the largest terrorist attack ever, is said to have cost only between 300,000 and 500,000 dollars (Hoffman 1999; Levitt 2002). Others point out that this problem of tracking very small amounts of 'new terrorist' money is further compounded by the way these small amounts are transported from one place to another using alternative flexible financial channels. They argue that most of the 'new terrorist' financing does not flow through the normal international financial banking system but uses other means of storing, sending and receiving the money needed for maintaining terrorist cells and planning and perpetrating new terrorist attacks (Raphaeli 2003). These include informal financial networks such as *hawalas*[10] or other informal money-by-wire arrangements which allow the anonymous sending of money without precise documentation on identity or location. It has been estimated that *hawala* transactions involve billions of dollars (El-Qorchi 2002), for example it is thought that 2.5 to 3 billion dollars enter Pakistan alone through the *hawala* system every year compared to just one million through the normal formal financial channels (Wechsler 2001).

Apart from these informal channels it is also possible to consider the physical movement of currency as a way of providing 'new terrorist' cells with the financial means of carrying out attacks. As 'new terrorism' is so cheap the financial needs can easily be covered by the amount of cash a tourist, business man or other visitors can bring into a country without having to declare or report the money at customs (Basile 2004). In the case of the United States this amounts to 10,000 dollars[11], in Germany it is 10,000 Euros[12] and in the UK prior to 2007 there was no legal requirement to declare cash whatever the amount or currency.[13] Furthermore, some claim that terrorist groups have shifted some of their assets away from money and have now invested in commodities such as gold and precious stones especially diamonds which are even harder to trace and can also be physically brought over the border in the form of jewellery (Shultz and Vogt 2003b: 378).

In addition some argue that apart from the way of transferring funds from one place to another the actual sources of 'new terrorism' financing are very varied. Terrorist groups generally rely on a number of different financial sources and '[t]hese include a mixture of ideological, religious, criminal and business sources, which often mingle and merge, so that it becomes difficult to determine the provenance of any particular terrorist funds in any given case' (Winer and Roule 2002: 90). So funding is generally considered a combination of legal and illegal sources such as gifts and donations from rich individuals, supporters or Diaspora and charities, legitimate businesses as well as the sale of drugs, illegal trading with weapons and counterfeit goods and other trans-national criminal activities on top of the potential for state sponsorship of terrorism (Raphaeli 2003).

At the same time, states may not implement measures aimed at combating the financing of terrorism as vigorously as others due to their well-established privacy laws or their high economic dependence on their financial service sector and their role as a tax haven making money by providing financial privacy for their customers (Weintraub 2002). And even among states which agree on the importance of tackling the financing of terrorism there can be clear disagreements regarding the classification of groups linked with terrorism. 'Inconsistent definitions and regulations will naturally lead terrorist groups to reroute their finances through the most lenient countries, by passing the restrictions imposed by others' (Bensahel 2006: 38).

'No policy' policy and negotiating: An impossible option?

So while we can find arguments for and against the use of military or judicial policies to deal with 'new terrorism' other options are not really discussed as they remain outside of the option considered as a possibility by policy makers. One rarely comes across the policy suggestion of doing absolutely nothing about 'new terrorism'. As the predicate 'new' automatically makes it appear necessary to have 'new' counter-terrorism measures. If there is something new about terrorism today surely old anti-terror policies will not be enough to deal with such a threat. The idea of a 'new' kind of terrorism automatically makes it appear logical that something has to be done as the threat posed now is something not witnessed before. The construction of 'new terrorism' calls not only for something to be done, but this has to be something new as 'old' counter policies are implied to be incapable of dealing with the menace of 'new terrorism'. No policy maker or government talks about doing nothing against 'new terrorism' and even in academia the voices are marginalised (Mueller 2006). One does not often encounter the idea of doing nothing against terrorism in the literature and the usefulness or the uselessness of such an idea is not really seriously discussed. It does not fit into the 'new terrorism' discourse. Nevertheless, a concrete 'no-policy policy', 'where the declared policy is that there is no official anti-terrorist policy distinct from ordinary criminal justice policy', may be a possible option even against 'new terrorism' (Crelinsten and Schmid 1992: 323).

As Clark McCauley (1991: 137) points out 'doing nothing in response to a terrorist challenge might actually be the best policy'. Although this may seem absurd to us following the attacks of 9/11 and the idea of 'new terrorism, a 'no-response response' does warrant consideration to illustrate how the concept of 'new terrorism' limits what we consider as possible counter options. As McCauley (1991: 137) argues: 'Doing nothing also does not mean giving up on regular police and intelligence work under existing laws: it means doing nothing new, nothing different from what the same threat or violence would provoke if perpetrated by criminals without political purpose'. Although this policy is outside of the established counter-terrorism discourse, this seemingly nonsensical option could have a number of clear advantages. First of all one could argue that it prevents the political infighting and struggle about a new way of dealing with terrorism. Although this may seem a fairly minor point, disagreement about how to deal with terrorism can cause immense friction, especially among different countries when one decides to go to war with a terrorist organisation or limits civil liberties. Related to this a 'no-response response' may not have the same direct costs as many of the new counter-terrorism measures implemented to combat 'new terrorism'. A military campaign, the implementation of new laws and new security technology all involve the use of limited resources such as time, effort and money. A 'no-response response' saves the sometimes vast resources such new initiatives would require.

In addition to the loss of actual resources one may argue that such a response, or rather lack of response, avoids the possible loss of civil liberties and the restrictions of individual rights and freedoms which many of the new anti-terror policies mentioned above are said to entail. It would not directly undermine the democratic institutions and principles of the state. Similarly, there is no 'collateral damage'. It thereby may avoid one of the key problems of terrorism: the spiral of violence where one terrorist action leads to an over-reaction by the state which in turn legitimates the next terrorist action. Terrorist organisations thereby cannot gain more sympathy, support and recruits as a result of the states indiscriminate over-reaction. As Clark McCauley (1991: 138–139) points out, such a policy option 'seizes the moral high ground by recognizing that non-combatant victims of terrorist violence are martyrs for the legitimacy of the state in the same way that terrorists are martyrs against the state'. Importantly, a 'no-response response' could refuse a central reason for terrorism: recognition. One may hold that not doing anything deprives the terror group of recognition as an enemy as any government action in response to terrorism confers a certain status to the responsible group. As Jarrold Post (2008) points out, recognition is not only an important source of identity and self-esteem for the individual member, but is also essential for the group to gain sympathy, supporters and new members.

Similar to the idea of a 'no-response response', the suggestion of negotiating with and accommodating 'new terrorists' is not considered as an option. Considering the fanatical and religious nature of 'new terrorism', some point out that 'appeasing al-Qaeda is difficult in theory and impossible in practice' (Byman 2003c: 147). In general negotiations with and concessions to 'new terrorist' are considered to be highly problematic. As Peter Neumann (2007: 128) points out: 'The argument against negotiating with terrorists is simple: Democracies must never give in to violence, and terrorists must never be rewarded for using it', as addressing grievances and proposing concession to terrorist groups can send the message that terrorism works. Talking to a terrorist group automatically involves a form of recognition. '[A]ny type of parley invariably suggests that the terrorist group has been implicitly recognised by the government as a valid negotiating partner' (Reinares 1998: 356). Negotiations and concessions can be interpreted as a victory or a reward for those who threaten terrorism, thereby creating incentives for further terrorism (Clutterbuck 1992). So, although negotiations and concessions can in short term alleviate for example a hostage situation, they are also considered in the long run to encourage the perpetrator and others with similar interests to use more terrorism and violence in the future (Sederberg 1995: 299).

Talking to terrorist groups is considered a political risk which can lead to political embarrassment or even the loss of government legitimacy. A number of scholars argue that if democratically elected governments allow political change because of violent terrorist acts or the threat of such acts by minorities they risk losing their intended purpose of representing its majority voters. Negotiations with and concessions to terrorists discredit those who use peaceful constitutionally acceptable means of achieving their political goals. If a well-armed minority willing to use terrorism can impose its will on the majority then the legitimacy of the elected government will undoubtedly suffer (Reinares 1998: 356). At the same time others point out that it will reduce the motivation in the majority population to deal with real social grievances (Heymann 2001/2002: 28). Similarly, while negotiations and concession can be seen as a weakness of the government, the refusal of such policies can be considered a sign of strength (Reinares 1998). The idea is that by denying negotiations and concessions and refusing to address the grievances of the group terrorists have no incentive for further violence. By not engaging with terrorists the government can send the message that terrorism does not work. In other words terrorism becomes pointless as it fails to achieve anything (Netanyahu 1995).

Apart from this Navin Bapat (2006: 214) points outs that '[t]he central obstacle to negotiation between target and terrorists is the perceived inability of terrorists to form credible commitments'. There is a concrete lack of trust as there is no way of enforcing and punishing defection from the negotiated agreements. 'New terrorist' groups face no costs for breaking the agreed commitments as they are outside of any institutional control mechanism (Leeds 1999). After all terrorists groups could be simply using the time spent negotiating to rearm or reorganise themselves for the next wave of terrorist violence. 'Buying time in the face of an aggressive government counter-terrorism campaign can be immensely valuable to them' (Byman 2006: 408). And even if the 'new terrorist' leadership do intend to stick to their negotiated agreements one can argue that it is not clear how much control they have of the group and whether the rank and file of the organisation will follow their orders. So negotiations could lead to an internal spilt within the terror group and result in the creation of a new more radical terrorist organisation. So the network like structure of 'new terrorism' automatically excludes negotiations and talks with terrorists as it is unclear who to talk to. With the absence of a hierarchical structure and a clear leadership which is able to talk with one voice for the organisation negotiations seems impossible (Toros 2008a).

One of the most important reasons why negotiations with 'new terrorists' are considered absurd is the lack of negotiable political motives. As Fernando Reinares (1998) points out, the terrorists' aims and ambitions are not necessarily always explicit and even those demands which are articulate often appear far too vague. They are 'emotionally charged enough to serve as the raw material for slogans, but not a basis for serious transactions' (Reinares 1998: 355). Even if 'new terrorists' do have political demands, they are considered to go beyond acceptable reform and are not a realistic option for government as they are simply too extreme to accommodate (Gurr 2003). Zartman (2003) argues that fanatical 'new' or what he calls absolute terrorists are beyond negotiation and impervious to political argument as they have nothing to negotiate about. 'It is not only the suicidal tactics, but the unlimited cause that makes for truly absolute terrorism. When the cause is world social and political revolution, it becomes an unattainable millennial dream used to justify total indiscriminate tactics' (Zartman 2003: 444). For example, democratic governments cannot remove certain ethnicities from the country, eliminate a certain state, stop western cultural influences or impose a certain religious faith on all of its population.

Although addressing the root causes of terrorism is generally considered to be a good idea in the media, a number of scholars in Terrorism Research have pointed out that it is actually very difficult to establish a concrete link between a root cause and the act of terrorism, as grievances that fuel terrorism are generally multi-causal rather than deriving from just on issue (c.f. Ross 1993; Crenshaw 1981). They argue that the pursuit of terrorism may not only be down to political grievances but serve some other purposes such as a purpose in life, a feeling of importance and power, a certain exciting lifestyle or even boredom (Post 2008). If terrorism is the only thing members of such groups have learnt, finding alternative occupations once the struggle is over will be difficult (Horgan 2005; Crenshaw 2000). Not only are cause-and-effect relationships difficult to prove in their opinion, but it is important to note that social grievances are constantly changing and are a dynamic evolving factor (Pillar 2001a: 30). Authors such as Laqueur (2001a: 119) stress that one must consider that resolving one grievance can create new ones. So while concession to a terrorist group can reduce their use of violence it can provoke new violence from the now disaffected members of society. As Todd Sandler (2003: 793–794) points out, 'efforts to rectify one social wrong do not eliminate new injustices tomorrow. In fact, tomorrow's injustice may stem from addressing yesterday's injustices'.

Especially 'new terrorists' are considered to be beyond negotiation and the idea of concessions is not considered an option. Not only is it difficult to talk to 'new terrorists' due to their clandestine network structure, but the lack of rational political demands makes negotiations nonsensical. As we have seen 'new terrorists' do not want a place at the negotiating table, they want to blow the table up. Therefore the possibility of negotiations and concessions are not debated and are sidelined as they do not fit into the constructed phenomenon of 'new terrorism'. Appeasement options do not make sense when the 'new terrorist' is so uncompromising and negotiations are pointless if these organisations do not have concrete 'rational' political motivations. In other words '[t]he ideology of the 'new terrorism' conjures up the terrorist threat as a force that cannot be bargained with' (Burnett and Whyte 2005: 14). So it has become almost 'conventional wisdom' that regimes should never bargain with terrorists (Sederberg 1995: 295). Although the usefulness of negotiations in a hostage taking situation is generally accepted if only to buy time and wear out the hostage takers, talking to terrorist organisations outside of these circumstances and giving in to their demands is considered a bad idea (Zartman 1990; Miller 1993; Kim 2008). Nevertheless, governments have in the past frequently abandoned this idea of no negotiations when confronted with 'old terrorists'. And some scholars point out that there are examples where negotiation has worked: for example the political-military wing of ETA (ETA-PM) in the early 1980s, the Fronte di Liberazione Naziunale di a Corsica (FLNC) in 1997 (Reinares 1998) and more recently the negotiated peace with the Provisional IRA in 2005. In fact one may argue that not talking to terrorists is also a risky business as a refusal to negotiate with a terrorist group can strengthen radical elements within the organisation by indicating that non-violent means of engagement offer no hope of success. A number of scholars have investigated this phenomenon of negotiations with terrorists and argue that the tough stance by the government of 'no negotiations with terrorists' fails to convince these groups that states will not in the end negotiate after all (Atkinson et al. 1987; Sandler and Scott 1987).

So maybe there is point in reflecting on the possibility of talking to 'new terrorists' which are not generally taken into consideration. But what are some of the possibilities and maybe even advantages of talking to 'new terrorists' such as al-Qaeda if we question the dominant construction of the phenomenon? There are only a handful of scholars who reflect on the possibility of negotiating with 'new terrorists'. According to Harmonie Toros (2008a) there are at least three different arguments for engagement with terrorists. Firstly and quite simply, negotiations can eliminate the reasons for terrorism by offering an alternative means of voicing the groups grievances. Taken to the extreme, if governments give terrorist groups exactly what they want they could eliminate the causal factors, grievances and perceived injustices and therefore the need for continuing terrorism (Crenshaw 1995: 23). Importantly, negotiations force the terrorist organisation to clearly articulate their demands and could therefore even serve intelligence purposes. 'Talks can provide additional information on a terrorist group's true priorities and on which members of its leadership have the most influence' (Byman 2006: 406). Some would argue that 'new terrorists' cannot articulate clear demands, as they lack such clear political motives. They do however not consider that this understanding not only reflects 'new terrorism' but also constitutes it as well. So we construct 'new terrorism' as something which cannot be negotiated with, without reflecting that this understanding and our resulting policy of not talking actively contributes to new terrorism 'being' non-negotiable. Maybe 'new terrorism' does not 'really' lack political demands but the understanding of it being beyond negotiations stops these demands from being articulated. The continuous refusal to negotiate with al-Qaeda upholds and strengthens our construction of a 'new terrorism' which lacks clear political demands.

Secondly, negotiations could encourage dissent and divisions within the terror organisation which could culminate in the group's implosion (Crenshaw 1991) or at least strengthen the more moderate faction of the group which favours non-violent means. Furthermore, talks aimed at addressing the perceived grievance for which the terror group is allegedly fighting can influence the group's constituents. If the group's violence persists, despite the government's attempt to address the group's grievance, it may lose support and sympathy. Getting the terrorist organisation directly involved in politics can damage the group's credibility and its image when it fails to produce the promised goods (Byman 2006: 405). It is possible that some of these policies would at least reduce the number of recruits of a terrorist group with specific grievances. Similarly, concessions could be used to prevent people who still are indifferent from growing sympathy for the group's cause and accepting the legitimacy of their grievance. At the same time passive supporters of the group are encouraged to defect and become indifferent or even supportive of the government (Sederberg 1995: 307).

Thirdly, Toros (2008a) points out that engagement could ultimately lead to the transformation of the terrorist group and the rejection of violence and the acceptance of non-violent political debate. 'In a mirror process to the naming-isolating-radicalizing process used by states against "terrorists", one can envisage the possibility of a negotiating-including-legitimizing process' (Toros 2008a: 415).

Conclusion

The chapter hopes to have given an insight into some of the counter-terrorism options which are considered as options against 'new terrorism'. These include both military and judicial means but exclude other options which do not fit into the construction of what 'new terrorism' is. The concept of 'new terrorism' automatically calls for new counter-terrorism measures. It is predicated to be 'new' and thereby it renders 'old' counter options outdated and inappropriate. In particular the characteristics of 'new terrorism' make both policy options of seeing terrorism as war and as crime viable considerations. Although there is a debate over which of these two options is the better suited for the task of defeating terrorism, it is only these two options which are considered appropriate.

As we have seen the characteristics of 'new terrorism' fit into both of these categories: war and crime. If we consider the excessive violence of 'new terrorism' and the possible threat of WMDs a military response becomes understandable as most people link a high number of deaths in a conflict to a concept of war. As Michael Stohl (2008: 12) points out, 'the 'new terrorism' argument has been used to justify many new counter-terrorism measures, many of which involve increasing levels of force based on the unproven arguments and assumptions that the 'new terrorists' are not interested in coercive bargaining or creating fear in the target population, but simply death and destruction'. If we consider the clandestine network structure, the more complex nature of their 'new terrorist' attacks and the fact that groups do not take credit anymore they are surely harder to investigate. Combine this with the idea that 'new terrorism' is partly funded by crime and it makes sense to call for laws assigning more intelligence and police powers to investigate such phenomena. While some characteristics of 'new terrorism' make some options seem more viable they also make other options appear nonsensical. For example the idea that 'new terrorism' is fanatical and religiously motivated and lacks clear political motivations makes negotiations absurd.

The following chapter will draw out some of the underlying problems of terrorism research which have so far been indicated in Chapters 1 and 2. It will do so by firstly addressing a question which naturally arises out of the first two chapters: How do we know if the new counter-terrorism policies designed to combat 'new terrorism' are working?

3
Materialist Terrorism Studies: Researching the Unresearchable?

> 'The general public and the political leadership tend to perceive the threat of terrorism as a greater problem than the available data would indicate' (Falkenrath 2001)

Having examined the characteristics of 'new terrorism' and analysed some of the resulting counter-terrorism possibilities, this chapter brings these two aspects together to illustrate some of the main problems of doing terrorism research. The chapter will outline what could be considered materialist terrorism research by firstly examining a question which naturally arises out of the first two chapters of the book and which features prominently in both politics and academia: Are the countermeasures designed to deal with 'new terrorism' effective? This question and the first part of the chapter, although interesting on its own, is meant to serve as an example to highlight and exemplify the difficulties materialist terrorism research is currently facing. It will first illustrate traditional materialist approaches to dealing with the question of counter-terrorism effectiveness and then highlight some of the inherent difficulties and weaknesses of such analysis. Following this, the second part of the chapter will continue to draw out and generalise some of the methodological problems terrorism research has when investigating the subject of terrorism. This will be divided into a section which examines traditional terrorism research and a section which investigates the recent rise of critical terrorism studies. Throughout, the chapter sets the stage for Chapter 4 and constructivist terrorism studies by illustrating that terrorism research, both traditional as well as critical, are fascinated with 'hard facts' and primary sources while they somewhat neglect or underplay the discursive phenomenon of terrorism and the implications of a 'new terrorist' which is socially constructed.

Measuring counter-terrorism effectiveness

One aspect which illustrates the problems of terrorism research very well is the question of whether any of the counter-terrorism measures mentioned in Chapter 2 are really effective against 'new terrorism' described in Chapter 1. One is left here with the problem of how to measure the effectiveness of counter-terrorism, a question which is clearly embedded in the wider debate among scholars, politicians and in the media on whether the United States and its allies are winning or losing the 'war on terrorism'. And surely this is an essential, policy relevant question. It is generally considered to be of utmost importance to identify good and bad counter-terrorism policies and establish which policies are actually working, especially when the inadequate measures of effectiveness can contribute to complacency, the wrong allocation of scarce resources and eventually to horrible surprises (Byman 2003a: 411). However, 'if we look for precise evaluations of the effectiveness of antiterrorist policies we find it is surprisingly thin on the ground' (Townshend 2002: 133). As Bruce Hoffman and Jennifer Morrison-Taw (2000: 3) point out, 'relatively little research has been devoted either to broad, systematic, comparative analyses or to developing a methodology to evaluate the success of these countermeasures and their relevance to other countries with similar problems'.

Materialist terrorism research

The United States and many of it allies have spent billions on counter-terrorism since the attacks of 9/11 and as we have seen exactly demarcating the policy area of counter-terrorism is difficult, as measures implemented in the name of fighting terrorism are very different.[1] It has been estimated that the money spent in the US on increased security measures in response to 9/11 by both the public and private sector will amount to roughly $72 billion per year (Hobijn 2002). Official government figures point out that, between the fiscal years 2002 and 2005, US funding for homeland security increased by 39 per cent from $33 billion in 2002 to $46 billion in 2005. For the fiscal year 2006, President George Bush requested nearly $50 billion for activities associated with homeland security excluding direct military action.[2] Similarly Germany decided to spend an additional $1.5 billion on counter-terrorism shortly after 9/11 and the United Kingdom has since spent more than $10 billion on fighting terrorism (Haubrich 2006: 415–416).

Democratic governments around the world are generally required to justify their spending to their citizens. As with many other policies, bureaucracies and government agencies are held accountable for the cost-effectiveness of their expenditure. For example, in the US the Government Performance Results Act of 1993 calls for agencies to provide 'assessment of the results of a program activity compared to its intended purpose' in a quantitative or qualitative manner. In other words they have to give evidence of their performance and measure their progress against their aims.[3] Similar laws exist in most other democratic states and in response governments and the respective agencies involved in combating terrorism try to provide evidence of their measurable and effective progress.

Traditionally, governments and their agencies have often used simple material indicators to highlight 'success' in the 'war on terrorism', such as the number of attacks and casualties, arrested leaders, killed terrorists or the amount of terrorist money which has been frozen since 9/11 (Pillar 2001a: 80). The US government has repeatedly highlighted that it has killed or captured two-thirds of al-Qaeda's top leadership and has frozen over $200 million of terrorist financing.[4] By September 2004 it had charged 350 individuals with terrorism related charges and convicted over 185 people. It has disrupted alleged terrorist cells in New York, Washington, Oregon, North Virginia, North Carolina, and Florida. Furthermore, its military campaigns and the toppling of the regimes in Afghanistan and Iraq are presented as measures of success in the war on terrorism.[5] At the same time it is possible to point to terrorist attacks, which were aborted or intercepted due to the counter-terrorism work of governments, as a measurement of counter-terrorist effectiveness. These have included the botched bombing of a US airline by the Shoe Bomber Richard Reid in December 2001, the foiling of an attempted truck bomb attack in Singapore aimed at embassies, the airport and financial district, or the failed effort to bomb US embassies in Rome and Paris (Rogers 2003). George Bush in October 2005 declared that the US and its allies had stopped ten major attacks since 9/11, including attacks with hijacked aeroplanes in 2002 and 2003 (Sanger 2005; Kehaulani Goo 2005), and in the UK the mayor of London, Ken Livingston, reported that since 9/11 government authorities have foiled ten terrorist attacks on London alone (Milne 2005).

Parallel to government attempts to highlight the effect of their counter-terrorism measures, traditional terrorism research has also tried to deal with the topic of measuring effectiveness. Some point out that the number of fatalities generally give a good impression of the success of terrorist activities and is therefore a good way of assessing the effectiveness of counter-terrorism measures (Morag 2005: 310). Other scholars such as

Jonathan Stevenson believe that the effectiveness of counter-terrorist measures and the victory in the war on terrorism 'is likely to reveal itself over time as a negative – the relative absence of terrorism – gradually confirmed by an increase in arrests and convictions and by more probative intelligence' (Stevenson 2004: 92).

Nevertheless there seems to be a gap in the literature as there 'is almost a complete absence of high quality scientific evaluation evidence on counter-terrorism strategies' (Lum et al. 2006: ii). A 'concrete methodology for studying a state's ability to cope with wide-scale terrorism remains to be developed' (Morag 2005: 308). Those who have attempted to assess the effectiveness of counter-terrorism measures have done so predominantly by using time-series and intervention analysis. They believe that a successful counter-terrorism measure reduces the amount of terrorist violence and therefore that, if the level of terrorist incidents is plotted over time and against some policy indicators, it is possible to see whether the measure is effective or not (Hewitt 1984: xii). The central argument in other words, is that certain effective counter-terrorist policies will produce a change in the terrorist's modus operandi, which will be visible in the pattern of incidences. Here it is assumed that terrorists groups act in a rational materialist way; that they reflect and substitute certain types of action with others when faced with excessive difficulties. They believe terrorists to be rational actors and place great emphasis on them being a 'homos economicus'. Terrorists have a certain limited budget and try to maximise the effect of their resources. Measures taken to raise the cost of certain types of terrorist activities lead terrorists to use other types of tactics where costs have not risen (Sandler and Enders 2007).

One of the first studies to use economics in the analysis of counter-terrorist measures was conducted by William M. Landes, who in 1978 used ordinary least squares regression techniques to examine the aircraft hijackings in the US during 1961–1976. He showed with econometric methods that the use of sky marshals and metal detectors had had a significant positive effect on the probability of apprehension and a significant negative influence on the number of offences committed. The data indicated a steep drop in skyjackings after these security measures became operational in January 1973. In the US, there were 27 incidents of skyjackings in 1972 and only one in 1973 (Landes 1978). Other studies with a similar materialist understanding of terrorism which have also used economic calculations to measure effectiveness include Jon Cauley and Eric Im's (1988) use of intervention or interrupted time series analysis to evaluate the impact of metal detectors, fortified embassies and the UN convention on preventing attacks on protected persons; Walter Enders, Todd Sandler and Jon Cauley's (1990) examination of UN conventions and international responses to hijackings using a refined application of intervention analysis; and Bryan Brophy-Baermann and John Conybeare's (1994) paper on short- and long-term effects of Israeli retaliation attacks. Other studies include the evaluation of US air raids on Libya and their effectiveness against terrorism by Henry Prunckun and Philip Mohr (1996), and the intervention analysis of Basque terrorism in Spain by Carlos Pestana Barros (2003), which evaluates the effectiveness of policies against ETA using time series data from 1968 to 2000. More recently, Asaf and Noam Zussman (2005)[6] have evaluated the effectiveness of counter-terrorism policies by examining Israeli targeted assassinations of terrorists and the reaction of this on the Israeli stock market and Benjamin Zycher (2003) examines counter-terrorism policies in a benefit/cost framework on the basis of moderate, severe and nuclear terrorist attack scenarios in the United States.[7]

One of the most famous rational materialist econometric assessments of the effectiveness of counter-terrorism measures, however, is Walter Enders and Todd Sandler's (1993) vector-autoregession-intervention analysis. Enders and Sandler examined a number of counter-terrorism measures, including retaliatory raids, fortification of embassies, metal detectors and anti-terrorism laws. Their idea is that terrorists act according to a consumer-choice model, where they 'maximize utility or expected utility obtained from the consumption of basic commodities, produced from terrorist and non-terrorist activities' (Sandler and Enders 2004: 311). One type of terrorist action can be substituted with an alternative kind of attack if it creates the same basic commodities. To turn out these basic commodities, terrorists have to select between terrorist and non-terrorist actions, while having to deal with only limited resources. If they choose to follow the violent terrorist route they have to decide what kind of attack they want to perpetrate. Enders and Sandler (2005) point out that each type of attack has a 'price' that depends on how much time is involved to plan and execute the attack, the resources needed and the likelihood of the attack being successful. This again all depends on what the target is, the level of violence sought and where the attack will take place and what security measures are in place there. So the 9/11 attacks had a higher per-unit price than the London tube bombings because more resources were needed, the location was better protected and the target was more significant. The price of a certain terrorist attack depends highly on the resources governments have implemented to stop such an attack. Therefore, Enders and Sandler highlight that if one wants to assess the effectiveness of counter-terrorism policies, it is important to take into account the possible substitution of attack types due to this 'price' rise (Sandler and Enders 2005).

Problems for materialism in terrorism research

A materialist approach to establishing counter-terrorism effectiveness faces three interrelated difficulties: *how* and *what* kind of data should one gather and how could one *interpret* this data for the purpose of evaluating counter-terrorism. Governments, and until very recently terrorism research, have predominantly focused on hard quantitative data and thereby ignored many of the qualitative aspects. Success in counter-terrorism was generally expressed with the help of indicators which were easily accessible and quantifiable. For example, government officials have pointed to the decline of the number of terrorist incidents as a sign of a successful campaign against terrorism. This was the case in press conferences for the publication of the US State Department's annual report *Patterns of Global Terrorism 2003*.[8] It was announced that the number of terrorist attacks had fallen and that this was a clear indicator that the United States was winning the 'war on terrorism'. Regardless that this proved to be wrong due to a statistical error in their calculations and that the number of attacks actually was higher than in the previous year, thereby according to their logic indicating the failure of their policies, the number of terrorist incidents can say little about the effectiveness of existing counter-terrorism measures. There are many different reasons for why the numbers of incidents can decrease. For example, terrorists may be saving up their resources for a devastating attack, trying to give governments a false sense of security and aiming to encourage complacency, reduce their vigilance and thereby increasing the government's vulnerability. They may also be in a phase of recruiting and training new members or buying new weapons to strike another day. At the same time a terrorist group which is actually in decline may opt to attack more frequently and more violently in order to prove to governments, supporters and the general public that they remain a force to be reckoned with, despite these attacks really representing the last twitches of a dying organisation (Probst 2005: 318).

Similarly, when considering for example the terrorist 'body count' as an indicator of an effective counter-terrorism measure, one has to keep in mind that the overall size of a terrorist group is often unknown and many of those captured or killed are low-level recruits who can be replaced easily. Even, when one is able to eliminate two-thirds of the top leadership, the rank and file of the group may grow, and as a result decentralise and become more resilient. Indeed, a terrorist group that loses members to arrest or targeted killings may actually increase in overall size if the crackdown generates a backlash. For example, the Provisional IRA capitalised on indiscriminate British crackdown to gain recruits (Pillar 2001a: 217–235). In fact, measuring terrorism with numbers or statistics may be to a certain extent contradictory. Statistics are supposed to give an insight into general trends and patterns. However, the rare, random-like and uneven nature of terrorism and the fluctuation of incidents run counter to the idea of trends and patterns, something that might have been realised by the US government when it renamed its annual publication *Patterns of Global Terrorism* to *Country Reports on Terrorism*. Although governments often proclaim the effectiveness of their policies in the absence of further attacks and it may seem logical to consider a decrease in terrorist activity as an indicator of effective counter-terrorism, the asymmetric non-linear nature of terrorism, which aims to surprise its victims, can mean that terrorists are bidding their time and preparing for a bigger more devastating attack. If a large attack happens in one country, as was the case with 9/11, the Madrid and London bombings, 'although there have been none of that magnitude in preceding or later years, a time series based on the number of incidents is of little value' (Frey and Luechinger 2003: 4).

The determination to measure success in a quantitative numerical form is further undermined by the difficulty of gathering statistics and figures on terrorism. For example, the organisations and governments collecting the data have different definitions of what constitutes terrorism, making consistent counting impossible. Government figures are considered biased as they count incidents using a definition of terrorism which reflect their political ideals and policy concerns, while non-governmental organisations generally have to use media reports to compile their databases, therefore only including incidents which make it into the mainstream news (LaFree and Dugan 2007; Ellis 2008). For this reason most domestic terrorism in countries such as Sierra Leone, Sri Lanka, Algeria or Colombia are ignored or reported very unevenly. At the same time it is difficult to judge whether an attack can be attributed to terrorism or whether it is part of a continuing civil war in the country (Crenshaw 1992: 4). Most databases are incomplete with gaps and cover different time periods, and some even change their criteria for counting terrorist incidents halfway through.[9] For example, the MIPT Terrorism Knowledge Base covers international terrorism incidents from 1968 to 1997 and from 1998 it claims to include international and domestic incidents.[10]

This, together with the rareness of terrorism incidents, makes the use of risk management or cost benefit calculations awkward. While the number of other social phenomenon such as crime are high and their occurrence is fairly frequent, incidents of terrorism, especially large attacks, are in comparison very rare. Richard Falkenrath (2001) believes that data on terrorism is not really appropriate for quantitative analysis, on which risk assessments predominantly rely. Apart from the limited poor quality data on terrorism, one of the main problems is that the 'probability' variable in the risk calculation is extremely difficult to measure. Terrorism is not a random phenomenon. Unlike other traditional subjects dealt with in risk management such as natural disasters, accidents or public health, terrorism is less prone to conforming to statistical patterns. Terrorism is caused by humans and they decide when and how to attack. This decision is not made randomly but is made after careful but subjective consideration and depends on, and is influenced by, interpretations of external factors such as government decisions and actions. Terrorists attack deliberately in a form which does not conform to a pattern in order to surprise the opponent. As Falkenrath (2001: 175) points out '[m]ost estimates of the probability of an event are based on some understanding of their past frequency. Simple applications of this frequency theory of probability can fail spectacularly when the possible event has occurred only rarely or never at all'.

Even if probability and risk could be calculated, the cost benefit calculation of reducing the risk of terrorism faces grave difficulties. Although one can calculate the direct cost of certain anti-terrorist policies such as new x-ray machines or explosive detectors at airports, there are a number of hidden costs such as the value of the lost time of travelers (Frey and Luechinger 2004). Roger Congleton (2002: 62) has calculated that if each airplane passenger in the US spends half an hour longer at the airport due to increased security measures, the hidden cost of these measures would be around $15 billion per year. On the benefit side, calculations are even more difficult and more issues have to be taken into consideration. As Sandler and Enders (2004: 314) point out, one way to estimate a portion of this benefit would be to calculate the reduced loss of life attributable to airport security measures – for example fewer people killed in skyjackings and bombings. If the net number of such lives saved, after adjusting for substitution into other life-threatening terrorist actions, can be measured, then the average value of a statistical life, although morally highly questionable, could be applied to translate these lives into monetary value. One would have to also add the reduced financial losses in the form of destroyed planes and buildings as well as other even further removed considerations, such as the recession in the airline industry and increased insurance premiums to name but a few. All of these financial values face great measurement difficulties as 'it is difficult to confirm the absence of an occurrence and assign causality to that absence' (Malvesti 2002: 20). We can only really guess the number of terrorist attacks that are prevented by counter-terrorist measures. Some have argued that in order to tackle a question like this, one would have to set up two worlds, one in which nothing is done to combat terrorism and one where measures against it have been implemented. Furthermore, in order to find out exactly which measures are effective, one would have to create a large number of different worlds where only one counter-measure as well as a large number of combinations of measures would be tested (Tudge 2004). 'What seems to transpire [...] is that in securing a country against global terrorism, efficiency metrics such as 'number of lives saved' or 'cost per life saved' are not adequate to assess the priority of one policy option over another' (Haubrich 2006: 419).

A far larger problem of counting for terrorism research is the fact that only a few hundred people are generally killed each year by international terrorism. A number of scholars have pointed out that more people in the West are killed by lightning, accidents caused by deer, allergic reactions to peanuts or drowned in the bath and toilet than are killed by terrorism (Mueller 2005a; Hardin 2004). And it is clear that compared to fatalities due to war, heart and lung disease, cancer or simple traffic accidents, the number of direct terrorist victims seems minuscule (Schneider 2003; Mueller 2006). The US alone suffers around 40,000 fatalities each year through traffic accidents and worldwide there are around 1.2 million people killed in traffic each year (World Health Organization 2004). 9/11 killed around the same number of people that die in traffic accidents around the world every day. There are clearly many other more acute things people should 'rationally' worry about than terrorism (Jackson 2005; Mueller 2007). This is highlighted by Benjamin Friedman (2004: 33), who argues that telling 'Kansan truck drivers to prepare for nuclear terrorism is like telling bullfighters to watch out for lighting. It should not be their primary safety concern'.

The materialist approaches mentioned above seem to neglect the idea that for terrorism violence is only the means to the end of spreading the psychological effect of fear. And fear can be considered one of the main components of terrorism (Altheide 2006). The risk of directly being the victim of a terrorist attack is tiny; coconuts falling from trees kill more people each year (Mueller 2005b: 525). The perception of threat, or risk, and any resulting fear from such perceptions, bears no relation to what

Table 3.1   The ten leading causes of death in the US in 2001

Causes of death	Deaths	Percentage of total deaths
All Causes	2,416,425	100.0
1. Diseases of heart	700,142	29.0
2. Malignant neoplasms	553,768	22.9
3. Cerebrovascular diseases	163,538	6.8
4. Chronic lower respiratory diseases	123,013	5.1
5. Accidents	101,537	4.2
6. Diabetes mellitus	71,372	3.0
7. Influenza and pneumonia	62,034	2.6
8. Alzheimer's disease	53,852	2.2
9. Nephritis, nephrotic syndrome and nephrosis	39,480	1.6
10. Septicemia	32,238	1.3
Terrorism	Aprox.3000	0.12

Data taken from Anderson and Smith 2005

rationalists would consider to be the 'actual risk' as the 'general public and the political leadership tend to perceive the threat of terrorism as a greater problem than the available data would indicate' (Falkenrath 2001: 170). For scholars in the field of risk perception the question of why people fear terrorism more than, for example, cancer is nothing new and it generally acknowledged that this 'false sense of insecurity' (Wenar cited in Mueller 2005c) constitutes natural human behaviour. There is a sometimes very wide disparity between the public perception of risk and the risk indicated by the statistics compiled by experts. The reaction to dangers does not seem to match the numerical odds.[11] This perceived threat and fear of terrorism is reflected for example in the reduced number of people flying following 9/11. To illustrate this perception of risk more graphically, Michael Sivak and Michael Flannangan (2003) have calculated the probability of being killed in a domestic US non-stop flight in a major US airline, in a ten-year period, as about eight in one hundred million. At the same time, the probability of being killed while driving on a rural interstate highway in 2000 was about 4 in a billion per kilometre. From this they conclude that driving the distance of an average US domestic flight is 65 times more risky than flying, and for flying to become as risky as driving, airplane disasters on the scale of 9/11 would have to happen once a month.

This section hopes to have shown that 'measuring the effectiveness of combating terrorism is a thorny issue' (Ross 2006: 204) as methodological problems persist and social and qualitative aspects of terrorism appear to be sidelined. The unsatisfactory materialist answer often given highlights the number of attacks and casualties or looks at the quantity of arrested or killed terrorists (Pillar 2001a: 217–235). However, different to a traditional military campaign, there is no enemy capital to take over or industry to destroy (Byman 2003b). Though this measure of success may be appealing and easy, a 'body-count' or 'number of incident' approach ignores one of the key social components of terrorism: fear. Realising this neglect a materialist approach may now attempt to measure fear and suggest that counter-terrorism is effective when it reduces the level of fear of terrorism. So far fear has not been an issue in measuring the effectiveness of counter-terrorism measures but some rationalists would argue that one has to realise that not only those killed are victims of terrorism, but those who fear it as well (Friedman 2004: 29). Fear in a society is a real cost as people stop flying, avoid large gatherings, and spend time and money to reduce their anxiety. If fear is one of the main components of terrorism, should not the effectiveness of counter-terrorism measures also be assessed by the level of fear they reduce? The obvious problem one faces is how to 'measure' or gauge fear. Considering that the rationalist economic measurements have difficulties, sociological and psychological empirical measurements will seem even less exact. Estimating the feeling of fear in a society and of individuals due to terrorism seems impossible. 'A special difficulty here consists in the problem of quantifying and monetizing fear and its consequences, a problem that has yet to be seriously engaged in the relevant literature' (Sunstein 2003: 132–133).

The methods of studying terrorism

The difficulties of establishing the effectiveness of counter-terrorism are indicative of an underlying and larger methodological problem of studying terrorism. The next two sections want to outline these problems in more detail and indicate how both traditional terrorism research and critical terrorism studies propose to solve these methodological difficulties which hamper their field of enquiry. They will both offer their perspectives on what they consider to be the appropriate methods of 'good' terrorism research.

Traditional terrorism research

As we have seen a vast number of books and a lot of research has been conducted on the issue of terrorism and counter-terrorism, but how

does one evaluate good, bad and ugly terrorism research? As Michel
Wieviorka (1995: 597) points out, for a long time '[b]ooks and articles by
self-appointed experts on this subject were far from brilliant. The best
studies were usually written by journalists, not by social scientists. Most
analyses were superficial and ideological'. More recently, Marc Sageman
(2008: 14) asserted that 'most terrorism experts come from the fields of
journalism or intelligence analysis, have never taken an introductory
course in social science methodology, and lack a basic understanding of
the scientific method'. A large number of scholars point out that this
weak and unscientific methodology is clearly visible in the concrete lack
of primary source research, which many would regard as an essential part
of political science or really any science (Schmid and Jongman 1988;
Merari 1991; Sinai 2007; Silke 2001, 2007; Weinberg and Eubank 2008).
They would consider first-hand, face-to-face investigations as essential
for any scientific and objective investigation of the nature of the terrorists and their organisations. Even prior to the rise of the 'new terrorism'
debate scholars in the 1980s noted that '[w]ith a few clusters of exceptions there is, in fact, a disturbing lack of good empirically-grounded
research on terrorism' (Gurr 1988: 116).

Prior to 9/11 only around 11 per cent of all articles published in the
main terrorism journals between 1990 and 1999 contained significant
amounts of primary source interviews as the vast majority relied on secondary information (Silke 2004b). As another leading terrorism scholar
argues: 'The pre-9/11 literature on terrorism has been criticized for its
over-reliance on recycled secondary sources and for academics being
ensconced in ivory towers, instead of field research and talking to actual
terrorists' (Ranstorp 2009: 17). Some even go as far as claiming that
'*not* talking to terrorists seems to have become established as source of
scholarly credibility [... and that] terrorism studies seems to have placed
a premium on *avoiding* first-hand contact with the subjects of their
research' (Brannan et al. 2001: 7, emphasis in original). But even after
9/11 and the vast increase in the terrorism research being conducted the
situation remains the same as '[p]rimary source material is seldom examined and cited, defying the most basic tenet of social science research'
(Schulze 2004: 163; Horgan 2004). As Marc Sageman points out, 'there
is no substitute for careful scrutiny of primary sources, field research,
and analysis of court documents (in which suspected terrorists challenge
government claims)' (Sageman and Hoffman 2008). Brian Jenkins (cited
in Hoffman 2004: xviii) has compared terrorism researchers to 'Africa's
Victorian-era cartographers' who mapped the continent from afar without ever having seen it. So 'the field as a whole still suffers from a lack of

empiricism and remains too reliant on the regurgitation of existing material' (Fussey and Richards 2008). Similarly, Brendan O'Leary and Andrew Silke (2007: 393) point out that 'much of what is written about terrorism [...] is written by people who have never met a terrorist, or have never actually spent significant time on the ground in the areas most affected by conflict'.[12]

Actually, it is often very difficult to say whether scholars are conducting primary research or not, as they often fail to explain where they managed to get their information from. It is often down to the reader to accept the knowledge which is being presented as true without the possibility of verification. For example, one of the leading experts on 'new terrorism', Rohan Gunaratna (2003a, 2006), claims knowledge about the inside of al-Qaeda. Nevertheless, he fails to back up and reference many of his claims and where he does use references it is impossible to scientifically verify them. For example, one encounters rather comical footnotes which read: 'Interview, Al Qaeda member, March 2001' (Gunaratna 2003b: 50) or 'Interview, former Al Qaeda member, Europe, 2001' (Gunaratna 2003a: 334). Nevertheless, he is considered to be 'one of the few qualified to talk with authority about Al Qaeda'.[13] The privilege of inside-information has also been claimed by a vast number of other scholars who have done interviews with al-Qaeda members or associates (Bergen 2001; Fielding and Fouda 2003; Musharbash 2006), or even infiltrated the organisation (Sifaoui 2004; Nasiri 2008).

While some seem to have had access to al-Qaeda more directly, it is safe to assume that most of what has been written about this organisation draws uniquely on secondary material such as books written by others, media reports or intelligence information. The latter, in particular, are interesting, because in terrorism research they are often treated as if intelligence reports were primary material (c.f. Burke 2003; Gunaratna 2003a; Jacquard 2001; Koch 2005; Reeve 1999). Although the reports may be based on primary sources such as successful agent infiltration, the reports themselves are secondary information for scholars as they interpret other people's first-hand information. Taken one step further and considering that most intelligence is collected through informants rather than agent infiltration, this information can then really only be considered tertiary material. As Jeffrey Sluka (2009: 144) points out '[t]his is not objective social science, because no effort is made to establish the validity or verify the reliability of these mostly secondary data and interpretations received from 'official' sources which it would be naïve or biased to accept at face value as objective and reliable'. As Edna Reid (1993) argues, such second-hand research on 'new terrorism' has great implications: rather than providing new insights based on direct observation, this kind of research re-produces the views of others, wrong or false we do not know. This leads to a rather incestuous field of knowledge, where one scholar quotes the unverified views of another and thus contributes to the circulation of the ever-same 'facts' or rather beliefs about 'new terrorism'.

The reasons for these investigative difficulties (Silke 2004a; Ranstorp 2007a) and the lack of primary source enquiries are obvious: terrorists are generally considered to be violent, ruthless and dangerous, and therefore there is a certain level of risk for the safety of the researcher (White 2000; Ranstorp 2007b; Toros 2008b). 'Academic researchers have been threatened, kidnapped, attacked, shot and killed for attempting to research terrorism' (Silke 2004b: 189).[14] Not only does the researcher face the dangers of direct violence when suspected of spying for the government or collaborating with an illegal group, but things can get hairy when either party in the conflict considers the presentation of their side of the argument as unfavourable (Sluka 1995; Kovats-Bernat 2002). In addition, there is the danger of 'being unknowingly used as a pawn by governments monitoring armed groups' (Toros 2008b: 286) or simply being caught between the lines and ending up as a collateral damage statistic. Although this claim of personal risk has been disputed by some authors such as John Horgan (1997, 2008), the perceived threat and feeling of unease and nervousness when conducting interviews with members of a terrorist organisation must have a certain effect on the willingness of academics to conduct such research.

Another reason for the lack of primary research, as indicated in the first part of this chapter, is the fact that information on the 'real' nature of a terrorist organisation like al-Qaeda is hard to come by. The clandestine nature of terrorism makes access to it as a subject very difficult in any kind of systematic manner often associated with doing scientific research (Silke 2001: 2). Much of the information available on the issue provided either by intelligence sources or (former-)terrorist would not really meet what is considered to be a certain scientific standard of academic research. The possibility of verification, an aspect which is generally assumed to be of the utmost importance for establishing scientific knowledge and representativeness, is considered questionable. Some go as far as claiming that 'in situ studies of groups, structure and processes, for example, are inconceivable modes of research on terrorism' (Merari 1991: 89–90). Ariel Merari goes on to argue that even if you do conduct interviews with a captured or repentant terrorist, the conditions do not really 'represent the "normal" terrorists' habitat' and that he or she may not be a representative sample of the real terrorist group (Merari 1991). Hence, it is the characteristics of the research object that serve as an explanation for the failure to study it in a more direct way normally considered central to social scientific analyses. Still terrorism studies longs for primary source research and criticises the general heavy reliance in the terrorism literature on secondary data such as media reports. As Alex Schmid and Albert Jongman famously claimed in 1988: 'There is probably few areas in the social science literature in which so much is written on the basis of so little research' (Schmid and Jongman 1988: 177). Over twenty years later little seems to have changed and as John Horgan (2008: 73) points out that it 'is unfortunate that much academic research on terrorism, despite (or perhaps because of) its often prescriptive nature, remains often misinformed, skewed in nature but perhaps most significantly, often unsupported by empirical enquiry'. At the same time the critics question the neutrality and objectivity of many researchers. 'Terrorism itself is an emotive subject and researchers have traditionally not been overly concerned with remaining objective and neutral in how they view the subject and its perpetrators' (Silke 2001: 2). Andrew Silke (2001: 6) further criticises the use of the media in terrorism research as the 'media reports rarely aim to be entirely neutral on the subject'.

Critical terrorism studies

If primary sources really are that important and at the same time so difficult and dangerous to access, maybe there is not much to be expected from terrorism research. If only a small fraction of the research fulfils the field's self-proclaimed standards of quality, one is left with the question of whether the discipline overall has failed? In response to the many problems terrorism research is facing, a number of scholars have called for a 'critical turn' in terrorism studies (Gunning 2007a; Jackson 2007a; Jackson et al. 2009). Academics involved in this effort have organised a number of workshops and conference-panels, created a working group at the British International Studies Association,[15] and launched a new journal (*Critical Studies on Terrorism*) devoted to addressing many of the shortcomings of what they refer to as 'orthodox terrorism research'.

What are the main points of critique? First, the orthodoxy is criticised for treating terrorism in the form of al-Qaeda as a new phenomenon, i.e. for lacking sensitivity for terrorist experiences in other countries, contexts and time periods (Gunning 2007b; Breen Smyth 2007). Second, conventional terrorism studies is found to ignore research on terrorism in other fields such as anthropology, sociology, psychology and peace and conflict studies (Gunning 2007a).[16] Third, terrorism studies is said to be uncritical of the role of the state in perpetrating terrorism itself or at least contributing to the conditions which foster terrorism by non-state groups (Blakeley 2007). Some argue that this uncritical state perspective and the emphasis on state-centric security notions are partly due to the close connections between traditional terrorism research scholars and governments (Herman and O'Sullivan 1989; George 1991). Fourth, the orthodoxy is criticised for poor research methods and equally poor theoretical foundations (Blakeley 2007). If theory is used at all, it is informed by rationalism and positivism, while constructivism is virtually unheard of (Jackson 2007b). Fifth, conventional terrorism studies is criticised for producing only problem-solving theories, i.e. for treating terrorism as an objective problem which terrorism research should contribute to solve. This, as one of the main proponents of the critical turn suggests, disregards 'the extent to which the status quo – the hierarchies and operation of power and the inequalities and injustices thus generated – is implicated in the 'problem' of terrorism' (Jackson 2007b: 245).[17]

This critique is important and suggests the way forward for terrorism studies, which should become more historical, interdisciplinary, state-sceptical, theoretical, constructivist and reflexive. While in agreement with all of these points, there is a sixth point of critique which is not as convincing: Orthodox approaches are criticised for being over-reliant on secondary information instead of basing their research on primary sources (Jackson 2007b: 244). 'The most enduring of criticisms of the field is the accusation of the dearth of primary research and the resultant derivative nature of many research findings' (Breen Smyth 2009: 195). As Zulaika and Douglass (1996: 179) point out: 'One characteristic of the work of terrorism experts is the very prohibition upon personal discourse with its subject. Authors writing about terrorism must abide by this taboo. It is telling that one can claim expertise regarding 'terrorists' without ever having seen or talked to one'. Traditional terrorism research is criticised for being 'unreliable, invalid, biased, and propagandistic' as it 'simply does not fit the grounded reality of the political violence we have studied' (Sluka 2009: 139).

Critical Terrorism Studies believes that '[f]ieldwork can re-inject life into research on terrorism' (Toros 2008b: 286). Yet, this is hardly an original observation. Conventional scholars, as we have seen above, are well aware that a lack of first-hand information apparently hampers the quality of their work (Horgan and Boyle 2008; Weinberg and Eubank 2008). In fact, critical terrorism scholars sound very conventional when they claim that interviews with terrorists, for example, are pivotal to good scientific research (Gunning 2007a: 378), or when they concede that collecting primary data is difficult, but maintain that nonetheless these problems 'must be negotiated and overcome if the credibility of research is to be maintained' (Breen Smyth 2007: 262). They argue that primary research on terrorism in the form of interviews (Breen Smyth 2008; Jackson 2008b) or 'engagement with those involved in "terrorist" activity' is something of a taboo which needs to be overcome (Breen Smyth et al. 2008). In this respect critical terrorism studies believe that 'primary research is crucial, since it can expose the gaps in understanding, and the culture and political bias and misinterpretations in government, intelligence and media accounts' (Breen Smyth 2009: 195). In other words: 'Primary data is a crucial reality-check' (Breen Smyth 2009: 196).[18]

Admittedly, there are important differences between the advocated primary source research of critical and orthodox terrorism studies and the way they approach the terrorist actor. While the latter assumes that there is an objective truth about the terrorist that a neutral observer can find out, such epistemological assumptions are generally not to be found among the former. In fact, critical terrorism studies acknowledges the intersubjective and constructed nature of terrorism knowledge (Jackson 2007b). So while traditional terrorism research tries to establish for example the structure, strategies and financial means of terror organisations, critical terrorism studies is interested in the individual motivations and experiences of terrorists. In other words, they want to understand terrorist subjectivity, their mind-sets and world views, 'their humiliations and desires' (Zulaika and Douglass 2008: 32). They want more primary research because they want 'to learn about him or her' (Zulaika and Douglass 2008: 32). Against conventional scholars' objectivity and neutrality they put their own subjectivity and empathy. Yet, despite their differences, conventional and critical terrorism approach have one important commonality: They both put their analytical focus on the terrorist actor and primary sources. In both approaches primary information – talking to or doing fieldwork among terrorists – is assumed to enable scholars to better explain (conventional approaches) or understand (critical approaches) terrorism. Without denying that such work can prove fruitful, the next chapter will argue that such an approach ignores the discursive processes by which the terrorist is constituted in the first place.

Conclusion

As we have seen in the first part of this chapter terrorism research is faced with a number of difficulties: It is obsessed with numbers and 'hard facts' while it ignores the social aspects of terrorism. As Gary LaFree and Laura

Dugan note 'whether a case is classified as terrorism ultimately depends on a process of social construction. That terrorism is not simply "out there" to be counted in the same way that we might count rocks, trees, or plants' (LaFree and Dugan 2004: 55). While most of the other social sciences have come under the influence of constructivism, terrorism research has until recently remained a bastion of rational objectivism. The socially constructed nature of terrorism, visible for example in 'disproportionate' level of fear, has so far been ignored. The second part of the chapter has shown that there is not that much difference between critical and traditional terrorism studies when it comes to celebrating the importance of the terrorist actor and primary sources. Indeed, one can argue that critical terrorism scholars are also fascinated with getting first-hand information on the terrorist actor, while at the same time disregard the intrinsic value of secondary sources for the study of terrorism.

This poses a problem for the critical terrorism studies project, as the preference for primary sources seems to conflict with the call for a more reflexive and constructivist research agenda. It is difficult to call on the one hand for more reflection on how knowledge on the terrorist is being produced and at the same time argue that more first-hand information is needed (as if this was to bring us closer to the truth about the terrorist organisation). And it is tricky to call for a constructivist approach to terrorism – which would entail shifting the focus from the terrorist to the social construction of the terrorist – and still maintain that primary sources such as interviews are necessary. From a constructivist perspective, not the terrorist himself or herself is the primary source that can be studied, but the texts and practices which constitute the terrorist actor. As Wieviorka (1995) points out, 'the notion of terrorism can be seen as a social product: an image, psychological representation, or social conception. Accordingly, it is necessary to examine the processes whereby a society (or certain intellectual or political circles, for example) forms such an image'. The next chapter will examine what such a constructivist kind of terrorism research could look like by illustrating the importance of discourse and in particular the role of predicates and metaphors in the construction of 'new terrorism'.

4
Constructivist Terrorism Research: The Role of Discourse and Predication

'[W]e all make terrorism what (we say) it is' (Onuf 2009)

While over the last 20 years most of the social sciences, including International Relations, have come under the influence of constructivism, this (meta-)theoretical perspective seems to have passed Terrorism Research by. Terrorism Research does not seem bothered by the 'latest' developments in IR, nor does IR theory seem interested in the subject of terrorism.[1] This is a shame as both disciplines have something to offer to the other. While IR would gain insight into a subject which has recently dominated much of international politics, Terrorism Research would greatly gain from the theoretical understandings and insights of a discipline which has continuously struggled to explain political violence. Nevertheless, terrorism researchers seem comfortable in their small enclave devoid of political theory. They are concerned with questions such as: What is terrorism? What causes it? How is it organised and financed? What are its motives? They are predominantly interested in the terrorist actor, which may appear natural. Indeed, what should they investigate if not the terrorist (organisation)? And what better way to do it than having direct contact with the terrorist and reporting these primary observations? As we have seen first-hand information and primary sources are still thought to be the best way of doing research and accessing the truth about 'new terrorism' and groups such as al-Qaeda. This chapter wants to directly address this state of affairs by introducing theoretical ideas and questioning terrorism research's fascination with objectivism, primary sources and the terrorist actor. It will argue that the focus on the terrorist actor and the use of primary sources in terrorism research is maybe not the only way forward for terrorism studies. It will propose a constructivist terrorism research where terrorism and the terrorist are a social construction, hence a social fact produced in discourse.

As we saw in the last chapter, both conventional and more critical approaches regard direct access to 'the terrorist' as the gold standard of good terrorism research. Here, terrorism research bears a strong resemblance to cultural anthropology. Both seek to find out about people who seem to function according to a logic that escapes Western minds, who are difficult to access and possibly even dangerous to investigate. In anthropology, this has resulted in two kinds of academics: The first consists of adventurous scholars who live for months among their informants, thus being able to learn about their research objects directly. The second kind – sometimes dismissed as 'veranda anthropologists' (Malinowski 1959) – keeps a safe distance to its research objects, relies on secondary information rather than going native, and observes from afar. In terrorism research on al-Qaeda, the adventurous group of first-handers includes scholars such as Rohan Gunaratna (2003a, 2003b, 2006) and Bruce Hoffman (2003, 2004b), who among others (Della Porta 1995b; Coogan 1995; Bowyer-Bell 2000, Horgan 2005) have managed to get inside information on a terrorist organisation. While this research provides important and interesting interpretations of al-Qaeda, it suffers from a major weakness: the interpretations are presented as objective truth, as mimetic descriptions of what al-Qaeda is and correct explanations of what it does. Yet, in the light of a constructivist epistemology, this ignores the scholars' own role in the process of producing knowledge. Even researchers who have direct access to primary sources need to interpret those sources, as data does not speak for itself. What is more, when conducting interviews with members of al-Qaeda, scholars do not receive objective accounts but only specific interpretations of the phenomena in which they are interested. Hence, they are dealing not with the objective truth about al-Qaeda but with al-Qaeda members' discursive constructions of themselves. Scholars thus interpret interpretations.

In any case, as we have seen, most of what has been written on al-Qaeda and 'new terrorism' is based neither on interviews nor on field research conducted inside the organisation. Rather, it builds on less-direct information – it is 'veranda terrorism research'. Among the sources used are already existing studies of al-Qaeda, media information and intelligence reports. And obviously, this lack of primary research further aggravates the problem identified above, as it adds another layer of interpretation. Studies of this kind which predominantly use secondary information are interpretations of how others (e.g. intelligence staff or field-researching terrorism scholars) have interpreted al-Qaeda members' self-interpretation. And yet, despite these various filters, information in such studies is presented as though it provided objective accounts of the reality about al-Qaeda and the new terrorist actor (Zangl and Zürn 2003). Although Critical Terrorism Studies raises a number of important and valuable criticisms of the conventional approach, it does not sufficiently deal with terrorism research's major problem: its preoccupation with the terrorist actor and the use of primary sources. It wants to take the terrorist's subjectivity into account, but suggests that engagement with the terrorist actor as primary source is in fact the way forward (Jackson 2007a,b; Gunning 2007b; Breen Smyth 2007).[2] Without denying that such work can provide important and interesting insights, the next section will argue that it attributes too much importance to the terrorist actor and 'primary sources' while neglecting the discursive processes by which terrorism is constituted in the first place. This book does not by any means want to suggest that previous research both traditional and critical should be discarded or that it is inferior to a constructivist understanding of terrorism. The whole purpose of the following sections and chapters is to outline *a possible* rather than *the* alternative way of conducting terrorism research. If we accept that terrorist groups such as al-Qaeda are social constructs (Turk 2004: 271), which does not mean that they only exist in our heads, then the traditional kind of research 'Inside Al Qaeda' (Gunaratna 2003a) with all of its problems becomes just one interpretation among many. The chapter proposes that researchers, in addition to these 'objective' accounts, could analyse the social constructions and the discursive processes through which particular interpretations of al-Qaeda become common knowledge. So rather than looking directly at al-Qaeda this kind of research could examine those who are involved in the construction of al-Qaeda. This could be anybody who says or writes something about 'new terrorism' such as politicians, terrorism experts or the media.

The rest of the chapter will be structured as follows: The next section will very briefly introduce the reader to the idea of what constructivism as a (meta-) theoretical approach to International Relations is all about. The second part will illustrate what a constructivist terrorism research project might look like and what role discourse plays in such a study, while the third will be directly concerned with the methodology of metaphor analysis which is to be applied in Chapter 5.

A constructivist perspective on international politics

Nicholas Onuf (1989) was one of the first to introduce the term 'constructivism' to International Relations. Yet, it has to be made very clear that there is not one constructivism in IR and that there is generally no agreement on whether to refer to constructivism as a method, an approach or a theoretical orientation. What is clear is that constructivism is not a 'theory' to the same extent that neo-realism is a theory of IR. Rather, there is a vast number of different approaches which can be roughly classified as constructivist meta-theoretical approaches rather than a 'theory'. This does not make summarising the main aspects of 'constructivism' any easier. However, if one had to break down these approaches to a number of core assumptions one would probably mention the following.[3]

Firstly, while many other IR theories place emphasis on material aspects of international politics, constructivism is interested in social relations. Above all constructivism is a social 'theory'. 'Fundamental to constructivism is the proposition that human beings are social beings, and we would not be human but for our social relations. In other words, social relations *make* or *construct* people – *ourselves* – into the kind of beings that we are' (Onuf 1998: 59, emphasis in original). If there is such a thing as a central tenant of constructivism in IR it must be the understanding that international reality is a social construction. The social world of international politics is not a physical or material object as it does not exist on its own. The international system is constituted by ideas and not by material things; it is a set of understandings and meanings or a system of norms which has developed within a particular historical context. All kinds of relations between human beings, including international relations, are not the result of material conditions but consist of ideas and thoughts. Alexander Wendt (1992: 136–137) says 'a fundamental principle of constructivist social theory is that people act towards objects, including other actors, on the basis of the meaning that the objects have for them'. The social world is not part of nature. It does not follow natural laws equivalent to those of physics or biology. In a socially constructed world all social phenomena and relations depend on a web of meaning and practices which constitute them (Kratochwil 1989). Although these meanings and practices can be very stable, they are never permanent or fixed objects as they invariably change over time and space. It is important to consider that these ideas 'are embedded not only in human brains but also in the "collective memories," government procedures, educational systems, and the rhetoric of statecraft' (Legro 2005: 6). In other words they 'include ideas that are intersubjective (that is, shared among people) and institutionalized (that is, expressed as practices and identities)' (Hurd 2008: 301). So, in contrast to a materialist understanding, the social world is not a given. It does not exist outside of human thought and independently of people's ideas. However, as Kratochwil (2000: 91) notes, 'hardly anyone [...] doubts that the "world" exists "independently" from our minds. The question is rather whether we can recognize it in a pure and direct fashion [...] or whether what we recognize is always already organized and formed by certain categorical and theoretical elements'. It does not question the possibility of thought-independent existence of things but it does question their language-independent observation of these things. 'What counts as a socially meaningful object or event is always the result of an interpretive construction of the world out there' (Guzzini 2000: 159). Normative or ideational structures shape the behaviour of social and political actors such as individuals and states. Whereas neo-realists would emphasise the material structure and the distribution of capabilities, constructivists would generally argue that a system of shared ideas and values also has structural characteristics. This structure also has a huge influence on the actions of actors in the international system. As Wendt (1995: 73) points out 'material resources only acquire meaning for human action through the structure of shared knowledge in which they are embedded'. Mirroring Wendt's (1995) example of British and North Korean nuclear weapons, a purely materialist understanding of international politics would find it hard to explain why the possible acquisition of WMDs by al-Qaeda is considered more threatening than the existing WMDs of France or the UK.

Secondly, one should mention that in contrast to other IR theories and materialism, constructivism is often contrasted to rationalism. While rationalists consider actors to be rational entities who attempt to realise their interest and minimise their risk, constructivists believe that the identities of actors are constituted by the institutionalised ideas and norms of the social environment in which they exist and act. The identity of an actor is not a given, he or she can pursue his/her interests 'rationally' but does not have to. Rationalists hold that interests are exogenously determined prior to social interaction while constructivists believe that interests are endogenous to interaction. Interests here are the consequence of actors' identities. While rationalists would see society or international politics as a place in which to pursue their interests rationally, in other words as a strategic realm, constructivists consider it to be a constitutive realm in which actors are generated as social and political agents. In rationalism subjects are said to be guided by a logic of consequences in which rational actions are supposed to maximise the interests of the actor. In constructivism actors rather focus on what they consider to be legitimate behaviour, in conformity with norms and shared understandings. They are guided by a logic of appropriateness (March and Olson 1989).[4] So identities are a central aspect of constructivist IR theories. Constructivism considers these identities as fundamentally important as they inform interests and ultimately actions. As Wendt (1992: 397) points out, actors acquire identities through the participation in collective meaning. While rationalists consider interests to be exogenously determined, in other words they have a set of pre-existing preferences, constructivist are interested in how certain interests develop on the basis of certain identities. For them, '[i]dentities are the basis of interests' and it is essential to understand that 'actors acquire identities – relatively stable, role-specific understandings and expectations about self – by participating in ... collective meanings' (Wendt 1992: 397–398). Relating this back to the notion of terrorism one could point to the label of 'terrorist' as an example that norms or rather the breaking of norms has an influence on identity attributions. Furthermore, the idea that identities are not fixed but in constant flux may be visible in the transformation of illegitimate 'terrorists' such as Jassir Arafat, Gerry Adams or even Nelson Mandela to legitimate politicians.

Thirdly, constructivism generally assumes that structure (the institutions and collective meanings that make up the context of international actions), and agents (those who operate as actors in this context) are mutually constituted. In the case of terrorism, Onuf (2009: 54) points out that the 'co-constitution of agents and structures implies that we all make terrorism what (we say) it is'. In other words, the ideational structures condition the identities and therefore the interests of actors, but these structures would not exist if the actors did not act out the practices these structures prescribe in interaction with other actors. Institutionalised ideas 'define the meaning and identity of the individual actor and the patterns of appropriate economic, political, and cultural activity engaged in by those individuals' (Meyer et al. 1987: 12), and it 'is through reciprocal interaction that we create and instantiate the relatively enduring social structures in terms of which we define our identities and interests' (Wendt 1992: 406). The co-constitution of agents and structure in constructivism means that actions by actors contribute to the making of institutionalised ideas and norms of the international system, while these ideas and norms contribute to socialising, defining and influencing the actors in this system. 'Both the institutions and the actors can be redefined in the process' (Hurd 2008: 304). One could here consider the example of al-Qaeda not as an organisation but as an 'ideology' or rather an ideational structure which influences the behaviour of actors or 'members' within this structure while the behaviour and actions of these actors influence the ideational structure which is al-Qaeda.

Finally, in addition to this construction of reality on the ontological side one has to take note of the construction of knowledge on the epistemological side of International Relations. 'In a nutshell, constructivism, as understood here, is epistemologically about the social construction of knowledge, and ontologically about the construction of social reality' (Guzzini 2000: 160). And here one comes across a major dividing line in the approach between more moderate and radical proponents of constructivism which is clearly mirrored by continued controversy about the suitable methods of 'scientific' research in a socially constructed world (Checkel 1998; Adler 2002; Pouliot 2007; Lupovici 2009). Both moderate and more radical constructivists generally agree that the social world of international politics is not an external reality or something which exists independently of the ideas of actors involved in it, governing 'laws' of this world cannot be discovered and explained by positivist or behaviouralist scientific research or theory. As the social world is not part of nature and there are no natural laws of society or international politics, the study of international politics cannot be an objective 'science' in a positivist sense. Both are therefore sceptical about a final truth about the social world which continues to be true over time and space. Nevertheless, while more moderate constructivists do make 'truth claims about the subject they have investigated ... while admitting that their claims are always contingent and partial interpretations of a complex world' (Price and Reus-Smit 1998: 272), more radical scholars reject the idea of truth claims altogether. They would argue that there is no neutral ground on which to decide what is true and what is not. 'What we call truth is always connected to different, more or less dominant, ways of thinking about the world' (Jackson and Sørensen 2007: 167). In other words, the more moderate constructivist such as Wendt (1992, 1995, 1999) believe that the socially constructed international system has patterns which can be generalised and on which one can formulate falsifiable hypotheses. According to this point of view, there are underlying, generalisable rules which govern international relations and which can be identified through detailed scientific research. More radical constructivists hold a more post-positivist understanding and claim that the researcher cannot be fully autonomous and neutral to the subject of study. They are not so much interested in revealing these generalisations but in investigating how certain identities and with them how certain actions become possible and ultimately how these understandings become dominant through language (Fairclough 1992; Zehfuß 1998; Fierke 2007).

This book will follow this more radical constructivist understanding and in the next section explicitly address and give examples of the importance of language and the role of discourse in the construction of reality, knowledge and terrorism. As Onuf (1998: 59) points out, 'saying is doing: talking is undoubtedly the most important way that we go about making the world what it is'. Here social reality is considered a discursive construction, and the central task of research is to find out how reality gets constructed in discourse. In this view, '"things" do not have meaning in and of themselves, they only become meaningful in discourse' (Waever 2004: 198).

Constructivist terrorism studies and discourse analysis

Above, we have drawn a comparison between terrorism studies and cultural anthropology. Terrorism studies' natives are the terrorists, and its goal is to describe and explain a particular terrorist group's social structure, its culture and motivations, and last but not least its practices. As mentioned above, in terrorism studies (as in anthropology), fieldwork of some kind or another is considered the best method for achieving this goal and focusing on the terrorist himself or herself is the best way of finding out about an indigenous group of terrorists. This assumption explains the preoccupation with primary sources within terrorism studies. However, it is not quite correct that cultural anthropology still fancies primary sources above everything else. Against the background of a more general constructivist turn in the social sciences, Clifford and Marcus (1986) in the 1980s launched a powerful attack on cultural anthropology's traditional mode of inquiry, on the entire idea of finding out by going native. Instead, they argued for a more reflexive approach that inquires into the social production of the native, not least by anthropologists themselves. As a result, numerous studies have analysed how 'the other' has been constituted in Western academic (especially anthropologist), political and media discourses (Said 1979). This book suggests a similar shift of perspectives in terrorism studies. For such a shift to become possible, however, it is necessary first to accept that terrorism is a social construction, a discursive rather than a material fact. This does not mean that such a constructivist perspective denies the 'real' existence of 'new terrorism'. There are real people who conduct real actions, but what these people and their deeds mean is a matter of interpretation. And, it is this interpretation in discourse which constitutes a certain group of people as proponents of 'new terrorism'.

If terrorism is a social construction, the terrorist himself or herself does not have to be the primary source for terrorism scholars. The terrorist is a consequence of discourse and vice versa. Hence, the primary source of terrorism research can be the discourse in which the social construction of terrorism takes place, that is, the discourse that constitutes a particular group of people as 'terrorists'. In the case of al-Qaeda, for example, this would be the post-9/11 Western discourse on 'new terrorism'. Clearly, what members of al-Qaeda say, what they do, and how they present themselves feeds into this 'new terrorism' discourse, but it is always mediated by Western interpretations.[5] Of course the constructions of al-Qaeda in the Western terrorism discourse will not be disconnected from al-Qaeda itself, but the discourse certainly does not simply mirror any kind of 'reality' or 'truth' about the organisation. The discourse gives al-Qaeda's words and deeds a certain kind of meaning, and it is this meaning that constitutes our relevant reality. This is obvious if we consider counter-terrorism. Counter-terrorism policies are not based on objective knowledge about al-Qaeda, but rather on our understanding of al-Qaeda that has been produced in political, scientific and media discourse. Hence, any understanding of our counter-terrorism policies should take into account the discourse through which our understanding of al-Qaeda was constructed.

This book is by no means the first to advocate a constructivist approach to the study of terrorism. In fact, a constructivist understanding of terrorism seems fairly common in neighbouring disciplines such as sociology (e.g. Turk 2004) or psychology (e.g. Harré 2004). Yet, until quite recently, the field of terrorism studies itself remained remarkably untouched by the constructivist turn in the social sciences and has stuck to the idea that there is an objective reality of terrorism that terrorism studies needs to uncover. Critical terrorism scholars seem to be in agreement with the constructivist notion of terrorism (e.g. Gunning 2007b: 377; Breen Smyth 2007: 265). Jackson (2007b: 247), for example, suggests that 'terrorism is fundamentally a social fact rather than a brute fact' and critical terrorism studies 'rests (...) upon an understanding of knowledge as a social process constructed through language, discourse and intersubjective practices' (Jackson 2007b: 246). Nevertheless, as we have seen critical terrorism studies remains preoccupied with primary sources and the terrorist actor. Surely critical terrorism scholars are aware of the fact that what terrorists say in interviews has a rhetorical and narrative dimension and thus is constitutive rather than reflective of reality (Zulaika and Douglass 2008: 29; Jackson 2007b: 246). Yet, they appear to neglect the idea that the terrorist's self-representations only become relevant as they become the object of interpretations in the Western discourse. What we make of the terrorist is what matters, not what he or she makes of himself or herself. Although these two perspectives are connected, the self-representation of the terrorist always has to be interpreted, it does not speak for itself. Hence, critical terrorism scholars' focus on the terrorist – even if it is on the terrorist's constructions of reality – may be misleading, because it looks for terrorism in the 'wrong' place. A similar critique has been raised by Ken Booth, who is also sceptical of the psychologizing or individualizing tendencies of critical terrorism studies. He emphasizes that while 'the terrorist subject ... is certainly available for psychological insights ... the most fundamental questions that confront us are political' (Booth 2008: 70). He points out that it 'is not possible to stand on neutral ground as far as terrorism, terrorists, and terrors are concerned, so the first task of a critical theorist is to show reflexivity in this regard' (Booth 2008: 71). Along this line Jeffrey Sluka (2008: 168) points out that a subjective understanding 'considers "terrorism" as a political or cultural construct, holds that the most important fact is that people do not act on the basis of what is real or true, but rather on the basis of what they believe to be real or true'.

So there are exceptions and a small number of scholars have even shown interest in the role of language and terrorism (Zulaika and Douglass 1996; Collins and Glover 2002; Silberstein 2002). Most recently and prior to the rise of Critical Terrorism Studies one of its main proponents Richard Jackson (2005) in his book *Writing the War on Terrorism* analysed US discourses on terrorism with a view to finding out how these discourses have constituted both terrorism and counter-terrorism. He argues that at 'the most basic level, the practice of counter-terrorism is predicated on and determined by the language of counter-terrorism'. 'Language and practice, in other words, are inextricably linked; they mutually reinforce each other; together they co-constitute social and political reality' (Jackson 2005: 8–9). He investigated the discourse on the 'war on terrorism' by examining the word used by senior US government officials to describe the reasons for and the progress of the 'war on terrorism'. For one this includes the words used to describe and explain the events of 9/11; the words used for the description of the 'terrorist' other and the American identities; the way the threat is described as catastrophic and how the response is essentially good and just. This book subscribes to many of the assumptions proposed by Jackson but suggests two important alterations. Firstly, as we will see in the next section, it has a far less instrumental understanding of discourse than suggested by Jackson (2005). Secondly, the proposed field of discourse is far less elite and state centric than that of Jackson.

Jackson suggests that discourse 'is designed to achieve a number of key political goals' (Jackson 2005: 2) and that language is 'deployed to maintain power' (Jackson 2005: 25). Therefore discourse 'has a clear *political* purpose; it works for someone and for something; it is an exercise of power' (Jackson 2005: 2, emphasis in original). For Jackson words are deliberately and meticulously chosen by the political elite to achieve a number of key political goals. Discourse is 'constructed and employed for specific purposes, most importantly, the creation, maintenance and extension of power' (Jackson 2005: 19). For him the 'war on terrorism' 'is an elite-led project' where the elites 'provide the primary justification and overall vision' (Jackson 2005: 26). This view of discourse as something that can be used and manipulated is shared by another critical terrorist scholar, Jeroen Gunning, who suggests to analyse how '"terrorism" discourse is used to discredit oppositional groups and justify state policies' (Gunning 2007a: 377). While such an understanding of discourse may correspond to the common sense understanding, this chapter wants to offer an alternative understanding of discourse which is less instrumental and where discourse is 'above' the individual discourse participants.

This brings us to the second important alteration, closely related to the first: As a result of this understanding of discourse, Jackson focuses predominantly on a particular type of discourse participant, namely political elites. He explicitly focuses 'on the speeches, interviews and public addresses given by senior members of the Bush administration' (Jackson 2005: 26). This focus is justified, he claims, by the 'fact' that 'these speeches represent the source of the discourse' (Jackson 2005: 26) and by the 'fact' that 'the "war on terrorism" is an elite-led project' (Jackson 2005: 26). However, Jackson does nothing to substantiate this claim. Surely, no one would deny that the political elite is important, but it is quite something else to state that they are the 'source of the discourse', that they – and here is the connection to the first criticism – have initiated and now control the discourse at their own will. As the proponents of critical terrorism studies themselves are eager to point out (Breen Smyth 2007: 260), the post 9/11 discourse on terrorism is not entirely new. Rather, it builds upon former discourses of terrorism and it intersects with other discourses (on Islamism, for example). Hence, it is impossible to identify any single 'source' of this discourse. And talk of the discourse as an 'elite-led project' seems to overestimate the agency of actors. The political elite, like anyone else, is bound by discourses. What the elite perceives, believes, says and does is pre-structured by discourses. Hence, it is former discourses on terrorism which have shaped the political elites' understanding of 9/11, making certain kinds of political action possible while excluding others. While the political elite may have the ability to opt for one reaction rather than another, the array of possible reactions has already been severely restricted by the discourse. The elite chooses from a very limited set of options, thus one can hardly speak of the 'war on terrorism' as an 'elite-led project'. If anything, we could conceive the political elite as a 'discourse-led project'. The elite-focus of Jackson's research is not only indicative of a discourse-approach that seems to underestimate the power of discourse (and overestimates the power of actors), but also of the possibility that critical terrorism studies is more conventional than it would like to be seen. Not only does it share with the mainstream a fascination with primary sources, but also a state-centric view. It is one of the 'core commitments' (Jackson 2007b: 246) of critical terrorism studies to overcome terrorism research's traditional 'state-centrism' (Breen Smyth 2007: 261). Yet, one could suggest that a 'sceptical attitude towards state-centric understandings of terrorism' (Jackson 2007b: 246) should also entail a shift of focus towards other segments of discourse, e.g. civil society's or popular culture's terrorism discourse.

The approach detailed in this and applied in the next chapter, in contrast, seeks to overcome the state-centrism of both conventional and critical terrorism studies by focusing on popular rather than elite discourse. It does so through an analysis of the popular press, as it seems important to examine the 'social' part of the 'social construction' in discourse. If one is interested in examining the social construction of a phenomenon then surely it makes sense to examine the medium which many members of society interact with. The normal average person does not read government press-releases, presidential speeches or parliamentary debates. Most people get their information from the media. The *Bild* in Germany and *The Sun* in the United Kingdom here are particularly interesting because they are among the largest national newspapers in Europe. They both greatly influence the national discourses on new terrorism. The suggested approach therefore places less emphasis on the political elite and 'high data' but on the 'low data' (Weldes 2006) found in the tabloid press.

The next section will examine in detail how such a discourse analysis of tabloids could be conducted by focusing on metaphor analysis as the methodological approach used in the next chapter. It will show what metaphors are and how they differ from other linguistic devises. Importantly it will outline what metaphors do, how they work in discourse and finally how one can conduct a metaphor analysis. Thereby, it will illustrate a particular understanding of metaphors which places emphasis on the predicative role of a metaphor and illustrate how metaphors shape our understanding of the world.

Metaphor analysis and the predication of 'the terrorist'

The analysis of metaphors is by no means a radically new or innovative enterprise. In fact it has become very popular. Metaphor analysis has its own association, conferences[6] and its own journals[7] and can be found in a vast number of different academic disciplines such as psychology, sociology and anthropology (Glucksberg 2001). Wayne Booth sarcastically calculated that by the year 2039 'there will be more students of metaphor than people' (Booth 1978: 49). Even in political science, a subject which continuously seems to lag behind other subjects in the race of cutting edge innovation, metaphor analysis could be metaphorically considered as an 'old hat' (Landau 1961; Miller 1979; Zashin and Chapman 1974; Rayner 1984). As a response to its growing popularity in other fields, metaphors also began to take hold in International Relations (Chilton 1996a; Milliken 1996; Campbell 1998; Chilton and Lakoff 1999). And even here metaphor analysis cannot really be considered marginal anymore (Beer and Landtsheer 2004a; Little 2007; Kornprobst et al. 2008; Carver and Pikalo 2008) with a growing number of research applying metaphor analysis to aspects of international politics such as European integration (Chilton and Ilyin 1993; Hülsse 2003a; Drulák 2006; Luoma-aho 2004), immigration (Santa Ana 1999; Charteris-Black 2006; O'Brian 2003) and, one of the generally most conservative realms, security policy (Chilton 1996b; Thornborrow 1993; Murtimer 1994) and war (Paris 2002; Hartmann-Mahmud 2002).[8] Even some of the leading IR scholars such as Richard Little (2007: 23) seem to accept the importance of metaphors for international politics as 'metaphors have the ability to transform the meaning of an established concept and they also play an essential role in comprehending aspects of the world that are new or that we do not understand'. As Petr Drulák (2006: 500) points out, the 'analysis of metaphors has greatly enriched our understanding of international relations'. Surprisingly the issue of metaphors and terrorism has received far less attention and appears to have been neglected.[9]

But what exactly is a metaphor? The Oxford Dictionary of English (2005: 1103) describes a metaphor as 'a figure of speech in which a word or phrase is applied to an object or action to which it is not literally applicable'. In an etymological sense the term 'metaphor' comes from the Greek word '*meta*' meaning beyond or above and the word '*pherein*' meaning carrying or bearing. And Sam Glucksberg (2001: 3) has pointed out that '[f]rom this deceptively simple root, metaphor has come to mean different things to different people, so much so that specialists in the area are often temporarily confounded when asked for a definition of *metaphor* (emphasis in original). Andrew Ortony (1979: 3) has argued that '[a]ny serious study of metaphor is almost obliged to start with the works of Aristotle' as '[h]is discussion of the issue, principally in the Poetics and in the Rhetoric, have remained influential to this day'. According to Aristotle metaphors are a transference, naming one thing in terms of another (Jordan 1974; Foss 1996; Mahon 1999). Metaphor 'consists in giving the thing a name that belongs to something else' (Aristotle 1982: 1457b). A couple of hundred years later and around a thousand kilometres to the north-west Cicero similarly stated that metaphors happen 'when a word applying to one thing is transferred to another, because the similarity seems to justify the transference' (cited in Purcell 1990: 39).

The general idea of what a metaphor is has more recently been discussed by a vast range of different scholars from very different disciplines using a varying degree of complexity to express their understandings. In fact, '[m]etaphor has by now been defined in so many ways that there is no human expression, whether in language or any other medium, that would not be metaphoric in *someone's* definition' (Booth 1978: 50, emphasis in original). For example, Kenneth Burke (1945: 503) quite simply believes metaphors to be 'a device for seeing something in terms of something else' and Susan Sontag (1989: 93) describes metaphors as 'saying a thing is or is like something-it-is not'. Paul Ricoeur (1978: 80) argues that 'metaphor holds together within one simple meaning two different missing parts of different contexts of this meaning' and most recently Jonathan Charteris-Black (2004: 21) has defined a metaphor as 'a linguistic representation that results from the shift in the use of a word or phrase from the context or domain in which it is expected to occur to another context or domain where it is not expected to occur, thereby causing semantic tension'. So metaphors do not simply substitute one term for another, but create a strong perceptual link between two things (Bates 2004).

Most of these 'definitions' mentioned above which focus on the transference of something to something else would however include a large number of other linguistic tools such as analogies, similes and metonymy. 'Analogies' make comparisons between one thing and another and involve an inference that if two or more things are the same in one aspect they are probably the same in others. While metaphors draw comparisons from different realms of experience (across-domain comparisons), analogies generally draw comparisons from the same realm of experience (within-domain comparisons) (Vosniadou and Ortony 1989: 7). Nevertheless, they are similar to metaphors as they involve understanding something in terms of something else (Juthe 2005). As Keith Shimko (1994: 660) points out, in 'a purely cognitive sense, there is very little difference between analogies and metaphors. Indeed, because the dynamics of analogical and metaphorical thought are alike, many cognitive psychologists usually fail to distinguish between the two (not because they cannot, but because doing so is often unnecessary)'. An example of a historical analogy is the comparison between the events of 9/11 and Pearl Harbor. In contrast, a 'simile' explicitly uses the words 'as' or 'like' to compare two things. Although, like metaphors and analogies, it makes a comparison, it is different because it allows these two things to remain distinct from each other despite their similarities. The first of the following sentences is an example for a simile while the second is a metaphor:

'Al-Qaeda is as well armed as an army'.
'Al-Qaeda is an army of terrorists'.

While metaphors involve two things that are similar but also different from each other in our conceptual system, metonymies involve two things which are closely related to each other in our conceptual system. With metonymies one uses one thing, for example 'Washington', to stand for another thing such as 'the American government'. For example:

'Washington decided to impose sanctions on Sudan'.
'Bin Laden attacked New York and Washington on September 11th'.

Metaphors and metonymies both involve a substitution of one term for another but metaphors are based on similarity while metonymies are based in contiguity. In the case of metonymies, the things which are compared have a 'stand-for relationship' within a single conceptual domain while the elements in the case of metaphors have a 'is-understood-as relationship' between two conceptual distant domains (Kövecses 2002: 227).

Despite these differences, most scholars especially in political science and IR generally adopt a very broad definition of metaphor to include these other linguistic devises such as analogies, similes and metonymy. Metaphor has become an 'all-purpose connector term' (Zashin and Chapman 1974; Gozzi 1999: 55). This is understandable as the general idea of understanding something with the help of something else is central to all these linguistic tools. This book will follow this tradition and use 'metaphor' inclusively for all types of transference of meaning from one concept to another which thereby predicate something in a certain way. As we will see the aspect of predication is central here.

Essentially, the definition one adopts depends very much on what one considers metaphors capable of and maybe it will become clearer what a metaphor is when examining what metaphors actually do (Glucksberg 2001:3). Traditionally metaphors were on the one hand considered 'convenient labels that accurately describe the nature of world politics' (Chilton and Lakoff 1999: 56). On the other they were deemed to be a purely rhetorical tool which replaces one word with another and serves little purpose but to make speech sound nice (Chilton 1996a: 359; Charteris-Black 2004: 25). '[M]etaphor has been considered a mere ornamental use of language, a pretty turn of phrase rippling along on the surface of discourse' (Gozzi 1999: 9). In other words, a metaphor was seen as 'superficial stylistic accessory' and a way of decorating discourse without affecting its meaning (Beer and Landtsheer 2004b: 5). Traditional terrorism research would probably think of metaphors in this way and consider them unimportant, seeing them as only words and rhetoric and therefore irrelevant for political analysis on a subject of such life-threatening importance.

In contrast to this rhetorical understanding of metaphor, cognitive linguistics goes further and argue that metaphors are more than just words. In particular, Lakoff and Johnson (1980) are among the most influential scholars in this respect as they have managed to export the study of metaphor from linguistics into other disciplines such as psychology, sociology and political science. For them, the 'essence of metaphor is understanding and experiencing one kind of thing in terms of another' (Lakoff and Johnson 1980: 5). In their groundbreaking book 'Metaphors We Live By' they argue that metaphors structure the way people think and that the human conceptual system as such is fundamentally metaphorical. '[T]he way we think, what we experience and what we do everyday is very much a matter of metaphor' (Lakoff and Johnson 1980: 297). They believe that metaphors make humans understand one conceptual domain of experience in terms of another by projecting knowledge about the first familiar domain onto the second more abstract domain. 'Metaphors [...] are devices for simplifying and giving meaning to complex and bewildering sets of observations that evoke concern' (Edelman 1971: 65). The central idea here is that metaphors map a source domain, for example WAR, onto a target domain, for example TERRORISM, and thereby make the target domain appear in a new light. Sometimes the source and target domain are referred to as 'tenor' and 'vehicle' or as 'primary subject' and 'secondary subject'

(Cameron 1999: 13; Black 1979). This idea is commonly captured in the following way:

TARGET DOMAIN (A) IS SOURCE DOMAIN (B)
TERRORISM IS WAR
TERRORISM IS CRIME

Here we have to distinguish between two kinds of metaphors: the *metaphoric expression* and the *conceptual metaphor*.[10] The conceptual metaphor, in our case TERRORISM IS WAR or TERRORISM IS CRIME, involves the abstract connection between one 'conceptual domain' (Lakoff 1993: 208–209) to another by mapping a source domain (WAR) and a target domain (TERRORISM). Mapping here refers to 'a set of systematic correspondences between the source and the target in the sense that constituent conceptual elements of B correspond to constituent elements of A' (Kövecses 2002: 6). 'Thus, the conceptual metaphor makes us apply what we know about one area of our experience (source domain) to another area of our experience (target domain)' (Drulák 2005: 3). Conceptual metaphors do not have to be explicitly visible in discourse. However, metaphorical expressions are directly visible and represent the specific statements found in the text which the conceptual metaphor draws on. For example:

'The West is facing a *terrorist army* led by Osama bin Laden'
'Osama bin Laden and his *lieutenants* are planning an attack'

Here the metaphors 'terrorist army' and 'lieutenants' are two different metaphorical expressions which both draw on the same conceptual metaphor of TERRORISM IS WAR. In other words: 'The conceptual metaphor represents the conceptual basis, idea or image that underlies a set of metaphors' (Charteris-Black 2004: 9).

The metaphorical formula A IS B applied to the conceptual metaphor mentioned above is, however, slightly misleading and not totally accurate as it suggests that the whole target domain is understood in terms of the whole source domain. However, this cannot be the case as concept A cannot be the same as concept B. The mapping between the two domains is only ever partial as not all characteristics of concept B are transferred to concept A. In fact, it is commonly accepted in the realm of metaphor analysis that through the use of metaphor 'people make *selective distinctions* that, by highlighting some aspect of the phenomenon, downplay and hide other features that could give a different stance' (Milliken 1996:

221, emphasis in original). Similar to media framing, they draw attention to certain aspects of a phenomenon and invite the listener or reader to think of one thing in the light of another. Thereby, and this is central to the whole book, they influence policy and in our case counter-terrorism policy. Metaphors 'limit what we notice, highlight what we do see, and provide part of the inferential structure that we reason with' (Lakoff 1992: 481). As Chilton and Lakoff (1999: 56) point out, metaphors 'are concepts that can be and often are acted upon. As such, they define in significant part, what one takes as 'reality', and thus form the basis and the justification for the formulation of policy and its potential execution'. Metaphors structure the way people define a phenomenon and thereby influence how they react to it: they limit and bias our perceived policy choices as they determine basic assumptions and attitudes on which decision-making depends (c.f. Milliken 1996; Chilton 1996a; Mio 1997).

These assumptions have lead to two distinct types of metaphor analysis. The first which is in line with many aspects found in Critical Discourse Analysis (CDA), takes the premises mentioned above and argues that metaphor analysis can reveal the hidden agenda, ideology, thought or intentions of the person using the metaphors (Fairclough 1992: 194; Musolff 2000: 4). Among these Jonathan Charteris-Black (2004) has developed a critical approach to metaphor analysis which argues that metaphors are potentially powerful weapons as they can influence the way we perceive a certain social reality. Metaphors have the potential to influence human beliefs, attitudes and consequently their actions. Critical metaphor analysis therefore wants to 'demonstrate how particular discursive practices reflect socio-political power structures' (Charteris-Black 2004: 29). The second kind of metaphor analysis does not try and reveal these secrets and the thinking behind the metaphor but concentrates on the reconstruction of how these metaphors shape and effect reality (Tonkiss 1998; Hülsse 2003a, 2003b, 2006). Rather than asking the question of who is responsible for cer-tain metaphors and why these metaphors are used, this approach focuses on the 'reality' which follows from these metaphors. This is in line with the kind of discourse analysis which has been put forward by, among others, David Campbell (1998), Roxanne Lynn Doty (1993), Jennifer Milliken (1999), Ole Wæver (2005) or – more recently – Lene Hansen (2006). Drawing on Michel Foucault, these scholars share a concept of discourse which is 'above' individual dis-course-participants. Discourse constitutes actors and structures what they can meaningfully say or do. Accordingly, actors have very limited agency. Rather than being able to use words intentionally and manipulate discourse to further their own purposes, they are themselves inextricably bound up with discourses that leave them little room for individuality. What they say and what they do is to a large extent determined by discourse. Seen in this light, it hardly makes sense to ask about the use of discourse by particular actors. Instead, the main focus is on how discourse shapes the world, i.e. the actors, their self-understandings, and their actions. This book follows this strand of researchers and wants to examine the 'reality' which follows from the use of certain metaphors rather than the reasons for that use.

Obviously we have to be careful when talking about the idea that metaphors shape or cause politics and in particular counter-terrorism policy as they are only one among many linguistic devices, even taking a broad understanding of the term, which play a role in the discursive construction of reality. As Andrew Anderson (2004: 91) points out '[w]hen metaphors are said to *cause* political phenomena, political science often objects' (emphasis in original). 'The nature of metaphor does not lend itself easily to rigorous demonstrations of causality. Metaphorical power may exist, but it is hard to nail down' (Beer and Landtsheer 2004b: 7). It is therefore very important to realise that metaphors do not cause a certain counter-terrorism policy in a positivist sense where the metaphor is the independent and the policies are the dependent variable.[11] Metaphors do not entail a clear set of policies, but open up space for policy possibilities. Metaphors offer a discursive construct which frames the situation in a certain way. 'Metaphors are more likely to influence policy indirectly through their impact on the decision maker's general approach to an issue; they will be part of the conceptual foundation, not a detailed policy map' (Shimko 1994: 665). As metaphors help construct reality in a certain way they are able to define the limits of common sense, the limits of what is considered possible and logical while excluding other options from consideration (Hülsse 2003b: 225).

So how does one actually carry out metaphor analysis? There are a number of scholars who offer a range of different detailed plans of how to carry out a metaphor analysis (Gibbs 1999; Schmitt 2005). Although their emphasis vary the key components remain similar. First, one selects a text or rather a series of texts such as works or speeches of a particular author or politician, news reports or television programmes (Ricoeur 1981). Second, the researcher starts identifying narrative elements which provide the context for metaphors such as actors, actions or settings. Third, one starts collecting the metaphorical expressions used in this corpus to talk about the narrative elements. In a fourth step one notes common and recurring metaphors and organises them into clusters which are then generalised into conceptual metaphors underlying the discourse. The frequency of the different conceptual metaphors is crucial as an indicator for their importance in the discourse. The more common the metaphor is, the more influence it is bound to have on the construction of reality and ultimately on policy (Charteris-Black 2004: 34; Drulák 2008: 112). In the final step these metaphors are inductively interpreted. This interpretation is intuitive and undoubtedly subjective (Lule 2004: 182).[12] But there have been a number of suggestions of how such an interpretation of metaphors could be carried out in a 'scientific' and controlled way. For example Ronald Hitzler (1993: 230) has used what he refers to as 'artificial stupidity' while Rainer Hülsse (2003b: 228) takes up Umberto Eco's (1994) suggestion to interpret a metaphor like someone who would encounter it for the very first time. This without doubt is a difficult endeavour as 'metaphors are typically culturally-loaded expressions, whose meaning has to be inferred through reference to shared cultural knowledge' (Littlemore 2003: 273). Therefore there is a danger that people from one cultural background do not understand a metaphor from another especially if they attribute different associations to the source domain (Charteris-Black 2003; Deignan 2003). So the interpretation of metaphors is predominantly down to the intuition of native speakers and individual analysts embedded in the corresponding cultural sphere (Pragglejaz Group 2007: 25).

The metaphor analysis in the following chapter wants to avoid the charges of being arbitrary in two ways. Firstly, it focuses solely on the most common metaphors, and secondly it reassures the intuitive interpretation with the help of dictionaries. The assumption is that dictionaries store common knowledge about a phenomenon (Pragglejaz Group 2007). So if we want to know about the social construction of terrorism in discourse, we can examine the metaphors used and establish the kind of source and target domains of the underlying conceptual metaphors by checking the meaning of these metaphors in dictionaries. For example, the 'commando' metaphor is important in the terrorism discourse after 9/11, so to find out how this particular metaphorical expression constitutes the terrorist actor one consults the definitions of 'commando' provided in dictionaries. One here can find following definitions:

'A soldier specially trained for carrying out raids' (Oxford Dictionary of English)

'A military unit trained and organized as shock troops especially for hit-and-run raids into enemy territory' (Merriam-Webster)
'An amphibious military unit trained for raiding' (Collins English Dictionary)

These definitions of the metaphor 'commando' construct him or her as something military, elite, well trained and deadly. Ultimately, words such as soldier, military unit and troops automatically come to mind and with these connotations one thinks of those actors as being involved in war. Obviously the definitions dictionaries offer vary to a certain extent but they represent a legitimate spectrum of interpretations which avoids the accusation of interpreting metaphors arbitrarily. As Rainer Hülsse (2006: 404) points out, with such techniques which spell out 'what appears to be obvious, i.e. the deautomatisation of the usually automatic projection from source to target, one can reconstruct the reality constructions of metaphors'.

Conclusion

This chapter has called for a constructivist turn in terrorism research and has illustrated how such an approach might look like by outlining the (meta-) theoretical underpinnings and developing a metaphor approach to the study of terrorism. Constructivist terrorism research is not so much interested in how the terrorist really is but how he is talked or written to be. Therefore, primary sources in the traditional sense and the focus on the terrorist have been replaced with the analysis of discourse and metaphors in particular which constitute the 'new terrorist' in a certain way. Metaphors are particularly important makers of social reality because they project familiar worlds onto unfamiliar phenomena and thus constitute the new in terms of the old. Here terrorism is not a fact but a social construction. This does not mean that terrorism only exists in our heads. Terrorists are real people who really kill others. Nevertheless, acts of terrorism and the terrorist actor have to be interpreted via discourse, they do not speak for themselves. The understanding of discourse proposed here differs to Critical Discourse Analysis and the approach of Richard Jackson as it is not instrumentalist and therefore does not solely focus on the political elite as the driving force behind discourse. In the next chapter the book will apply this theoretical and methodological approach to a popular media discourse on terrorism and examine the predicative construction of 'new terrorism' by looking at the metaphors found in the *Bild* and *The Sun* newspapers from 2001 to 2005. These two popular media outlets could be considered to be particular influential in this respect as their reporting on al-Qaeda and 'new terrorism' shapes the reality of many people in Germany and the United Kingdom. Therefore analysing the discursive constructions in the tabloid press could be a promising way to study 'new terrorism' and examine the changing conceptions of a terrorist organisation such as al-Qaeda.

5
The Tabloid Terrorist in the *Bild* and *The Sun*

'Metaphor is a solar eclipse. It hides the object of study and at the same time reveals some of the most salient and interesting characteristics when viewed through the right telescope' (Paivio 1979)

This chapter will apply the methodological understandings developed in the previous chapter to illustrate how metaphors map source onto target domains and how this predicates the action of terrorism and the terrorist actor in the German *Bild* and the British *The Sun* newspapers. So far metaphor and predicate analysis has predominantly been applied to elite discourses or what can be called 'high data'. So for example the focus has been on speeches by leading politicians (Ferrari 2007) or on government statements or documents (Hülsse 2003a) from one country. Although there has been some investigation of media reporting (Pancake 1993; Zinken 2003; Lule 2004) and quality press newspapers (Flowerdew and Leong 2007), analysis of popular tabloid newspapers from different countries has so far been neglected.[1] The central idea behind analysing the media rather than the political elite is that the media, and in particular the widely read tabloid media, give an insight into the construction of terrorism possibly held by large portions of the general public and the metaphoric 'Joe the plumber' or his German female equivalent 'Erika Mustermann'. Furthermore, it is important to note that it was not the political elite but the media who were the first to metaphorise the events of 9/11 as war. George Lakoff (2001), one of the leading scholars on metaphors, has pointed out that the Bush administration first used a 'crime' metaphor to describe the attacks of 9/11 but then quickly replaced these with a 'war' metaphor. In the case of the US Shoma Munshi (2004: 49) points out that:

> CBS's Dan Rather was one of the first to introduce the context of battle, calling the incident 'the new face of war'. Jeff Greenfield of CNN compared the numbers of casualties at Pearl Harbor to the potential casualty counts in New York. As September 11 wore on, framing the events in the context of Pearl Harbor started gathering momentum, and the phrase 'day of infamy' was used liberally throughout the coverage. By the morning of Wednesday, September 12, headlines in the New York Post declared 'Act of War' and the Daily News declared 'It's War'.

Metaphors provide a means of analysing news coverage as 'metaphors provide colourful and accessible means of explaining abstract notions' (Charteris-Black 2005: 16). Consequently this chapter wants to disregard the 'high data' of the political elite and investigate the 'low data' (Weldes 2006) produced by the tabloid press in Germany and Britain in order to get an insight into the social construction of 'new terrorism' in two different countries and cultures. Therefore, it will focus on the predication and metaphorisation of 'new terrorism' in the *Bild* and *The Sun* newspapers by analysing one month of articles following five large attacks perpetrated by al-Qaeda: 9/11 in 2001, the bombings in Bali in 2002, the attacks in Istanbul in 2003, the train bombings in Madrid in 2004 and the London tube attacks in 2005. These events were chosen not only due to their fairly large nature and their focus on a western target, but also because they offer a fairly regular timeline which indicates the regularity of the predicative constructions of 'new terrorism'. The time frame of one month after each incident for selecting articles was chosen as further research beyond this time period did not add further kinds of conceptual metaphors.

The chapter offers a brief insight into how 'new terrorism' has been constructed from 9/11 to the London bombings without claiming that these kinds of constructions are how al-Qaeda are seen today or how they will be considered in the future. Overall this chapter, as well as the book in general, are supposed to give an insight into what a theory orientated and in particular a constructivist kind of terrorism research could look like and how discursive constructions of terrorism can influence countermeasures. In pursuit of this aim, the first part of this chapter will examine the predicative construction of 'new terrorism' in the German *Bild* newspaper after 9/11, the bombings in Bali and Istanbul as well as the attacks

in Madrid and London. The second part will mirror the first by studying
the discursive constitution of terrorism after these events in the British
The Sun newspaper between 2001 and 2005. Throughout these two parts
the focus will be on metaphorical expressions which indicate five different dominant conceptual metaphors. This will include the predication
of 'new terrorism' as WAR, CRIME, NATURAL, UNCIVILISED EVIL and
DISEASE. Although the section will indicate trends and certain fluctuation in the number of metaphorical expressions, the most important
consideration is that these conceptual metaphors can be found more or
less consistently in both Germany and the UK and throughout the time
period between 2001 and 2005. The chapter will then be rounded off by
a conclusion which summarises the main findings of this investigation
and draws out a number of similarities and differences between the discursive construction of 'new terrorism' in Germany and Britain. Thereby
the chapter hopes to set the stage for an investigation of what policies
are made appropriate and logical for countering such 'new terrorism' and
which policy options appear non-sensical.

The tabloid terrorist in the German *Bild* newspaper

The *Bild* is of particular interest to the discursive construction of terrorism in Germany simply because it is the largest national newspaper
with over eleven and a half million readers. Therefore it is widely accepted
that the *Bild* has great influence on the perception of many people in
the country (Alberts 1972; Klein 2000; Gabrys 2008). It is also the paper
which is quoted most commonly, and it has frequently taken the top
slot in a national agenda-setting ranking conducted by Media Tenor.[2] It
can therefore be considered one of the most important agenda setters
in Germany, able to not only influence the national discourse but to
actually set the national debate.

9/11: 2001

The terror attacks on the 11th of September 2001 in New York and Washington commonly referred to as 9/11, which killed over 3,000 people
are considered to be the most dramatic example of 'new terrorism' and
the dawn of a new era. And unsurprisingly the media reactions around
the world to the events of 9/11 were massive. The *Bild* newspaper in Germany was no exception as it reported extensively for several weeks and
months and thereby actively participated in the construction of what
'new terrorism' and al-Qaeda was and therefore also, so the central idea of
this book, how best to counter this 'new' threat.

One of the most dominant conceptual metaphors in the *Bild* after 9/11 was TERRORISM IS WAR. Apart from the famous metaphor 'war on terrorism' or 'war on terror' there are a large number of other metaphorical expressions which strengthen this understanding of TERRORISM IS WAR by mapping military source domains to the target domain of terrorism.[3] Firstly, 9/11 is likened to events in the Second World War by explicitly connecting the terrorist attacks with the surprise attack by the Japanese in 'Pearl Harbor'[4] and the use of kamikaze tactics. Most notably this is visible in the references to the attack as a 'kamikaze attack'[5] and the actors perpetrating the attacks as 'kamikaze flyer',[6] 'kamikaze pilots'[7] or 'kamikaze assassins'[8] or the airplanes used to crash into the targets as 'kamikaze-weapons'[9] or 'kamikaze-flights'.[10] Apart from this historical analogy, there are a vast number of other metaphorical expressions: For example, Osama bin Laden is said to have 'declared war'[11] on the West and the scene of the attack in New York is described as a 'war zone'.[12] Like a general bin Laden is conducting a 'terror-war'[13] in which he 'orders'[14] his 'private army'[15] made up of 'soldiers'[16] to attack. The West is said to be facing a 'terrorist army'[17] consisting of 'death-troops'[18] or 'terror-troops'.[19] But these 'armed forces'[20] are not simply made up of normal soldiers, the terrorist is a 'veteran'[21] in other words 'an ex-member of the armed forces'[22] or even 'a soldier who has seen considerable active service',[23] someone who has fought a war in the past and who is 'battle hardened'[24]. They are constructed as 'warriors',[25] as elite soldiers, 'terror-'[26] or 'suicide-commandos',[27] so 'a soldier specially trained for carrying out raids'[28] or 'an amphibious military unit trained for raiding'.[29] This military style construction of the terrorists is further strengthened by other metaphorical expressions. For example, the terrorists are said to be supported by 'terror-strategists'[30] and 'terror-logisticians'.[31] According to the Merriam-Webster Online dictionary 'strategy' can refer to 'the science and art of military command exercised to meet the enemy in combat under advantageous conditions' and 'logistics' refers to 'the aspect of military science dealing with the procurement, maintenance, and transportation of military matériel, facilities, and personnel'.[32] Furthermore, throughout the discourse the terrorists are generally described as heavily armed, they have an 'arsenal'[33] of automatic weapons, military style assault rifles such as the AK 47s, rocket propelled grenades as well as high-tech surface to air missiles.[34] In addition the military construction of al-Qaeda is reinforced by the idea that they are said to have a 'command center'[35] and 'military bases'[36] in Afghanistan, and by the idea that they use 'camouflage':[37] 'the disguising of military personnel, equipment, and installations by painting or covering them to make them blend in with their surrounding'.[38] In line with this military construction of terrorism in the *Bild* after 9/11 one finds a large emphasis of the terrorist leadership and in particular Osama bin Laden. The famous network structure of 'new terrorism' is still largely absent and the constitution of terrorism seems to here focus on a military-like hierarchical structure in which bin Laden gives the 'orders'.[39] For one, this seems supported by the metaphors used as synonyms of the person Osama bin Laden himself by which he is constructed as the ultimate leader of a hierarchical structure who is in full control of his organisation. He is frequently referred to as a 'top-terrorist',[40] 'terror-chief',[41] 'terrorist-leader',[42] 'terror-boss'[43] and 'senior-terrorist',[44] all of which imply a hierarchical structure. In addition to this military-like hierarchical structure some metaphors also further imply strategic goals with the use of 'strategist of terror'[45] and large financial resources such as the terms 'terror-emperor'[46] and 'terror-sheik'[47] as well as his pioneering role in the form of 'godfather of terror'.[48] This appears to be sustained further by the analysis of the predication of the actor Osama bin Laden who throughout the discourse is constructed as 'directing'[49] and 'ordering'[50] terrorist attacks.

A second conceptual metaphor one encounters when analysing the construction of new terrorism in the *Bild* after 9/11 is TERRORISM IS CRIME. Interestingly, however, is the fact that these kinds of metaphors are far less frequent than those of the conceptual metaphor TERRORISM IS WAR. One does encounter metaphorical expressions such as 'criminal',[51] 'offender'[52] or 'murderer'[53] but they stand in no relation to the number of military style metaphors found in the discourse.

Interestingly, a third very dominant group of metaphors in the *Bild* discourse after 9/11 constituted terrorism as something natural. The conceptual metaphor TERRORISM IS NATURAL likened the events of 9/11 to naturally occurring phenomena such as a 'storm'.[54] In these terrorist storms the western shores are battered by high 'assassination-'[55] or 'terror waves'[56] which are inevitable. On of the most frequent metaphorical expressions here was the 'catastrophe',[57] which the Merriam-Webster Online dictionary defines as 'a violent usually destructive natural event'[58] or 'something very unfortunate'.[59] So, terrorism especially with terms such as 'terror-catastrophe'[60] is constituted as something natural which regrettably happens from time to time.

Rather less surprising than the conceptual metaphor TERRORISM IS NATURAL are metaphorical expressions which constitute terrorism as something essentially uncivilised and evil. Here the double conceptual metaphor TERRORISM IS UNCIVILISED EVIL is on the one hand indicated by simple metaphors such as 'evil',[61] 'barbaric',[62] 'monstrous'[63] or 'terror-monster'[64] but also by religious metaphors depicting terrorism as something 'satanic'.[65] Here the events of 9/11 are frequently described as an 'inferno',[66] i.e. 'any place or state resembling hell',[67] or even directly as 'hell',[68] 'flaming hell'[69] or 'apocalypse'.[70] Here Osama bin Laden is the 'devil'[71] and the attacks were 'diabolical'[72] and 'apocalyptic'.[73] The terrorists of 9/11 were 'riders of the apocalypse'.[74] The acts are considered 'terroristic barbarity'[75] committed by 'unhuman'[76] 'terror-beasts'.[77] At this stage the conceptual metaphor TERRORISM IS DISEASE is still very rare in the *Bild* as one only encounters a hand full of metaphorical expressions which constitute the attacks of 9/11 as 'insane'[78] or 'sick'.[79]

Bali bombings: 2002

'New terrorism' struck again in 2002 when on the 12th October bombs exploded in and outside of nightclubs on the island of Bali. Two hundred and two people were killed and over 200 others were severely injured in the attack. A third bomb exploded outside of the US consulate but caused only minor damage. Although the events in Bali are the reason for the analysis of the month long media discourse in 2002, the articles on terrorism examined also include reports on the Moscow theatre hostage crisis as this fell within the one month time period which was investigated.

In contrast to 9/11 there is a decline of the conceptual metaphor TERRORISM IS WAR and a rise in the proportion of TERRORISM IS CRIME to an extent that they can both almost equal in numbers. So we still have metaphors of war. The scene of the attacks in 2002 are still considered to resemble a 'battlefield'[80] on which one encounters 'troops'[81] of terrorists, 'combat troops'[82] or 'commandos'.[83] In the media discourse of the *Bild* the 'alliance against terror'[84] is still engaged in a 'war',[85] 'terrorism-war'[86] or 'anti-terror war'[87] against 'warriors'.[88] However, at the same time these metaphors of war are joined by metaphors of crime, so the 'battlefield' is now also a 'crime scene'[89] and the 'commando' is also an 'offender'[90] who commits 'murder'.[91] Terrorists are constituted as 'murderers'[92] who 'mug'[93] their victims and leave 'evidence'[94] of their 'crimes'.[95] The conceptual metaphor TERRORISM IS NATURAL which was fairly prominent after 9/11 has become less frequent. But one can still encounter metaphorical expressions such as 'catastrophe'[96] or 'terror-wave'.[97] Interestingly, there is a large proportional increase in the double conceptual metaphor TERRORISM IS UNCIVILISED EVIL. The acts of terrorism themselves are considered 'barbarism',[98] 'diabolical'[99] and the aftermath of the attacks are described as an 'inferno'.[100] Here the most common metaphor describes the situation as 'hell'.[101] One finds a large number of variations of the 'hell' metaphor including 'flame-hell',[102] 'fire-hell'[103] and 'terror-hell'.[104] And still the conceptual metaphor TERRORISM IS DISEASE and the 'mad terrorist'[105] is seldom in comparison to the other metaphors.

Bombings in Istanbul: 2003

2003 witnessed four bombings in Istanbul within one week for which al-Qaeda has claimed responsibility. On the 15th of November 2003 two bombs exploded outside of two synagogues, destroying the buildings, killing 27 and injuring over 300. This was followed by another bomb attack on the British consulate and an HSBC bank on the 20th of November. In total 57 people died and more and 700 were wounded in these two attacks.

In comparison to the other incidences of 'new terrorism', this attack with only ten articles received comparably little attention in the *Bild*.[106] In the *Bild* one can see a further decline of the conceptual metaphor TERRORISM IS WAR and an increase of TERRORISM IS CRIME. Although there are only very few metaphorical expressions which described the situation directly as a 'war'[107] and the arena of the conflict as a 'war zone',[108] the terrorist was still 'camouflaged'[109] and the attack was said to have been 'ordered'[110] or 'commanded'[111] by Osama bin Laden. The location of the attack is now established more firmly as a 'crime scene',[112] the possible perpetrators are 'suspects'[113] who are 'suspected of having committed a crime'.[114] The attacks themselves are 'criminal',[115] acts committed by 'rogues'.[116] After the attacks in Istanbul the conceptual metaphor TERRORISM IS UNCIVILISED EVIL with metaphorical expression, which describe the terrorists as 'hydras'[117] and the aftermath of the terror attack as a 'terror inferno'[118] and the perpetrators as having 'diabolical intentions',[119] is significantly lower than after Bali. Both TERRORISM IS NATURAL and TERRORISM IS DISEASE have completely disappeared from the discursive constitution of terrorism in the *Bild*.[120]

Madrid train bombings: 2004

Following the events in Madrid the indicated trend which shows a reduction of the conceptual metaphor TERRORISM IS WAR and an increase in the conceptual metaphor TERRORISM IS CRIME is further substantiated. One does still come across the occasional 'war'[121] metaphors such as 'military spokesman of al-Qaeda',[122] 'terror-troop'[123] or 'al-Qaeda warrior'[124] who are given 'terror-orders'[125] or are 'commanded'[126] to attack and who are especially 'drilled'[127] for such operations. However, in comparison to 9/11 these metaphors are far fewer in number and do not construct a military like terrorist to the same extent as the metaphors such as 'terrorist-army' or 'soldier' found after 9/11. Similarly there is a clear shift away from the military style hierarchical understanding of terrorism with a focus on the terrorist leader Osama bin Laden. Now there is far more emphasis on al-Qaeda as a network rather than as a hierarchy under the command of bin Laden. Even though a few remain such as 'al-Qaeda boss'[128] or 'al-Qaeda leadership',[129] they do not directly refer to bin Laden as explicitly as before.

So there is a clear shift away from a military to a criminal constitution of terrorism and al-Qaeda in the *Bild*. In this discourse the term 'murderer'[130] is often used as a synonym for the actor involved in terrorism and his act is referred to as 'terror-murder',[131] 'mass murder',[132] as a 'murderous strategy'[133] or a 'criminal assault'.[134] The actor is also repeatedly described as an 'offender',[135] and those assumed of committing or aiding the act are referred to as 'suspects'[136] or 'accomplices'.[137] Both of these terms in German are generally used in connection to crime rather than having a military connotation. The terrorist is constructed as someone whose act leaves behind 'terror-leads'[138] which can be followed and give an insight into who was responsible for the attack. The use of the term 'traces' or 'leads' appears to reinforce the construction of the act as something which can be investigated and 'solved'[139] by the police and the judicial system.

In a reversal to the events in Istanbul one again encounters the conceptual metaphor TERRORISM IS NATURAL and with it the metaphorical expression of likening the events to a 'catastrophe'.[140] Unsurprisingly one consistently encounters the conceptual metaphor TERRORISM IS UNCIVLISED EVIL: terrorists are 'barbaric',[141] 'diabolical'[142] 'Hydras'[143] who are responsible for 'infernos'.[144] Interestingly there is an increase of the conceptual metaphor TERRORISM IS DISEASE. The terrorist leadership is likened to a 'sick head'[145] in control of al-Qaeda which is metaphorised as the 'plague'.[146] Terrorism here is described as 'insane'[147] or as 'terror-lunacy'.[148]

London-underground bombings: 2005

In a sharp reversal to the events of 9/11 there are very few military style metaphors in the *Bild* discourse after the bombings on the London public transport system on 7th July 2005. Whereas there were fewer military metaphors in use after the Madrid bombings in comparison to 9/11, one finds even fewer in the aftermath of the tube bombings. So there is a far greater emphasis on the metaphorical expressions which constitute the terrorist as a 'criminal',[149] a 'murderous'[150] 'offender'[151] or at least a 'suspect'.[152] So the actors are now predominantly 'murderers'[153] who 'murder'[154] their victims. Their acts are now 'terroristic crimes'.[155] In addition the terrorist now is not only a 'murderer' but a 'killer',[156] he is not part of a 'terror army' or 'terror-group' but now part of a 'terror-gang'.[157] At the same time terrorist supporters are now considered 'accomplices',[158] in other words a person 'who helps another commit a crime'.[159] All these metaphorical expression constitute TERRORISM IS CRIME as the most dominant conceptual metaphor after the London bombings in the German *Bild* newspaper.

In addition to the conceptual metaphor TERRORISM IS CRIME one again finds metaphorical expressions which indicate that TERRORISM IS NATURAL. Here the attacks are metaphorised as 'al-Qaeda terror-waves'[160] which have hit London and left behind a 'zone of catastrophe'.[161] And again the conceptual metaphors TERRORISM IS UNCIVILISED EVIL and TERRORISM IS DISEASE can also be found in the discourse, as the 'barbaric'[162] attacks which were perpetrated by 'bomb barbarians',[163] who followed a 'diabolical terror plan'[164] to create an 'inferno'[165] or 'hell'[166] on earth, are constituted as a 'delusional idea'.[167]

The tabloid terrorist in the British *The Sun* newspaper

The Sun has approximately 7.9 million[168] daily readers and with around 3.15 million copies *The Sun* has the biggest daily circulation in the UK. In fact, it is the largest daily English-language newspaper in the world.[169] *The Sun* has dominated the tabloid newspaper market in the UK for almost 30 years and as Dick Rooney (2000: 92) points out: 'It can fairly be argued that *The Sun* has set the news agenda'.[170]

9/11: 2001

Similar to the *Bild* in Germany the military style construction of the terrorist actor and his act of terrorism is also very prominent in the British *The Sun* newspaper and there are a vast number of metaphorical expressions which indicate the conceptual metaphor TERRORISM IS WAR. Apart from the most obvious and explicit, the direct referral to a 'war'[171] in the two phrases 'war against terrorism'[172] or 'war on terror',[173] one encounters other metaphorical expressions which map the source domain WAR onto the target domain TERRORISM. For example Osama bin Laden is said to have 'declared war'[174] on the West, the attacks were 'acts of war'[175] and the remains of the World Trade Center are likened to a 'warzone'.[176] In addition to the direct reference to a 'war' there are a number of other metaphors which reinforce a military style construction. Similar to the *Bild* one frequently encounters metaphors in *The Sun* which refer to the Second World War. Here the events of 9/11 are likened to the German 'blitz'[177] on Great Britain or the Japanese attack on 'Pearl Harbor'[178] and this link is strengthened by the use of the term 'kamikaze'[179] in combination with the actor, act and means. The incidents on the 11th of September 2001 are described as 'kamikaze attacks'[180] as 'kamikaze horror'[181] or 'kamikaze plot',[182] which was perpetrated by 'kamikaze hijackers'[183] using 'kamikaze planes',[184] 'kamikaze airliners',[185] 'kamikaze jets'[186] or 'kamikaze flights'.[187] But the military style construction is also supported by a number of other metaphorical expressions found throughout the text in *The Sun*. In general the West is said to be facing al-Qaeda 'forces'[188] which are 'mobilising',[189] in other words we are confronted with a devoted 'army'[190] made up of 'footsoldiers'[191] and loyal 'lieutenants'.[192] Osama bin Laden and his 'comrades'[193] i.e. his 'fellow soldiers'[194] are said to have a huge devastating 'military arsenal'[195] and 'bases'[196] paid for with a 'warchest'[197] and overseen by his 'council of war'.[198] Fundamentally underpinning this militaristic construction of the al-Qaeda terrorist is the most common metaphor for Osama bin Laden as the 'terror war lord'.[199] And again one comes across the hierarchical constitution which considers bin Laden to be the ultimate 'terror-chief'[200] or 'terror-boss'[201] who commands his army from the safety of his 'command centers'.[202] 9/11 is frequently referred to as a 'strike'[203] which, according to the Merriam Webster dictionary, refers to 'a military attack; *especially:* an air attack on a single objective'[204] and the 19 hijackers directly involved in the 'assault'[205] are called a (kamikaze) 'squad'[206] in other words 'a small organized group of military personnel'.[207] This 'battle'[208] with the 'enemy'[209] al-Qaeda, 'a military adversary',[210] is said to have a 'front line'[211] and the dead of this conflict are not so much victims of a crime but 'casualties'[212] of war.

In comparison to the conceptual metaphor TERRORISM IS WAR there are far fewer metaphors which constitute terrorism as something criminal. One does encounter the odd metaphorical expression which considers the actors 'murderers'[213] or their acts as 'murder',[214] 'murderous'[215] or simply as a 'crime'.[216] Nevertheless, the metaphorical expressions which construct the conflict with al-Qaeda as a military style confrontation far outweigh those expressions which are part of the conceptual metaphor TERRORISM IS CRIME. In addition to the two conceptual metaphors TERRORISM IS WAR and TERRORISM IS CRIME one encounters two very common metaphorical expressions, 'catastrophe'[217] and 'disaster'[218] which indicate the conceptual metaphor TERRORISM IS NATURAL.

Another fairly dominant conceptual metaphor found in *The Sun* after 9/11 is TERRORISM IS UNCIVILISED EVIL. Terrorism is constituted as 'savage',[219] a 'barbaric act',[220] as pure 'barbarism'.[221] Here the terrorists are not only predicated as 'evil'[222] terrorists but they are metaphorised as the noun 'evil'.[223] Members of al-Qaeda and Osama bin Laden are 'inhuman',[224] they are considered 'hydras'[225] or 'monsters'[226] which have 'tentacles'[227] and live in 'swamps'.[228] And similar to the *Bild* there is a strong religious component to this conceptual metaphor as 9/11 is compared to an 'inferno',[229] 'Armageddon'[230] or to 'hell'[231] while the attacks themselves are 'doomsday attacks'.[232] The final conceptual metaphor to be found in the discourse following 9/11 is TERRORISM IS DISEASE. Here the terrorism is a 'wicked plaque',[233] predicated as 'insane'[234] or 'deranged'.[235] The terrorist is a 'maniac',[236] 'lunatic'[237] or 'madman'[238] perpetrating 'terrorist madness'.[239]

Bali bombings: 2002

Overall the predicative and metaphorical construction of terrorism after Bali bombings in 2002 have remained fairly consistent to those constructions found after 9/11. The dominant military style construction of new terrorism continues. Apart from the known metaphor 'war on terror' there are a large number of other metaphorical expressions which indicate the continued importance of the conceptual metaphor TERRORISM IS WAR. 'New terrorism' is likened again to the 'Blitz',[240] as the targets of terrorism are said to have been 'blitzed',[241] and so the experience of the Second World War is mapped onto the understanding of 'new terrorism'.[242] The bombings in Bali are still considered military style 'strikes',[243] an 'al-Qaeda operation'[244] which is part of a large 'al-Qaeda campaign',[245] in other words 'a connected series of military operations forming a distinct phase of a war'.[246] So terrorists are still 'waging'[247] a 'war'[248] against the West in which there are 'battles',[249] 'sieges'[250] and 'fronts',[251] and where the 'enemy'[252] is organised in 'squads'[253] which have received 'military training'.[254] As is typical of 'wartime',[255] 'casualties'[256] in this conflict are unavoidable.

Similar to 9/11 there are far fewer criminal metaphorical expressions such as 'murder',[257] 'murderous',[258] 'murderer'[259] or 'crime scene'[260] which are indicative of the conceptual metaphor TERRORISM IS CRIME. And again there are metaphors such as 'catastrophe'[261] and 'disaster'[262] which indicate that TERRORISM IS NATURAL. Similarly, the terrorists responsible for this 'inferno'[263] are still considered uncivilised[264] and 'evil'.[265] Osama bin Laden, who's 'tentacles'[266] are spread around the globe, is said to command 'evil followers'[267] or 'monsters'[268] 'without a soul'.[269] And with the Bali bombing these 'vile'[270] creatures, unrivalled in 'wickedness',[271] have created 'hell'[272] in 'heavenly'[273] paradise. This conceptual meta-phor TERRORISM IS UNCIVILISED EVIL is again joined by TERRORISM IS DISEASE as bin Laden's followers are not only 'evil', they are 'crazed'[274] 'lunatics'.[275]

Bombings in Istanbul: 2003

Similar to the *Bild* this incident of terrorism was reported on far less than any of the other attacks and therefore the overall number of meta-phorical expression is limited. Nevertheless terrorism after the bombings in Istanbul in 2003 is still predominantly considered a military style phe-nomenon in *The Sun*. There is still a clear dominance of metaphorical expressions which constitute the terrorist as the 'enemy'[276] and al-Qaeda as military style army made up of 'brigades'[277] and 'units'[278] which are waging a 'war of terror'.[279] This 'war'[280] still involves 'campaigns'[281] and 'battles'[282] and in this particular 'terror strike'[283] the terrorists 'blitzed'[284] the British consulate leaving behind a devastated 'battlefield'.[285] So overall the conceptual metaphor TERRORISM IS WAR is still more dom-inant than the conceptual metaphor TERRORISM IS CRIME with expres-sions such as 'murder',[286] 'murderous'[287] or 'murderers'.[288] Although the conceptual metaphor TERRORISM IS NATURAL was totally absent the other two TERRORISM IS UNCIVILISED EVIL and TERRORISM IS DISEASE could also be found in a limited number as the terrorists were constituted as 'evil'[289] 'maniacs'[290] who 'infest'[291] the world.

Madrid train bombings: 2004

After the train bombings in Madrid in 2004 the conceptual metaphor TERRORISM IS WAR remains the most dominant. Again there are links to the Second World War with the use of metaphors such as 'blitz'[292] or odd word combinations such as 'islamofascism'.[293] Terrorist attacks continue to be seen as 'strikes'[294] in a 'battle'[295] or 'operations'[296] in a 'war'[297] 'waged'[298] against the world in which there can be no 'armistice'.[299] This conflict is said to involve a 'frontline'[300] and 'fortresses'[301] in a fight against an al-Qaeda who's 'ranks'[302] are made up of 'death squads'.[303] The 'enemy'[304] is commanded by 'warlords',[305] the scenes of the bombings are 'war zones'[306] and those killed or injured are 'casualties of terror'.[307]

And again the metaphorical expressions indicative of the conceptual metaphor TERRORISM IS CRIME such as 'murderers',[308] 'murderous'[309] or 'criminal',[310] are comparatively much more seldom than those indicative of a military style construction of terrorism. Furthermore, in contrast to the bombings in Istanbul, the conceptual metaphor TERRORISM IS NATURAL reappears with expressions such as 'catastrophe'[311] and 'disaster'.[312] Similarly there is an upturn in TERRORISM IS UNCIVILISED EVIL: One here finds that the act of terrorism is predicated as 'barbaric'[313] and 'savage',[314] something committed by an 'evil'[315] 'Al-Qaeda monster'[316] which leaves behind a 'trail of slime'[317]. Like a spider terrorists have spun a 'terror web'[318] or a 'web of evil'.[319] Not only is terrorism evil, TERRORISM IS DISEASE as terrorists are 'maniacs',[320] 'madmen'[321] or 'nutters'[322] and terrorism is constituted as 'deranged',[323] 'lunacy'[324] or simply 'insane'.[325]

London-underground bombings: 2005

After the bombings and the attempted bombings of public transport system in London on the seventh and twenty-first of July there is a shift in the distribution of the conceptual metaphors. Although TERRORISM IS WAR is still the most dominant conceptual metaphor TERRORISM IS CRIME has increased. It should be noted that the events in London are still considered similar to the Second World War as the attacks are constituted as a 'blitz'[326] on London by 'Islamonazis'.[327] Although there are far less references to a 'war on terror'[328] there are still a large number of other metaphorical expressions which construct the terrorist as a military style actor. For example al-Qaeda is still made up of 'troops'[329] or 'suicide squads',[330] those in control are 'Al-Qaeda commanders',[331] their subordinates are 'second in command'[332] and their supplies are distributed by an 'Al-Qaeda quartermaster':[333] 'an army officer who provides clothing and subsistence for a body of troops'.[334] The London attacks themselves are still considered a 'siege'[335] or 'strikes'[336] by an 'enemy'[337] who is carrying out 'missions'[338] or 'operations'[339] which are part of a larger 'campaign'[340] in a 'war'[341] against the West. And in this 'warzone'[342] one typically encounters 'battlefields',[343] 'frontlines'[344] and 'casualties of war'.[345]

Interestingly the conceptual metaphor TERRORISM IS WAR is now closely rivalled by the conceptual metaphor TERRORISM IS CRIME. The 'casualty of war' is now also a 'victim'[346] of 'crime'.[347] The troops and squads are now also constituted as a 'gang'[348] or 'mob'[349] of 'criminals'[350] or 'murderers',[351] the battlefield is now also a 'crime scene'.[352] In addition to these two ways of predicating the location of a terrorist attack one also comes across the term 'disaster zone'.[353] This, together with other metaphorical expressions such as 'catastrophe',[354] 'disaster'[355] or 'waves'[356] of attack indicated the remaining relevance of the conceptual metaphor TERRORISM IS NATURAL.

In addition a significant proportion of the metaphorical expressions found in the discourse after the London bombings are part of the conceptual metaphor TERRORISM IS UNCIVILISED EVIL. Here terrorism is predicated as 'barbaric',[357] 'savagery'[358] or 'evil'.[359] It is a 'wicked',[360] 'inhuman'[361] act of 'barbarism',[362] likened to 'hell'[363] perpetrated by 'subhuman',[364] 'evil beasts'.[365] The four terrorists responsible for the 'monsterous act'[366] known as 7/7 are constituted as 'possessed'[367] 'monsters',[368] and maybe even the four 'horsemen of the Apocalypse'.[369] At the same time there also seems to be an overall increase in the metaphorical expressions which constitute TERRORISM IS DISEASE. Here the attacks are predicated as 'sickening'[370] 'madness'[371] committed by 'nutters',[372] 'maniacs',[373] 'lunatics'[374] or 'psychopaths'.[375] The terrorists are constructed as 'mad',[376] 'sick'[377] 'suicide nuts'[378] and 'crazed fanatics'[379] who have been 'infected'[380] by 'poisonous clerics'.[381]

Conclusion

The chapter does not claim to have covered all the metaphors in the texts and there are a number of other metaphors which did not find a mention here. For example, there are a very limited number of metaphorical expressions which liken al-Qaeda to a 'holding company' and bin Laden to its 'chairman' and therefore may constitute TERRORISM IS BUSINESS.[382] Other examples refer to al-Qaeda as a 'terror machine'[383] or a person which has a 'head' and a 'heart'.[384] The chapter tried to gather some of the most dominant metaphorical expressions and categorise these into conceptual metaphors in order to illustrate the discursive constitution of 'new terrorism' in the tabloid media in Germany and Great Britain between 2001 and 2005. The analysis of the *Bild* and *The Sun* newspapers revealed five distinct conceptual metaphors: TERRORISM IS WAR, CRIME, NATURAL, UNCIVILISED EVIL and DISEASE. And interestingly despite the fluctuations, the five conceptual metaphors can be found more or less consistently in both Germany and the UK over the five-year period.

The next and final chapter wants to examine the consequences of such discursive constructions. The central idea is that counter-terrorism options depend very much on the conception of terrorism (Schmid 1992; Daase 2001). As Brian Jackson points out, 'embedded within specific labels for al-Qaeda – group, network, movement – are very different answers to key questions for policy and counterterrorism design' (Jackson 2006: 242). So the chapter argues that the construction of the terrorist in public discourse such as the *Bild* or *The Sun* makes only certain counter-terrorism policies possible while other means of addressing the issue remain outside the options considered as a response.

6
Metaphors, Predicates and Policy Implications

'Metaphor is the dreamwork of language and, like all dreamwork, its interpretation reflects as much on the interpreter as on the originator'. (Davidson 1978)

The central notion of this chapter is that a certain predication of terrorism makes certain counter-terrorism policies more likely than others. It does not claim that the metaphors used to predicate 'new terrorism' in the tabloid newspapers the *Bild* and *The Sun* 'cause' particular policies in the sense of dependent and independent variables. As we have seen in the last chapter one cannot talk of a causal link between certain metaphors and policy. Nevertheless, metaphors do open up certain policy options as they promote certain belief systems and justify causes of action (Mio 1997; Hartmann-Mahmud 2002). Metaphor 'defines the pattern of perception to which people respond' (Edelman 1971: 67). This chapter does also not want to offer an overview of all the existing counter-terrorism measures both Germany and the United Kingdom have implemented but indicates that the construction of 'new terrorism' in discourse made certain response appear logical while others are considered absurd. It wants to show how military, criminal, disaster management and immigration measures as well as the absence of any engagement or negotiation policy fit the predication of 'new terrorism' in discourse.

The first part of the chapter will look at what policies are made possible by the predication of TERRORISM IS WAR and will examine Germany's and Britain's military response to 'new terrorism'. The second section will examine the notion of TERRORISM IS CRIME and illustrate some of the judicial responses in both countries while section three contemplates the idea of TERRORISM IS NATURAL and the 'resulting' option of disaster management. Part four and five will evaluate the predication of TERRORISM IS UNCIVILISED EVIL and TERRORISM IS DISEASE and indicate their predication of terrorism as something other and foreign calling for tighter immigration policies, and as something one can definitely not negotiate with. Where possible, these interpretations will be supported by public opinion polls which illustrate the general understanding of what 'new terrorism' is considered to be.

Terrorism is war

As we saw in the last chapter the conceptual metaphor TERRORISM IS WAR was prominent in the tabloid media discourses regarding 'new terrorism' in both countries especially after 9/11. But even in non tabloid media outlets one encountered metaphorical expressions which predicate terrorism as war (Haes 2002). For example, the German broadsheet newspaper *Süddeutsche Zeitung* headlined: 'Terror-War against America'[1]; the Christian *Rheinische Post* called the attack a 'War against Civilisation'[2] and even German left-wing newspapers such as *Die Tageszeitung* and *Neues Deutschland* opened with 'War against the USA'[3] and 'Terror-War against the USA'.[4] Similarly, in the UK the predication of terrorism as war went beyond *The Sun* as the leftwing *The Mirror* titled 'War on the World'[5] and the broadsheet *The Guardian* called the attacks 'a declaration of war'.[6] And without doubt the metaphor 'war on terror(ism)' was very dominant at the start of the 'campaign' (Smith 2002). However, the 'war on terrorism' is by no means the first occasion where the metaphor of war has been used to frame a certain issue or problem. Other examples include the 'war on poverty' 'waged' by the US government under Lyndon B. Johnson in the sixties and the 'war on drugs' under Richard Nixon in the seventies (Glover 2002). According to Keith Shimko (1995: 79) the reason for the metaphorical popularity of 'war' for issues which are deemed as threatening are simple: 'First, war is a widely and readily accessible concept; everyone knows what a war is. Second, war is a complex and multifaceted phenomenon. Since there are so many aspects of war, there are many dimensions along which something can be like a war'.

So how does the metaphor 'war' constitute terrorism and what policies does it make possible or logical? People associate a large number of things with war and these associations are included in the transference of the source domain 'war' to the target domain 'terrorism'. For example, this includes allocation of funds in the war effort. As Susan Sontag (1989: 99) argues '[w]ar-making is one of the few activities that people are not supposed to view "realistically"; that is, with an eye to expense and practical outcome. In an all out war, expenditure is all out, unprudent – war being defined as an emergency in which no sacrifice is excessive'. So the normal budgetary concerns and the idea of a cost-benefit analysis go out the window to a certain extent as the whole nation's industry has to be mobilised and sacrifices have to be made to ensure the ultimate victory.

War is not considered a normal state of affairs; it is an unusual period of time where unusual measures have to be implemented to stop the enemy from winning. Securing the borders of a country and preventing the enemy from entering makes sense in a war. As the enemy is usually another country, those from that country or region are suspected of automatically supporting the opponents cause. They are therefore treated with suspicion and subjected to different treatment than the own population. For example, in the Second World War it was normal to apprehend potential saboteurs from the country one was fighting. Here the incarceration of Germans and especially Japanese, and even second or third generation Japanese Americans, in camps was considered a necessary precaution (Cole 2003). The state of emergency in a war calls for such new legislation where checks and balances are reduced and civil liberties are restricted; both sacrificed in the war effort (Shimko 1995).

In addition, the war metaphor simplifies the issue which it frames. The problem is made manageable as it is reduced to a question of defeating the enemy and winning the war. Searching for the root causes of the problem is discouraged as critical voices are silenced. Criticism of the war becomes unpatriotic, cowardly and treacherous. The problem becomes apolitical, something which cannot be debated in the public realm. 'What feedback are we allowed in wartime? Acceptable questions include, "Are we winning?" "What weapons should be used to defeat the enemy?" "What war strategies should be applied?" We cannot ask if the war is necessary, or if the enemy is ourselves. We cannot back away saying that we were wrong' (Hartmann-Mahmud 2002: 429).

Most obviously, a military style constitution of 'new terrorism' calls for a military response. As early as 1987 Jeffrey Simon of the RAND corporation, a think tank not really known for its expertise on metaphor analysis, realised the importance of the war metaphor in the fight against terrorism: 'Equating terrorism with war effectively ends any debate over whether military responses are justified. If a nation is at war it must respond militarily to attack' (Simon 1987: 9). So the war metaphor influences the public's perception of the enemy and makes a military response appear logical (Bates 2004). The illustrative metaphor constitutes reality. As Sarbin (2003: 150–151) points out: 'An important feature of the war metaphor is that problems engendered by terrorist acts can be solved through the deployment of military forces'. So more than anything the public associates war with violence, insecurity and the application of military force to achieve victory and solve the threat of terrorism. If the problem is considered to have military dimensions a military solutions seems appropriate. Metaphors such as 'terror commando', 'terror army' or 'war on terror' outlined in the last chapter are all part of the language of war and thereby frame the issue of 'new terrorism' and the conflict with al-Qaeda as a war which can be won by military means (Shimko 1995; Kruglanski et al. 2007). These words may not cause a certain policy, but they increase the likelihood of a military response as it seems appropriate to the constructed image of 'new terrorism'. And obviously a military response entails violence and therefore casualties both at home and abroad are naturally accepted. Although sad and regrettable civilians always perish in a war where collateral damage is part of the fighting. So in a war on terrorism the death of innocent civilians due to the bombing of al-Qaeda 'bases' in Afghanistan is inevitable and ultimately an acceptable means of engaging the 'new terrorism': After all it is war!

Germany's military responses

Generally, the Federal Republic of Germany is not known for its military adventures abroad, at least not anymore. Following the Second World War Germany has continuously presented itself as a peaceful, diplomatic country, which nobody has to be afraid of; a soft power which strives for political solutions rather than military confrontation (Maull 1999). Nevertheless, following 9/11 Germany openly supported US military action in the fight against 'new terrorism' and quickly offered almost 4,000 troops in support (Hyde-Price 2003).

This chapter would argue that a military reaction was made possible by an understanding of 'new terrorism' as war which 'resulted' from the discursive construction of the phenomena in discourse. And it was this shared understanding of 'new terrorism' found both among politician and the general public which naturally led to a military response and made it appropriate. For example, Chancellor Gerhard Schröder stated that the 'attacks in New York and Washington were not only attacks on the United States of America; they were a *declaration of war* against the entire *civilised* world'.[7] However, the notion in favour of military action was only passed in parliament with a majority of only ten votes.[8] Even though the vote in parliament might suggest otherwise there was wide spread support for the participation in a military response as the seemingly tight decision was due to the fact that Chancellor Gerhard Schröder linked the proposal of military action to a question of confidence in his government. This meant that the opposition parties such as the Christian Democrats (CDU/CSU) and the Liberals (FDP) voted against the notion even though they supported the participation in military action (Maull 2001; Hyde-Price 2003).[9]

There was similar initial support for military action among the German population as a 'military contribution by Germany to the war in Afghanistan met with majority approval by the public' (Oswald 2004: 96). In the past support for military action abroad was generally very low, for example only 17 per cent supported military action in the first Gulf War in 1991 and only 19 per cent did so during the war in Kosovo. In September 2001 58 per cent favoured a German military participation in a war against terrorism (Katzenstein 2002a: 429). Similarly, a different poll found that 57 per cent of those asked held the opinion that the United States was right to use military force in response to 9/11 (Malthaner and Waldmann 2003: 124). A large number of other opinion polls support this construction of TERRORISM IS WAR after 9/11 (Noelle-Neumann and Köcher 2003: 990–994). One opinion poll found out that around two-thirds of Germany's population were in favour of supporting the United States militarily after 9/11.[10] A different poll suggested that 57 per cent of the population supported the activation of Article 5 of the NATO treaty (Noelle-Neumann 2002), other studies indicated that 65 per cent of the German population agreed with the military reaction of the United States[11] and over 50 per cent directly supported the deployment of German troops in the 'war on terrorism'.[12]

As a result of the political and public support, which is indicative of a shared understanding of terrorism as something war-like, Germany following 9/11 participated in a number of military counter-terrorism missions at a very early stage (Mauer 2007). The policies are evidence and the result of this interpretation of 'new terrorism' is war. The military policies include, for example, Germany's participation on *Operation Eagle Assist* which used NATO's airborne early warning aircraft (AWACS) to patrol North American airspace against potential 'kamikaze' terrorists. In response to the activation of Article 5 of the North Atlantic Treaty Germany contributed a third of the squadron's personnel (Miko and Froehlich 2004). In addition, Germany also actively participated in another NATO mission, *Operation Active Endeavour*, which was supposed to detect, deter and prevent the movement of 'new terrorist' 'troops' and hamper their activities especially the intention to obtain WMDs.[13] Here the German navy is taking part in a naval operation in the Mediterranean Sea and the Straits of Gibraltar by deploying frigates of the Bremen-Class and submarines as well as patrol boats to guard against the 'new terrorist' 'army'.

Germany's largest and most important military contribution to the 'war on terrorism' and evidence of a TERRORISM IS WAR understanding is, however, its allocation of up to 3,900 troops to *Operation Enduring Freedom* (Connolly 2001). The almost 4,000 soldiers for the fight against 'new terrorist' soldiers are made up of a number of different troops including both passive and more active elements directly engaging the 'enemy'. On the more passive side this involves around 250 military medics and an Airbus A310 MedEvac which provides medical airlift capability; 500 troops responsible for logistical operations and air transport as well as 450 support staff. The more active element of this force includes up to 800 soldiers together with *Fuchs* armoured vehicles which are capable of identifying nuclear, chemical and biological warfare 'arsenals' as well as a 1,800-strong naval force and around 100 special-forces troops.[14] Among these, the largest contribution to the fight against terrorism is the mission of the German Navy around the Horn of Africa (Roell 2003). Similar to *Operation Active Endeavour* this part of *Operation Enduring Freedom* is supposed to gather intelligence about terrorist activity around the Horn of Africa, safeguard international shipping routes and cut off the 'new terrorist's' supply chain to their 'military bases' (Clark 2002; Miko and Froehlich 2004).

Afghanistan, however, has been central to Germany's military involvement in the 'war on terrorism'. It has taken an active role in Afghanistan and participated in the 'war' with al-Qaeda and the Taliban and *Operation Enduring Freedom* by sending around one-hundred special-forces troops, *Kommando Spezialkräfte* (KSK, Special Forces Command) to Afghanistan (Leggemann 2003). Their mission was to destroy al-Qaeda 'command centres' and terrorist training facilities, to combat 'battle hardened', 'terror-commandos' and bring them to justice and stop other parties 'logistically' supporting terrorist activities (Mauer 2007: 74). Although details about the activities of Germany's special forces is difficult to verify it is assumed that the KSK took part in a number of operation such as Task Force K-Bar (*Combined Joint Special Operations Task Force – South*), the battle for Tora Bora and Operation Anaconda (Broomby 2002; Löwenstein 2008; Scholzen 2004).[15]

Apart from Operation Enduring Freedom Germany has also been actively involved in Afghanistan with the International Security Assistance Force

(ISAF) Mission which was initiated by the Bonn Agreement and sanctioned by Security Council Resolution 1386 in December 2001. On the 21st of December the Bundestag approved to send 1,200 German soldiers to Afghanistan as part of ISAF. These were deployed in addition to the 3,900 troops committed to *Operation Enduring Freedom* (Oswald 2004). The mandate for the ISAF mission has to be re-approved every year by the German parliament and since the first deployment the number of soldiers has risen to around 3,300. Between February and August 2003 Germany together with the Netherlands had joint command of the whole ISAF mission. By now it is the third largest troop contributor, and is in charge of Regional Command North where it assists the Afghan government with security and reconstruction in the provinces of Badakhshan, Baghlan, Takhar and Kunduz (Maaß 2007).

Overall the German counter-terrorism policies seem to fit the initial military style constitution of 'new terrorism' after 9/11 as Germany, in contrast to its (self)-image, became directly involved in the 'war on terrorism'. Actually as Miko and Froehlich (2004) point out, 40 per cent of German troops based abroad are in fact engaged in counter-terrorism. Its support of the United States and Germany's participation with almost 4,000 troops represent its 'most extensive military engagement since the Second World War' (Connolly 2001). In 2001 the Bundeswehr was given an additional 1.5 billion Marks exclusively for anti-terror programs (Clark 2002; Leggemann 2003) and in 'November 2004, the parliament approved an additional 114 million for future counter-terrorist operations of the army' (Szyszkowitz 2005: 53). As Peter Katzenstein (2002a: 429) points out, 'September 11 is a watershed because Germany assumed military responsibility in a worldwide context'. The German government and the German people initially went along with an interpretation of 9/11 as a 'war' (Katzenstein 2002a: 427).

Britain's military responses

Similar to Germany, Britain's military response to terrorism following 9/11 fits the conceptual metaphor TERRORISM IS WAR found in the discourse. The central idea is that the source domain 'war' mapped certain aspects of this phenomenon on to the target domain 'terrorism'. In other words, the military style construction imminent in the different metaphorical expressions such as 'terror-commando' or 'terror-army' made a military response appear appropriate. And this understanding is again visible both in the political elite as well as the public. Tony Blair, for example stated: 'Whatever the technical or legal issues about the declaration of war, the fact is we are at war with terrorism'.[16] Overall, the general public also seems to share this kind of understanding of 'new terrorism' as a number of opinion polls indicate that the United Kingdom's active participation in the 'war on terrorism' fits into the general public's understanding of what terrorism is and therefore how it should be fought. A survey in October 2001 found that between 67 and 74 per cent of those questioned supported or approved of the military action by the United States and Britain against Afghanistan.[17] Similarly, 57 per cent approved of sending British troops into Afghanistan to take part in the fighting on the ground.[18] In 2002 between 76 and 78 per cent of those questioned in Great Britain supported air strikes and attacks by ground troops against 'new terrorist' 'bases' and other facilities and 84 per cent even 'supported the use of one's own troops to destroy terrorist camps' (Worldviews 2002: 20–21). Even in 2004, 56 per cent in Britain still agreed that military action was the most appropriate way of fighting terrorism (Transatlantic Trends 2004: 18).

Now considering the concrete policy responses 'resulting' from these interpretations of 'new terrorism' as war one should note that Britain was the only other country apart from the United States to deploy forces from the beginning of *Operation Enduring Freedom* on the 7 October 2001, only 26 days after the terrorist attacks in New York and Washington (Donohue 2007). In the first few weeks this military operation to destroy the al-Qaeda 'army' included elements of all three military branches of the British Armed Forces: the Royal Navy, the Royal Air Force and the British Army. The naval element to face the military threat of the 'new terrorist' 'forces' was made up of a number of Royal Navy ships including an Invincible class aircraft carrier, a destroyer, a frigate and three nuclear powered submarines which contributed Tomahawk cruise missiles to the initial aerial bombardment of al-Qaeda 'command centres' and training facilities (Bamford 2004; Dorman 2003). The Royal Air Force also contributed sophisticated military hardware to what the British government codenamed *Operation Varitas* including VC-10 and Tristar tanker aircraft, Nimrod, Sentry and Canberra reconnaissance aircraft as well as Hercules air transport aircraft and Chinook helicopters against the 'new terrorists'' 'military arsenal' (Donohue 2007). The involvement of the elite special forces of the British Army, the Special Air Service (SAS) Regiment, are shrouded in secrecy but there are a number of reports which suggest their direct involvement in fighting the terror 'soldiers' and their 'lieutenants' in Afghanistan early on in the 'war on terror' (Bennett 2003: 265; Norton-Taylor 2002).

Slightly more confirmed is the involvement of other special forces of the British military. For example, the Special Boat Service (SBS), the

Navy's equivalent to the SAS, landed at Bagram airfield outside of Kabul to evaluate its condition[19] and in November 2001 Royal Marines 40 Commando, along with US Marines, took part in securing the airbase against 'mobilising' 'forces' of 'new terrorism' (Bamford 2004). Similar to the German KSK, British special forces also served on the 'front line' and participated in the 'battle' of Tora Bora in December 2001 against al-Qaeda 'troops' and around 1,700 British Royal Marines were involved in *Operation Anaconda* in between 2nd and 18th of March 2002 and the follow up operation *Operation Jacana* (Dorman 2003). The Ministry of Defence points out that '[t]heir role was to deny and destroy terrorist infrastructure and interdict the movement of al-Qaeda in eastern Afghanistan'.[20] Since the invasion the number of British forces in Afghanistan in support of Operation Enduring Freedom and the International Security Assistance Force (ISAF), named Operation Herrick, has continuously risen to around 8,300 in October 2008. [21] Around 7,300 of these troops are stationed in Helmand province in the south of the country and apart from the individual soldiers this also includes hi-tech military hardware such as Warrior armoured vehicles, Apache attack helicopters or Harrier jets to conduct 'operations' against terror 'war lords', 'commanders' and 'death squads'. Overall the cost of British military operation in Afghanistan over and above the planned expenditure on defence from 2001 to 2007 has reached about one and a half billion pounds.[22]

One could even debate whether the invasion of Iraq was/is linked to the 'war on terrorism'. As Laura Donohue (2007: 31) points out, '[t]he war with Iraq may be said to relate broadly to counter-terrorism concerns'. Both the political elite but also the media have emphasised a possible link between al-Qaeda and Saddam Hussein. Tony Blair for example stated that 'Iraq is not the only country posing a risk in respect to WMD. Over the past few weeks, we have seen powerful evidence of the continuing terrorist threat: the suspected ricin plot in London and Manchester' (Hewitt 2008: 42). But also the tabloid *The Sun* constituted TERRORISM IS WAR and explicitly linked Iraq and 'new terrorism' by reporting that 'an Osama bin Laden lieutenant sheltered by Iraq was linked to the ricin poison factory found in north London'[23] (Norton-Taylor 2005). In fact some polls indicate that 61 per cent believed that there was a link between Saddam Hussein and al-Qaeda.[24] Similarly, 61 per cent were totally or at least fairly convinced that Iraq had weapons of mass destruction and that these weapons may end up in the hand of terrorists if Britain did not deal with the issue now.[25] Even though there was widespread protest in the run-up to the war with Iraq, a large majority (66 per cent)[26] of the British population supported the military action.[27]

Terrorism is crime

In contrast to TERRORISM IS WAR the conceptual metaphor TERRORISM IS CRIME has become increasingly dominant throughout the media discourse on 'new terrorism'. While the idea of terrorism as war and crime has been presented as two distinct almost dichotomous categories in the literature on terrorism,[28] the metaphorical constitution of 'new terrorism' in discourse seems to include both understandings to a fluctuating degree. But what does this kind of predication of 'new terrorism' as crime do and what kind of policies does it make possible?

In contrast to the war the crime metaphors predicate 'new terrorism' as something rather ordinary. While the event of a war is something unusual, something which has a beginning and an end, crime is very common and can be considered almost a constant phenomenon in every society (Kruglanski et al. 2007). In comparison to war, crime is widespread and occurs very frequently and therefore anybody can be a 'victim' of crime not just the soldiers and those close to the front. Importantly criminals are part of society and crime is generally understood as something which happens inside a community, while war is something which involves engagement with the outside. 'Regardless of what country we live in, we are taught from childhood that people who are criminals live among us' (Kappeler and Kappeler 2004: 176).

Essentially, the predication of 'new terrorism' as crime automatically involves a moral judgement not inherent in the constitution of terrorism as war. While war can be a legitimate endeavour, crime cannot. One generally accepts the right to existence of a military adversary, while the criminal is considered a menace which lacks any kind of legitimacy. As Kappeler and Kappeler (2004: 176) point out 'the eradication and punishment of criminal behaviour is seen as a desirable and just goal'. The military adversary is similar to us only on the other side of the front, almost a like unit, which generally follows certain rules of engagement. The criminal on the other hand is deviant; he or she does forbidden things and does not adhere to rules. In fact, criminals by definition break rules and therefore have to be punished in some sort of way. Therefore, some point out that the 'policy of criminalization makes it hard for the state to negotiate with its armed opponents [...]. Just as it is inappropriate to deal with bandits, since the rule of law is thereby prejudiced, so, it is often supposed, it is inappropriate to negotiate with terrorists' (Gilbert 1994: 167). Others may disagree with this interpretation as there are ample examples of plea bargaining or reduced sentences in which the prosecution strikes a deal with the criminal.

What is clear, however, is that the conceptual metaphor TERRORISM IS CRIME in contrast to TERRORISM IS WAR most importantly calls for a judicial rather than a military response. As Peter Sederberg (1995: 299–300) points out, while 'the view that terrorism is war leads its proponents to favour repressive responses; the view that terrorism is crime leads its proponents to favour legal solutions'. This however, does not mean that the two understandings are dichotomously opposed to each other in all aspects. In fact both conceptual metaphors seem to overlap to a certain extent as a legislative response can make sense in both TERRORISM IS WAR and TERRORISM IS CRIME. For example, one encounters implementation of new laws such as a war powers act or emergency powers for police in both situations of war and situations of crime.

Germany's judicial responses

Similar to the conceptual metaphor TERRORISM IS WAR and the military responses, the understanding of 'new terrorism' as something criminal made a legislative response of Germany after 9/11 appear logical. And again the implemented policies are evidence and the result of this interpretation of 'new terrorism' as crime.

For example, the German government quickly passed a large number of new anti-terror laws and alterations to existing legislation against the terrorist 'criminal'. Most directly this is noticeable in the first two so-called security packages (*Sicherheitspakete*), the first of which is generally considered to be more repressive in nature while the second has a more preventative character (Hein 2004: 148; Bukow 2005). Security package one was adopted by the cabinet on 19 September 2001 and included a number of legislative changes. Most importantly this included changes to the penal code by adding a new section 129b to the existing anti-terror paragraph. Previously, the illegality of forming a terrorist organisation only applied to registered associations which were at least partly based in Germany. The new section now made it possible to prosecute foreign terrorist organisations and terrorist 'crimes' committed abroad by giving the police powers, even at a very early planning stage, to investigate 'suspect' terrorists and their 'accomplices' living in Germany but planning 'criminal' attacks against other countries. Furthermore, the first security package made changes to the law of associations (*Vereinsrecht*) by banning certain religious organisations considered 'suspect' extremist. The alteration was supposed to end the privileged position of religious groups and take away their ability to mask their extremist and anti-constitutional stances under the pretext of free religious expression.

Apart from this the first security package also included a number of other measures. For example, it included the allocation of an additional three billion DM for counter-terrorism in 2002 and in particular more funding and personnel for the security services and the classical crime fighting institutions such as the Federal Criminal Police Office (*Bundeskriminalamt*) and the Federal Office for the Protection of the Constitution (*Bundesamt für Verfassungsschutz*). In addition, the package tightened banking regulations, increased the security for public buildings and made improvements to air safety by introducing more careful checks and monitoring of airport personnel and placing security staff on selected Lufthansa flights to prevent further 'murder' (Lepsius 2004; Hyde-Price 2003; Mauer 2007).

This understanding of terrorism as something criminal is also visible in the second security package as it made adjustments to more than 100 regulations in 17 different laws and a number of administrative decrees (Katzenstein 2002b). It increased the powers of the intelligence and security services giving the Federal Criminal Police Office a stronger position as it does not have to rely on the police forces of the *Länder* for data collection anymore. At the same time the Federal and the *Länder* Offices for the Protection of the Constitution were given more competencies to access individual banking, employment, university and telephone records of suspected 'offenders'. Furthermore, the second package includes legislation which is supposed to improve the cooperation between local and regional police forces and prevent the infiltration of potential terrorist 'killers' into Germany and identifying those 'terror gangs' already in the country through biometric data on identity cards, passports and visa applications (Lepsius 2004). As Victor Mauer points out, although this prompted concerns about civil liberties and excessive intrusion, the 'new legislation reflects that the lion's share of counter terrorism against transnational terrorist threats is to be conducted on the law enforcement and intelligence fronts [...after all] terrorists are regarded as criminals' (Mauer 2007: 63). This general understanding of terrorism as something criminal is also visible very clearly in German public opinion. For example, in November 2001 over 70 per cent of the German population seemed to support the second security package.[29]

Britain's judicial responses

The mapping of the source domain CRIME to the target domain TERRORISM is also clearly visible in the policies implemented in the United Kingdom following 9/11. Although the British government had only just passed a new set of fairly substantial anti-terror laws in 2000 (Terrorism

Act of 2000),[30] there was an understanding that further legislation would be an appropriate means of responding to this kind of 'criminal' 'new terrorism' (Donohue 2007). As Sebastian Payne points out, the government could have responded to 9/11 without making new law, but the government chose to legislate (Payne 2002: 44).

The Anti-terrorism, Crime and Security Act 2001 (ATCSA) was the first piece of legislation aimed at dealing with the 'criminal' terrorist.[31] While parts of the act replace and supplement parts of the Terrorism Act of 2000 a fairly substantial part is new legislation which addresses a wide range of issues. For example the act establishes rules for the freezing of 'new terrorist's' property and funding, the management of information vital for counter-terrorism and amends asylum and immigration procedures which may be exploited by terrorists. Furthermore, the act includes laws for the security of the aviation and nuclear industry as well as the issue of WMDs and other dangerous substances such as toxins or pathogens which may be used in an attack by 'new terrorist' 'gangs'. Similar to Germany the act makes amendments to policing measures and generally enhances police powers in the United Kingdom. This for example includes an increase of investigatory powers, the storage of communication data, police and judicial cooperation and the specification of various new criminal offences (Walker 2003; Cornish 2005). Despite the fact that the act is fairly substantial in size as it consists of fourteen parts, passed relatively quickly in December 2001. This indicates that the legislation appeared appropriate to the threat and was in line with the discursive constitution of 'new terrorism' as criminal.

This understanding of TERRORISM IS CRIME was further substantiated by another round of legislation in 2005. The Prevention of Terrorism Act 2005[32] allowed the Home Secretary to issue 'control orders' against people 'suspected' of being involved in 'murderous' terrorism. These orders could include restricting individuals' access to mobile phones or the internet or even placing suspects under house arrest which required a lower burden of proof in comparison to normal incarceration. Following the London tube attacks in July 2005, the British government again introduced new anti-terror legislation which included further increased powers for law enforcement, new criminal offences relating to 'new terrorism' such as the glorification or encouragement of terrorism and new rules for immigration detentions (Beckman 2007). This criminal understanding of terrorism inherent in these laws was further enhanced and extended by the Terrorism Act of 2006[33] which proposed that the police should be allowed to detain 'suspected' terrorists for 90 days without charging them. Although this was reduced to 'only' 28 days, the Prime Minister

Gordon Brown has since tried to increase the number of days in detention without charge to 42 indicating the continued understanding of terrorism as something criminal. The opinion of the British public appears to further substantiate the belief that TERRORISM IS CRIME as opinion polls have continuously showed a very high support for new anti-terror legislation.[34] For example, between 64[35] and 72[36] per cent agreed that the police should have the powers to detain 'suspected' terrorists without charge for 90 days.

Terrorism is natural

The last chapter also indicated that the conceptual metaphor TERRORISM IS NATURAL was found throughout the discourse in the *Bild* and *The Sun*. The conceptual metaphor TERRORISM IS NATURAL and metaphorical expressions such as 'catastrophe' or 'terror wave' construct 'new terrorism' as something which is natural, in other words, normal, unstoppable and inevitable but also sudden and difficult to predict (Lakoff and Johnson 1980: 145–146; Pancake 1993). And although the concept of a natural terrorism seems unusual it has consequences on how we think about counter-terrorism. If terrorism is a 'wave' then cease fires and negotiations are non-sensical as one cannot persuade a wave from hitting the shoreline. As waves and catastrophes are a natural phenomena they are unstoppable, they will happen regardless of what is done to prevent them. If terrorism is a 'wave' the reasons for such 'waves' become unimportant as one cannot change the physics of their creation. The naturalisation of 'new terrorism' through these metaphors marginalises the question of what causes 'waves' of terrorism. What is clear is that we are not responsible for these 'waves'. If we cannot prevent the 'waves' from striking the coastline then it does makes sense to implement measures to alleviate the effects such 'waves' will have. One here can think of coastal defences such as big concrete sea walls, revetments or levees which are supposed to stop the waves of the sea penetrating the coast. Obviously terrorists do not only enter a country via the sea but the metaphorisation of terrorism as something natural as a wave holds within it the idea that 'new terrorism' can be confronted and held back by building big walls. Similarly the idea of terrorism being a 'catastrophe' immediately calls for *Katastrophenschutz* or disaster control measures which is able to effectively deal with the aftermath of a natural 'catastrophe' or terrorism. This among other things includes the implementation of support measures for the victims, the clearing or removing of the damage done but also the preparation of contingency plans in advance.

As with the other two conceptual metaphors mentioned above, the discursive construction of 'new terrorism' in the *Bild* and in *The Sun* as something natural has been followed by concrete policies which directly address the predication of TERRORISM IS NATURAL. While both these notions of building (coastal) defences and fortifications and preparing a country's disaster control services for terrorism are clearly visible in both Germany and the United Kingdom the next two sections will predominantly focus on the latter.

Germany's disaster management responses

In Germany the *Katastrophenschutz* or the disaster control service are part of the counter-terrorism effort and there are a number of measures and policies which substantiate the understanding of 'new terrorism' as something natural and unstoppable inherent in the metaphorical expressions such as 'catastrophe'. The German government has explicitly stated that international terrorism is an important aspect in their new disaster control system where the Bund (*Zivilschutz*), the Länder (*Katastrophenschutz*) and other relief organisations are to cooperate more closely. The government directly links the creation of the Federal Office for Civil Protection and Disaster Assistance (BBK) with the need for such an institution following 9/11 and an increased danger of terrorism.[37]

But there are also a number of other policies which confirm this link between natural phenomena and 'new terrorism'. For example, the events of 9/11, or should we rather say the metaphorisation of 9/11, has resulted in the purchase of around 650 new civil protection vehicles which included ambulances as well as 340 modern ABC recognition vehicles (Bundesministerium des Inneren 2005a: 150). Another example of this close association between natural disasters and 'new terrorism' is the German Joint Information and Situation Center (GMLZ), a joint centre of the Bund and the Länder which gathers and analyses information and assesses the security and safety situation in Germany. This includes natural phenomena such as flooding, forest fires, storms, environmental disasters as well as the 'catastrophe' of 'new terrorism' (Bundesministerium des Inneren 2005a: 145–146). Other policies include the German Emergency Planning Information System (deNIS) which is an open access internet portal which provides citizens and other agencies with information about possible threats and gives guidelines on how to behave in case of a natural disaster or a large 'wave' of 'new terrorist' attacks with both conventional or ABC weapons.[38] The Federal Government has also created a satellite-based warning system that can warn the population about the dangers of an imminent natural disaster or other 'times of crises and defence. For example, attacks involving planes or missiles demand a quick warning' (Bundesamt für Bevölkerungsschutz und Katastrophenhilfe 2009: 10). Similar to sea wall protecting the coast line against waves or natural disasters such as tsunamis the Federal Office of Civil Protection and Disaster Assistance is also closely involved in the protection of critical infrastructure against 'new terrorism' as '[n]atural hazards, bad accidents and terrorism might seriously damage or even destroy critical infrastructures which are important to society and to every citizen' (Bundesamt für Bevölkerungsschutz und Katastrophenhilfe 2009: 14).

In addition to these concrete policies there have also been other measures which fit the discursive construction of terrorism as something natural. For example the disaster management training has been expanded for members of the disaster relief services such as the fire services, the German Red Cross, the *Technisches Hilfswerk* (THW), other emergency and relief services such as the *Johanniter-Unfall-Hilfe*, *Malteser Hilfsdienst* and the *Arbeiter-Samariter-Bund* and now there is more emphasis on nuclear, biological and chemical incidences which may arise as the result of a 'new terrorist' 'storm' (Bundesministerium des Inneren 2005a: 149).[39] Among these participant organisations of the new crisis management and emergency planning training most used to be only responsible for 'normal' disaster relief rather than the 'catastrophe' of terrorism. For example, following 9/11 the THW, a governmental disaster relief agency, has established concrete deployment option in the case of a terrorist 'wave'.[40] Even the rescue services which deal with the aftermath of 'catastrophes' such as the *Johanniter* link the aspects of terrorism and natural disasters. For example the procurement of a new special disaster relief vehicle has been justified with the reference to the new threat of terrorism.[41] 'Especially disaster management has become more important given the new threat of terrorism and climate change' (Greiber 2007). And even the German Red Cross also considers itself to have a role in dealing with a 'catastrophe' of terrorism (Haneda 2004).

Britain's disaster management responses

As Paul Cornish (2005: 157) points out, '[i]n the United Kingdom, arrangements for consequence management are as much part of the defence against terrorism as other, more directly protective and preventative measures'. So apart from protective measures and physical security at prominent buildings and airports (Bamford 2004: 749) which are supposed to alleviate the damage of terrorist 'waves' one encounters policies which are explicitly designed to deal with the aftermath of a 'catastrophic' 'new terrorist' attack. The notion of preparing for an inevitable attack by 'new terrorists' is explicitly part of the 'United Kingdom's Strategy for Countering International Terrorism' Britain's' which was published in March 2009 (HM Government 2009). Here the government states that the aim of their 'Prepare workstream' of their CONTEST counter-terrorism strategy is 'to mitigate the impact of a terrorist attack where it cannot be stopped' (HM Government 2009: 118). The British government here aims to ensure that local, regional and national crisis management structures are in place and have the appropriate capabilities, equipment and training to effectively deal with different types of terrorist 'disasters' and that any critical infrastructure damaged or destroyed in an attack continues its functions or quickly recovers. Furthermore the strategy is to ensure that 'plans are developed and capabilities improved to respond to a terrorist incident and to deal with the consequences of the UK's highest impact terrorism threats as set out in the National Risk Assessment' (HM Government 2009: 121). Similar to natural occurring events, terrorism 'catastrophes' are considered inevitable and unstoppable.

This understanding of terrorism as something natural is further visible in the 2004 Civil Contingencies Act.[42] This act is the legislative centre piece the UK's policy of preparing for disasters as it provides the basis for the responses to emergencies both at local and regional levels by outlining the duty of the responders in assessing possible risks in their jurisdiction and prepare for these possibilities by testing and exercising emergency plans to deal with such situations. And apart from natural disasters the act explicitly names terrorism as one of the 'emergencies' it is supposed to prepare for. This mapping from source (NATURAL) to target domain (TERRORISM), which is also apparent in operational and organisational structures of institutions responsible for dealing with natural disasters such as flooding and disease control, are also explicitly responsible for handling possible and unstoppable terrorism 'waves'. For example, the Civil Contingencies Secretariat (CCS) which manages the Civil Contingencies Act and which is part of the Cabinet Office works 'in partnership with government departments, the devolved administrations and key stakeholders to enhance the UK's ability to prepare for, respond to and recover from emergencies'.[43] The CCS is responsible for the management of a nation-wide 'Resilience Program' which is supposed to reduce the risk from emergencies such as natural disasters in the form of severe weather, droughts, flooding, plant and animal diseases as well as terrorism and contamination through chemical, biological, radiological and nuclear material. The Resilience Program also provides information and guidelines for other government agencies and services, businesses and the public via its website on these different types of 'natural' disasters.[44] Most explicitly, the British government has sent out a booklet to all UK households with details of how to respond in the case of an emergency such as terrorism.[45]

In addition to this information on emergencies of all kind, the British government has also increased the professional competences of emergency responders and those responsible for emergency planning. For example, this includes the Central Government Emergency Response Training and courses at the Emergency Planning College. This preparation for the inevitable 'natural' disaster is strengthened further through the National Counter-Terrorism Exercise Programme which is supposed to test the abilities of the established disaster response planning and improve the ability of emergency services, the police and other key stakeholders to prepare for and respond to inevitable terrorist 'waves'. The programme is supposed to deliver three national live exercises per year. Interestingly, with regard to these exercises the BBC explicitly notes the metaphorical expression which constitutes TERRORISM IS NATURAL by citing David Blunkett's reference to 'catastrophic' terror attacks.[46]

Apart from natural disasters and terrorism the UK emergency planning is also very concerned with 'catastrophic' events such as an attack with chemical, biological, radiological and nuclear (CBRN) material. As the government points out: 'Specific and dedicated capabilities have been put in place in the emergency services to manage the terrorist use of chemical, biological and radiological materials' (HM Government 2009: 118). For example, this includes better equipment for emergency services such as Personal Protection Equipment suits for ambulance services and hospitals to operate in a contaminated environment and mobile decontamination units to clear the polluted areas and treat injured victims of such a 'disaster'. Other examples include chemical and biological air monitoring units in public places such as the London Underground, the establishment of regional smallpox response groups, the stocking of vaccines and antidotes and the organisation of diagnosis laboratories for contagious disease, high security treatment units and secure care centres (Cornish 2005: 158).

Terrorism is uncivilised evil

Overall the double conceptual metaphor TERRORISM IS UNCIVILISED EVIL is the third most prominent discursive construction in both the *Bild* and *The Sun*. This predication, however, is probably the most unsurprising of all, as the 'othering' function of depicting one's opponent as evil and uncivilised is very common and can be found on almost all violent conflicts (Fiebig-von Hase and Lehmkuhl 1997; Weller 2001; Geis 2006). Both uncivilised and evil have been included into one conceptual metaphor as they both are the primary instruments of 'othering'.

Both the 'evil' and the 'uncivilised' part of the conceptual metaphor do a number of things and predicate 'new terrorism' in a number of ways. Starting with the notion of the 'evil' terrorist one has to note that apart from creating fear the predication of the 'new terrorist' as evil automatically excludes the question of why these actors perpetrate these acts of terrorism as the answer is inherent in their evilness. Why did 9/11 happen? Why do terrorists do this? The answer becomes simple: because they are 'evil'. In other words, the predication of 'new terrorism' as 'evil' marginalised the grievances and political goals of these groups and the reasons for the violence are avoided as 'evil' terrorists kill for the sake of killing rather than for some concrete motive. Evilness becomes the ultimate justification for their act and at the same time provides a justification for extreme counter-measures. The predication of evilness through metaphors such as 'monster' leads to a direct and clear dehumanisation and demoralisation and therefore 'every form of terror attributed to them becomes not only permissible but defined as noble when we do it to them' (Sluka 2009: 145). The elimination of 'evil' and the infliction of extreme counter-measures such as military violence, detention without trial and torture becomes less shocking and begins to appear appropriate (Ivie 2004: 80). After all killing monsters is something noble and heroic.[47]

Most clearly, however, the 'evilification' of the 'new terrorist' reinforces the moral judgement already inherent in the term 'terrorist' (Bernstein 2005). Predicating the 'new terrorists' as evil leads to a concrete and clear polarisation as it outcasts the actor and his/her actions and dichotomises and antagonises them (the out-group) and us (the in-group) (Lazar and Lazar 2004). As there are only two sides to the conflict, good and evil, the construction of the 'evil' other automatically constitutes the self as the binary opposite 'good' (Ivie 2004: 80). 'Here the dichotomy between the in and the out-group is a religious and spiritual one, the "good" outcasting the "evil" from the moral order that is instituted by the good itself' (Bhatia 2009: 282). Furthermore, one should note that the predication of 'new terrorists' as 'evil' automatically also makes those who assist terrorists 'evil', as we tend to consider those who help evil also to be evil. This indiscriminate guilt by association is not the case with the metaphors such as 'soldier', 'beast' or 'barbarian': those who help barbarians are not automatically also barbarians. So the construction of terrorism as 'evil' creates only two camps. This polarisation leads to the situation where 'people and countries must choose which side they are on' (Rediehs 2002: 71). While the conceptual metaphor TERRORISM IS WAR implied the possibility of neutrality the predication of terrorism as evil eliminates this option. The dichotomy of good versus evil leaves no space for anything in-between.

When terrorism ceases to be 'only' a crime and becomes a sin the elimination of this evil through 'counter terrorism becomes, in a bizarre sense, a religiously sanctioned duty' (Leach 1977: 36). This sacralisation is directly visible in the religious metaphorical expression such as 'devil', 'diabolical' or 'apocalyptic' found in both the *Bild* and *The Sun*. But also in the much criticised metaphor of a 'crusade' against terrorism declared by President George Bush[48] (O'Brian 2003: 33) which constructs the conflict 'as a type of "holy war" between the forces of "Good" and "Evil"' (Sluka 2009: 145). This leads to the fact that the predication of evilness reduces the possibility of questioning the implementation of the 'appropriate' counter-measures. As Rediehs (2002) points out, by questioning the appropriateness of a particular response one risks being placed on the other 'evil' side of the conflict simply due to the fact that there is no other way of classifying someone who questions the good side's inherently 'good' and 'righteous' methods. Furthermore, this kind of predication does not only silence dissent and justify harsh counter-measures, it also automatically excludes other policies which do not fit the constitution of 'evilness'. Most obviously, one has to note here the impossibility of any kind of engagement or dialogue with 'new terrorists' if they are predicated as 'evil' 'devils' (Abdel-Nour 2004). As 'evil' cannot be reasoned with, negotiations and talks with 'new terrorists' such as al-Qaeda are considered absurd. We all know that one cannot trust Satan and we are told from a very young age that those who strike a deal with the devil end up in hell. So while the military style construction of 'new terrorism' mentioned above would include the possibility of coming to some kind of negotiated peace deal with the opponent, the additional predication of terrorism as 'evil' excludes such counter-terrorism possibilities from the policy options considered appropriate. The most obvious example of this overlap between TERRORISM IS WAR and TERRORISM IS UNCIVILISED EVIL is the metaphorical expression 'Axis of Evil' (Smith 2002; Heradstveit and Bonham 2007).

The process of 'othering' is also clearly visible in the metaphors which predicate terrorism as something uncivilised as the polarisation imminent in the dichotomous relationship of 'good' and 'evil' can also be found in the binary structure of 'civilised' and 'barbaric' (Motroshilova 2009). The 'uncivilised' part of the conceptual metaphor TERRORISM IS UNCIVIL-

ISED EVIL reinforces many parts of the 'evil' metaphor discussed above. As Robert Ivie (2004: 78) points out '[s]avagery is a multidimensional image of the enemy that contrast the civilized victim's rationality, morality, and peaceful purposes with the irrational and immoral behaviour of the uncivilized aggressor'. So while 'barbarians' are not unhuman 'monsters' or 'devils', they are still judged as 'inferior'[49]; they are considered a 'lower standard of human being' (Kappeler and Kappeler 2004: 182) As William Ryan (1976: 10) points out, barbarians 'are seen as less competent, less skilled, less knowing – in short less human' and almost animal-like. Therefore, one cannot trust a 'barbarian' as he or she does not adhere to the civilised notion of rational debate. One cannot peacefully engage with such an opponent in a dialogue as they will not adhere to any agreements or deals struck in negotiations. Therefore, similar to the 'evil' metaphors, the 'uncivilised' predication constructs the terrorist as someone who cannot be logically reasoned with and consequently there is no real point in talking to them. At the same time 'barbarians' are brutal, violent and primitive[50] and therefore only understand violence as an answer. So the predication of terrorism as 'barbaric' makes the use of violent counter-measures seem appropriate (Salter 2002: 163). 'Cultures and groups of individuals who consciously reject progress, technology, innovation and consumption are suspect. The creation of the uncivilized other has justified conquest and dominance of those who refuse to conform' (Kappeler and Kappeler 2004: 183). Considering the invasions of Afghanistan and Iraq in the 'war on terrorism', who in their right mind would reject the superiority of civilisation over barbarity and who would question the value of development, technology, freedom and democracy? 'By definition then, the notion of civilization rejects patterns and cultures that fall outside of these normative values' (Kappeler and Kappeler 2004: 183).

In connection to this, one importantly has to note that the origin of the term 'barbarian' as the word 'barbarous' itself comes from the Greek word *barbaros* which means foreign.[51] So the metaphor 'barbarian' constitutes terrorism not only as something 'other' but as something explicitly foreign; something that comes from outside one's own country or cultural hemisphere. Similar to the term 'islamist' the expression 'barbaric', gives the terrorist construction something foreign without assigning a concrete nationality. So in addition to the dehumanisation of the evil metaphors the terrorist actor is de-westernised. Interestingly, Marina Llorente (2002: 45) has noted that 'most violent acts by Westerners tend not to be labeled "barbaric". A good example is the case of Oklahoma City bomber Timothy McVeigh, whose action was not categorized in terms of "barbarism," presumably because he belonged to the "civilized" part of the world'. Therefore, one could also make the argument that the regular use of the term barbaric increasingly constructs the terrorist as something 'other' and generally alien and foreign, which then makes counter-terrorism measures such as tighter border and immigration controls possible and appropriate to keep such elements out. The understanding, inherent in the conceptual metaphor TERRORISM IS UNCIVILISED EVIL, of 'new terrorism' as something barbarian 'other' and foreign makes policies which target this otherness appear appropriate.

There is a substantial amount of research on the link between immigration and security and the role of the foreign 'other' (c.f. Doty 1998; Bigo 2002b; Huysmans 2006). Therefore due to a lack of space and time the next two sections cannot address many of the interesting points raised in the literature but will instead focus predominantly on Germany's and Britain's use of immigration policies against 'new terrorism'.

Immigration policies in Germany

The notion of linking 'new terrorism' to the foreign 'other' and with this to the idea of migration was visible in the political debate after 9/11 from the very start as politicians from both the conservative parties, the liberals and the social democrats immediately linked terrorism to immigration and called for tighter controls. Here the '[d]ifferences were in degree, not in principle' (Diez and Squire 2008: 574). And as a result of this shared understanding of 'new terrorism' as something foreign the German government implemented a number of seemingly appropriate counter-terrorism policies. As the conceptual metaphors found in the discourse mapped aspects such as barbarity and foreignness of the source domain UNCIVILISED to the target domain TERRORISM, it made counter policies which focus on the foreign 'other' appear logical and appropriate.

The most obvious means of stopping these 'barbarians' from entering the 'civilised' world is the securing of one's borders. And Germany has done precisely that, it has tightened its borders and increased resources for the Federal Border Guards (prior to 2005 known as the *Bundesgrenz-schutz*, BGS) responsible for protecting Germany borders from 'evil' 'savages'. Following 9/11 the budget for the border guards was substantially increased in 2002 by around 120 million Euros and it purchased new high-tech helicopters and patrol boats and recruited and trained more personnel to patrol Germany borders and embassies abroad against foreign 'new terrorists'. Air traffic security was also enhanced by training so-called sky-marshals and implementing new surveillance and security technology at airports. Additional financial resources were used to enhance the information and communication technology of the BSG, the technology used for checking (travel) documents and the improvement of the nuclear, biological and chemical technical services of the BSG (Bundesministerium des Inneren 2005b).

In addition to these physical enhancements at Germany's borders against the foreign terrorist 'barbarian' there are also a number of other policies which try and prevent the 'new terrorist' 'other' from entering the country or extract these 'uncivilised' elements if the first kind of policy should fail. As Imke Kruse et al. (2003: 132) point out, the anti-terror laws in security package one and two mentioned above had 'far-reaching implications for immigration and asylum policy'. And Thomas Diez and Vickie Squire (2008: 573, emphasis in original) argue that the 'Law on Fighting Terrorism (terrorismusbekämpfungs-gesetz 9 January 2002) devoted six of its 24 articles directly to non-citizens, *Ausländer* ('foreigners') generally speaking and asylum seekers more specifically'. This included the already mentioned banning of foreign extremist associations but also a number of other policies which indicate the understanding of 'new terrorism' as something 'other' and foreign. For example, foreigners considered to be a threat to society or those who have committed or supported violent acts are not permitted to take up residency or even enter the country and foreigners who give false information in visa applications 'pertinent to security' can now be deported. It is now also possible to deport foreigners who are considered to be supporting 'new terrorism' or inciting hatred if there is evidence that they pose a threat. In addition, seeking asylum has become more difficult and subject to more security checks. For example fingerprints of asylum seekers are taken and stored in a database and authorities can now use speech analysis to verify the origin of the immigrants to make sure they are not 'barbarian' (Kruse et al. 2003).

As Diez and Squire (2008: 573) point out, these policies are 'indicative of a direct linkage between terrorism and migration in the German case'. This link and the understanding of 'new terrorism' can also be seen in opinion polls as for example 79 per cent of the German population agreed with Interior Minister Schilly's idea following the train bombings in Madrid of making the deportation of suspicious foreigners quicker and easier.[52] The discursive construction and the mapping of uncivilised foreignness onto the 'new terrorist' makes policies against the 'savage' foreigner appear logical.

Immigration policies in Britain

Tightening immigration regulations, asylum and border controls have been a central aspect of British counter-terrorism since 9/11. Politicians in both the Labour and Conservative Party have continuously talked about 'new terrorism' in connection to immigration. A study by Jef Huysmans (2005) has examined parliamentary debates in the UK since 9/11 which have explicitly made the connection between terrorism and immigration, asylum or refuge. His findings show 'that asylum especially and migration more generally was an important element in the framing of the fight against terrorism' (Huysmans 2005: 2). Most dominantly this connection was made with the introduction of the Anti-terrorism, Crime and Security Act 2001 (ATCSA) in December 2001. The ATCSA explicitly deals with immigrations matters and links them to terrorism in part IV of the act, fittingly entitled 'Immigration and Asylum'. There are three main issues in this section. For one it deals with the retention of fingerprint data in asylum and immigration cases as well as 'an attempt to short-circuit any claim to asylum by making the tribunal focus upon the Secretary of State's reasons for denying the claim' (Walker 2003: 24). Although this measure has been dropped, one of the most controversial measures, was the provision of ATCSA which enables the UK Home Secretary to order the detention without trial of foreign individuals suspected of planning or intending 'savage' terrorist attacks in the UK or internationally (Payne 2002).

Similar to Germany, Britain has also responded to the 'barbarians' by locking the gates. In the name of fighting 'new terrorism' the government has created a new UK Border Agency (UKBA) which has integrated the work of number of different agency such as the Border and Immigration Agency and UKvisas into one central agency with more than 25,000 staff. And in order to prevent 'barbarians' from climbing the gates, the borders are directly manned by the UK Border Force. This force is aided in their task of protecting Britain by an electronic border system (e-Borders) which allows the screening, checking and risk assessing of passengers in advance so that any 'barbarian' can be identified prior to his or her arrival in the UK. Furthermore, to establish the 'foreignness' of people entering the country the UKBA is testing facial recognition gates which scan the faces of people and compares them to their biometric passports. Visa application now also requires the foreign applicant to provide fingerprints and a digital photograph which are then checked against existing data sets in order to establish whether the foreigner is an 'evil' terrorist 'savage' (HM Government 2009: 108–109).

Similar to this is also the introduction of the National Identity Scheme (NIS) which extends the use of biometric data through the creation of an identity register and identity cards. Although these identity cards are currently voluntary for UK citizens, they are compulsory for foreign nationals (Border and Immigration Agency 2008). As Diez and Squire (2008: 573) point out, 'it has been argued that the main policy device bringing together migration and security with reference to the 'terrorist threat' in Britain was the introduction of ID cards and the collection and administration of biometric data' (Diez and Squire 2008: 573). As 'barbarians', in contrast to 'monsters', are more difficult to identify as they look more or less human, an ID card can help find 'new terrorists'. So the mapping of foreignness from the source domain UNCIVILISED to the target domain TERRORISM makes the introduction of ID cards to identify the 'foreign other' seem appropriate.

This understanding in the UK of the 'new terrorist' as something uncivilised and foreign is also visible in public opinion polls. For example, in 2003 82 per cent of those questioned thought that it was certain or likely that 'terrorists linked to Al Qaeda are entering Britain as asylum seekers'[53] and a survey conducted after the London bombings in July 2005 showed that 88 per cent agreed with using 'tighter controls on who comes into the country' as a 'measure that could be taken to try and reduce the threat of further terrorist attack'.[54] In addition, other polls indicated strong support (62 and 74 per cent) for detaining foreign terrorist suspects indefinitely[55] and detaining 'all immigrants and asylum seekers until they can be assessed as potential terror threats'.[56]

Terrorism is disease

Finally, one also comes across the conceptual metaphor TERRORISM IS DISEASE. Here the terrorist actor and his or her act of terrorism are predicated as some kind of illness through metaphorical expressions such as 'insane', 'sick' or 'plague'. With regard to the conceptual metaphor TERRORISM IS DISEASE Ann Mongoven (2006: 413) points out that '[a]ssociating terrorism with disease undoubtedly has contributed to the acceptance of high civilian casualties in the war on terror'. She believes that '[c]ivilian losses become viewed as necessary amputations to protect the body from the malignancy of terrorists' (Mongoven 2006: 413). Importantly, one should consider the interpretation that disease, similar to the metaphor evil and uncivilised mentioned above, is something one cannot reason with. This is especially true when we consider the notion of 'madness' as a disease. While negotiations and cease fire agreements do make sense if we constitute the terrorist as a soldier in a war, they are absurd in a conflict with an army of 'lunatics' who lack the ability for rational thought. One can simply not trust the 'insane' be they soldiers or criminals. A psychological study by Emily Pronin et al. (2006) showed that peo-ple were far less likely to advocate the use of diplomacy against terrorists if these were depicted as irrational. Not only can one not negotiate with the insane or diseases such as cancer but many other illnesses such as the plaque are in fact contagious. So any kind of contact with the 'disease' of terrorism and 'disease riddled' 'new terrorist' may infect you. Therefore, 'new terrorists' should not be talked to but rather isolated and quarantined as '[c]ontact with them is polluting' (Zulaika and Douglass 1996: 62). Overall, the construction of 'new terrorism' as 'evil' or 'disease' rather suggests that certain policies such as engagement or negotiations are not considered as possible options.

In contrast to the other concrete policies mentioned above, it is obviously more difficult to indicate the non existence of a policy. However, one may gain some insight into the implications of the conceptual metaphor TERRORISM IS DISEASE when we consider concrete examples of suggested negotiation possibilities between the two sides in the 'war on terror'. One such event occurred in April 2004 when Osama bin Laden proposed a truce with European states. In an audio tape sent to the broadcasters *Al Arabiya* and *Al Jazeera* bin Laden proclaimed:

> I also offer a reconciliation initiative to them [Europe], whose essence is our commitment to stopping operations against every country that commits itself to not attacking Muslims or interfering in their affairs [...] The reconciliation will start with the departure of its last soldier from our country. The door of reconciliation is open for three months of the date of announcing this statement.[57]

Although the United States were not included in the first truce, a second message by Osama bin Laden in January 2006 was directly addressed at them:

> We do not object to a long-term truce with you on the basis of fair conditions that we respect. We are a nation, for which God has disallowed treachery and lying. In this truce, both parties will enjoy

security and stability and we will build Iraq and Afghanistan, which were destroyed by the war.[58]

In the following section the chapter will examine the reaction of both Germany and the United Kingdom to these suggested truce offers by 'new terrorists' such as Osama bin Laden.

Germany's no-negotiation stance

In Germany the 'truce' or 'reconciliation' offer of both these messages was soundly opposed by the government, experts, the media and the public. In response to the first ceasefire suggestion by Osama bin Laden Chancellor Schröder and a large number of other politicians vigorously rejected such a truce.[59] Overall the German government forcefully stated that '[t]here cannot be negotiations with terrorists and criminals like Osama bin Laden'.[60] Similarly, the second offer was rebuffed by the German government's claim that 'terrorists are no negotiation partners for the democratic world'.[61] And even German terrorism 'experts' such as Kai Hirschmann argued that the idea of a negotiated truce with al-Qaeda cannot be taken seriously and was indeed 'laughable'.[62] Following the truce offer the *Bild* newspaper affronted bin Laden calling him a 'megalomaniac bastard'[63] and told him in no uncertain words: 'Fuck you'.[64] Furthermore, the *Bild* believed that bin Laden was 'poisoning'[65] the minds and 'ridiculing'[66] Europe with his reconciliation offer. But also other media outlets rejected the truce offer. For example the *Frankfurter Rundschau* stated: 'No Negotiations with Terrorists'.[67] So the mapping of the source domain DISEASE onto the target domain TERRORISM through expressions such as 'madness', 'terror-lunacy' or 'plague' makes engagement and negotiations seem absurd and dangerous. Unfortunately, there seem to be no opinion polls in Germany on whether this truce offer by bin Laden should be considered and whether negotiations with al-Qaeda are indeed a possible option.

Britain's no-negotiation stance

Similar to Germany the British government announced that bin Laden's first truce offer to Europe was 'absurd'[68] and 'ludicrous'[69] as a number of government spokesmen stated that '[t]he idea of an armistice with a group that defines itself by violence is an absurdity',[70] and the peace offer was 'evidence for the confusion of Al Qaeda'.[71] Individual politicians also strongly rejected the idea of any kind of cease fire with such a terrorist group. For example, Foreign Secretary Jack Straw proclaimed: 'One has to treat such proposals by Al-Qaeda with the contempt they deserve. It is a murderous organisation which seeks impossible objectives by the most violent means'.[72] So negotiation with 'mad' 'new terrorists' such as bin Laden seem to be considered quite impossible. As Home Secretary David Blunkett put it: 'It is ludicrous to think that his suggestion has any sense of reality',[73] and even the Liberal Party leader Charles Kennedy points out that '[t]here can be no negotiation with Al Qaeda, and [that] bin Laden's truce offer was repellent'.[74] Even terrorism 'experts' seem to agree on this interpretation of al-Qaeda as Peter Bergen believes that 'this whole offer is, in a sense, sort of pretty ludicrous'.[75]

This kind of constitution of 'new terrorism' as something non-negotiable inherent in the discursive formation of TERRORISM IS DISEASE is also visible in the media. A number of newspapers both tabloid and broadsheet explicitly state that 'there can be no bargaining with terrorists'[76] as '[t]his is war without negotiation'.[77] In response to the truce offer *The Sun* similar to the *Bild* in Germany 'eloquently' responded in an article titled 'Peace off bin Laden' that the offer was 'bizarre', 'ludicrous' and 'absurd' and that 'evil' bin Laden should 'go to hell'.[78] Most explicitly the response to the truce was 'beggars belief' and that '[n]o one in their right mind would accept it', after all 'bin Laden is mad'.[79] This understanding of the irrational and mad 'new terrorist' was mirrored in a number of other media outlets. For example, *The Mirror* called the idea 'binsane',[80] while others simply called the idea of 'evil Osama' and his 'lunatic sect'[81] 'quasi-rational',[82] 'mad'[83] or 'insane'.[84] In this regard *The Express* most explicitly exemplifies this constitution of TERRORISM IS DISEASE and its automatic exclusion of a negotiation possibility with such 'insane' 'new terrorists' by stating: 'bargaining with madmen is folly'.[85]

Interestingly, again similar to Germany, there seem to be no opinion polls on the issue and whether a truce deal with al-Qaeda or negotiations with Osama bin Laden were a viable option or not. However, in a time where opinion polls seem to be conducted on almost every issue thinkable, the absence of such questions may actually say a lot about what 'new terrorism' is considered to be like: un-negotiable. Therefore, one could argue here that the absence of such polls indicates that the question of negotiating with al-Qaeda is not considered worthy of even being asked in the first place as the answer is so glaringly obvious.

Conclusion

Metaphors do not 'cause' policy! But metaphors do play a vital role in the discursive construction of 'new terrorism' and thereby automatically contribute to our understanding of how to react to such a phenomena. Although seemingly obvious, our reaction to 'new terrorism' depend strongly on how we perceive 'new terrorism' to be. Metaphors predicate 'new terrorism' in a specific way which then makes certain counter options appear more appropriate than others. This chapter has shown how a number of counter-terrorism policies in Germany and the UK fit the discursive construction of 'new terrorism' found in the media. The policies are evidence as well as the result of a specific understanding of 'new terrorism'. For example, understanding 'new terrorism' as a war calls for a military reaction, while the constitution of it as a 'crime' necessitates a judicial response. At the same time the notion of 'new terrorism' as something 'natural' and therefore inevitable suggests the implementation of disaster response measures to deal with the aftermath. Classical predications of 'othering' found the metaphors 'uncivilised' 'evil' imply the tightening of borders and immigration to keep the foreign 'other' out, while the concepts of 'evil' and 'disease' indicate the impossibility of engagement and negotiations with 'new terrorists'.

Conclusion: The Tabloid Terrorist and Future Research

'If we cannot hope ever to be perfectly right, we can perhaps find both enlightenment and refreshment by changing, from time to time, our ways of being wrong' (Wheelwright 1962)

This book does not claim to contain any 'truths' about 'new terrorism'. The book was based on the premise that 'new terrorism' is a social construction. So rather than being a brute 'fact', terrorism is constituted in language. It does not exist outside of discourse. Any kind of act has to be *interpreted* as terrorism for it to *be* terrorism and the words we use to describe and predicate acts we interpret as terrorism both reflect and influence our perceptions of the phenomena. The first part of this conclusion wants to briefly summarise the main argument of the book, while the second part will reflect on the implications of a constructivist approach on future terrorism research and indicate three potential research areas arising from this book which could be pursued in the future. This includes questions about the origins of particular understandings about terrorism, the role of popular culture in the construction of 'the terrorist' and finally the consideration of 'counter-measures', such as for example reconciliation, which conventionally fall outside of the options considered appropriate against the 'tabloid terrorist'. These three research areas are meant to serve purely as examples and should not be understood as 'the' but as 'a' future of Terrorism Research.

A constructivist approach to terrorism

What we call things has a huge effect on how we see them and, importantly, how we react to them. In order to illustrate the importance of language in the study of terrorism the book examined how certain constitutions of 'the terrorist' in the media discourse make certain counter-terrorism policies possible while at the same time excluding other options which do not fit the construction. In pursuit of such a constructivist kind of terrorism studies, the book in a first step emphasised the importance of words and small and seemingly irrelevant predicates such as 'new' in the constitution of terrorism by deconstructing the notion of 'new terrorism'. It questioned the newness of many of its established characteristics such as the religious motivations, the use of indiscriminate extremely violent tactics, the possible use of WMDs and the network organisation of 'new terrorist' groups such as al-Qaeda. The aim was not to establish the 'true' or 'real' nature of al-Qaeda-like terrorism, but to indicate the contested nature of knowledge on terrorism. In a second step, the book considered what counter-options would fit this social construction of 'new terrorism'. While counter-terrorism policies such as military and judicial responses as well as the use of intelligence and the tightening of security measures make sense against 'new terrorism', other options such as negotiations with 'new terrorists' are considered absurd and fall outside of the options considered as a response. Following this, a third step then brought the two previous parts together by asking the question of how to assess the effectiveness of these counter-terrorism measures in the face of 'new terrorism'. This, although interesting on its own, served the purpose of indicating some of the wider problems a materialist terrorism research perspective has when it focuses predominantly on material aspects of terrorism and counter-terrorism. Having here indicated the problems of a materialist terrorism research, the book then outlined an alternative approach to studying terrorism. It formulated a constructivist theoretical understanding and articulated a constructivist means of investigating terrorism through the use of discourse and in particular metaphor analysis. The central notion was that metaphors transfer certain characteristics of a source domain (for example war) onto a target domain (for example terrorism) and thereby give the target domain a certain meaning. Metaphors predicate phenomena such as terrorism and thereby have great influence on our reaction to acts of 'terrorism'. Following this idea, the book applied this constructivist methodology to the media discourse on terrorism and in particular to the tabloid newspapers *Bild* and *The Sun* as these are widespread and very popular and therefore greatly influence people's perception of the world in Germany and the UK. The book identified five distinct conceptual metaphors underlying the discourse which conceptualised 'new terrorism' as a 'war', as a 'crime', as something 'natural', as 'uncivilised evil' and as a 'disease'. The final part of the book then examined how these social constructions found in discourse made certain counter-terrorism policies in Germany and the UK appear logical and appropriate. So while an understanding of 'new terrorism' as something war-like made a military response of both Germany and the UK possible, an understanding of 'new terrorism' as something criminal called for a judicial answer. At the same time, the constitution of 'new terrorism' as something natural such as a 'wave' or a 'catastrophe' and therefore something inevitable made it logical to implement disaster management plans rather than trying to prevent these natural phenomena from occurring in the first place. In addition, we have seen that the notion of 'uncivilised evil', and with it the aspect of othering and polarisation commonly found in many conflicts, calls, among other things, for tighter border controls in both Germany and the UK as the 'uncivilised evil' comes from the outside. Finally, the idea of terrorism being a 'disease' such as 'madness' or the 'plague' suggests that contact and any kind of engagement is not only pointless, but dangerous.

Despite the fascination with words, definitions, labels and the media, constructivist theory has been largely neglected within the realm of Terrorism Studies. This book wanted to address this situation by bringing together literature on terrorism, constructivist IR theory and discourse analysis and show that social constructivism and discourse analysis have much to offer the study of terrorism. In particular, the book had two aims: firstly, it wanted to show that words in terrorism studies matter as it pointed out how words and in particular metaphors theoretically affect our perception of situations such as 'terrorist' attacks and thereby shape our understanding of an appropriate reaction to such events. Secondly, by doing so the book wanted to empirically demonstrate the influence of words on policy options in politics and illustrate that constructivist research can be policy relevant. Not in the sense that it explains policy outcomes in a positivist sense, but that it can suggest why and how ranges of policy options are opened and closed. The book is therefore relevant not only for the sub-field of Terrorism Research but for International Relations as a whole, as the suggested method of analysing the discursive constitution of issues in the media can be applied to a variety of political phenomena. In other words, beyond the direct application to the field of terrorism studies the book should also be considered an example of applied constructivist research.

The future of terrorism research

After years of regurgitating the same questions and answers many have become bored with the subject of terrorism, and following the research frenzy after 9/11 Terrorism Research by now is almost out of fashion (again). In a time of financial crisis and environmental degradation, terrorism is not the hot topic it used to be. Yet, the future of Terrorism Research is not as bleak as it may seem. The recent rise of a more critical terrorism research agenda is promising as it opens up the opportunity of contemplating alternative answers to traditional questions and, more importantly, it offers the possibility of asking new questions.

Where did the tabloid terrorist come from?

This book has predominantly focused on the 'realities' which follow certain discursive constructions. It has not enquired into where these particular kinds of understandings have come from and why certain constructions manage to become dominant while others fall by the wayside. However, if we are interested in the 'results' of using one metaphor rather than another, the logical next step would be to ask where these metaphors, and with them the understandings they facilitate, come from. In other words, one could ask: Why did the understanding TERRORISM IS WAR become dominant rather than TERRORISM IS BUSINESS? Why is there a shift for example in Germany from TERRORISM IS WAR to TERRORISM IS CRIME?

Although pinpointing specific reasons for the use of a certain metaphor or other linguistic devices over another will be extremely difficult if not impossible, the variations and shifts in the usage of particular conceptual understandings call for more reflection on the reasons for these differences. The question of why metaphors change could and has been addressed in a number of ways and one may briefly consider three possible explanations which could be substantiated by further research.

Firstly, a materialist understanding in line with more traditional approaches to studying terrorism would probably point to 'realities' and suggest that changes in metaphor usage reflect the reality of changed circumstances which the metaphors describe. As metaphors only reflect reality, the change of discourse has to be due to changes on the ground. However, in constructivist thought discourse cannot simply reflect reality but reality is constituted in discourse. This does not mean that there is no reality or that discourse is independent of the real world, but that such reality has to be interpreted as it cannot speak for itself.

A second more critical perspective on terrorism advanced by authors such as Richard Jackson (2005) would probably point to 'interests' of those using the metaphors as an explaining variable. In this conception the changes or shifts of metaphor usage would not be due to the realities on the ground but due to the changing interests of the influential elite. Politicians and/or the media would change their metaphorical language in order to manipulate the public audience and further their interests (Drulák and Königova 2007). Consistently using or changing metaphors, and thereby spreading their implicit understanding of phenomena, would be considered an explicit act of power to maintain or increase the power of those uttering the metaphors. In other words, metaphors are used by someone for something. For example, in the case of the 'war on terror' a number of scholars claim that discursive devices and narratives where used to serve the interests of the conservative political elite in the United States (Jackson 2005; Jarvis 2009b). Alternatively in this explanation the war metaphors could be due to the financial interests of the media printing them. So it was a conscious choice of the *Bild* and *The Sun* to print war metaphors as the notion of 'war' sells more newspapers than the notion of 'business'.

A third possible interpretation focuses less on agency but is rather interested in 'experiences'. Metaphors arise or change if the inferences they make by mapping one domain to another are supported by physical and cultural experiences (Ritchie 2003). As De Landtsheer and De Vrij (2004: 166) point out, new metaphors arise in a time of crisis precisely because they are 'powerful agents of cognitive framing'. For example, in the case of 9/11 a war metaphor in Germany made sense as it appeared to fit many of the characteristics of war experienced in the past. The number of casualties, the level of destruction and usage of aeroplanes as guided bombs made the source domain WAR appropriate. However, over time the war metaphors seemed increasingly at odds with the experiences of terrorism in Germany. With a lack of further 9/11-style attacks the experiences of war did not seem an appropriate means of conceptualising and understanding terrorism anymore. Metaphors of crime were better suited for capturing the general sentiment in Germany. Rather than experiencing terrorism as an exceptional state of affairs with high levels of death and destruction, terrorism was slowly considered something normal to every society. Crime metaphors were better at capturing the notion of terrorism as something which is there all the time without constantly affecting us. The difference to the first kind of explanations rooted in 'realities' is that metaphors are not exact mirrors of events. There is no one-to-one relationship between reality and metaphors as we cannot observe physical events directly but do so in a particular interpretative context and discourse. Discourse makes us see things in a particular way, but at the same time discourse is not independent of empirical events. For example, the lack of any 9/11-style terrorist attacks in Germany had an effect on the terrorism discourse in Germany. The inferences of a war metaphor were not supported by physical and cultural experiences anymore. The central idea of this explanation would be that experiences of empirical events shape discourse, and discourse shapes our experiences. In other words, discourse and experiences are mutually constitutive.

Popular culture and the Xbox terrorist

While this book examined the popular media discourse on terrorism in tabloids such as the *Bild* and *The Sun*, terrorism research may benefit from a more detailed investigation of other popular cultural discourses on terrorism.[1] So rather than only examining the western political elite (Jackson 2005; Jarvis 2009b) or the print media and their role in the construction of terrorism, future research may be interested in the portrayal of 'the terrorist' in literature, movies and TV series as cultural phenomena (Campbell and Shapiro 2007; Wilkins and Downing 2002; Boggs and Pollard 2006; Erickson 2008). This could not only substantiate further the constructivist understanding of terrorism presented in this book, but could also contribute to a cultural or visual turn in Terrorism Studies by including research from other disciplines such as sociology, anthropology, media studies, cultural and literary theory (Weldes 2003; Weber 2006; Holden 2006).

In particular, videogames may be of interest here, not only because they are one of the fastest growing media industries with an estimated worth of $33.4 billion in 2008 (Power 2007) and a revenue larger than Hollywood (Machin and Suleiman 2006), but because they have a huge socialising effect on those 'playing' them. Regardless of whether videogames promote violent behaviour in children and whether games such as *Counter-Strike* are responsible for the recent rise of violence and killing sprees at schools, games are now a large part of popular culture, the influence of which on international politics is fairly established (Weldes 2006; Grayson et al. 2009). What makes computer games even more interesting in this regard than literature and movies is their interactive nature where the consumer partakes in the telling of the story and the construction of the 'terrorist'. This is something which appears extra relevant considering the move away from simple linear story lines to more open ended games where the gamer controls more of the decisions.

The political implications of computer games have not only been realised by computer game research (King and Tanya 2006; Halter 2006; Bogost 2007) and language and communication studies (Machin and van Leeuwen 2005), but also by a handful of IR scholars (Der Derian 2001;

Campbell and Shapiro 2007; Power 2007). Even government institutions and 'terrorist' organisations seem to be aware of the increasing importance of videogames. For example, the US Army has released three official instalments of a popular 'first-person shooter' computer game called *America's Army*[2] as a public relations and recruitment tool. At the same time, Hizbollah has produced two games depicting the Lebanon war with Israel called *Special Force*,[3] which according to the producers are 'educational for our future generations and for all freedom lovers of this world of ours'.[4] While there are differences between games produced in the West and in the Middle East, the concept of these two games is the same: 'it has merely reversed the polarities of the narrative and iconographical stereotypes [...] by substituting the Arab Muslim hero for the American soldier' (Sisler 2008: 211–212). So the analysis of computer games may not only provide insights into the western cultural construction of terrorism, but also the 'terrorists'' construction of themselves.

Although the games mentioned above reflect very different political interests, the format of the videogame already carries within it a value and ideological message that military engagement is the best and only solution to conflict (Machin and Suleiman 2006). While especially Western videogames about terrorism such as *Delta Force* or *War on Terror* provide extensive amounts of information about technical equipment and weapons they do not provide a deeper understanding of the conflict, its causes and its outcome. As Vit Sisler (2008) points out, '[w]hen a game is set in a particular Middle Eastern country and based on real conflict, the retelling on the narrative inevitably reshapes its comprehension and evaluation, schematizing complex political relations into a polarized frame. [...] The militarization of the video game trope, having reinforced the polarized frame of the good Self and the evil Other, obviates any further explanation of the reasons for the conflict' (Sisler 2008: 209–210). So it may prove fruitful to investigate how the 'terrorist' is constructed in popular culture such as videogames and how this affects our understanding of him or her and with it the idea of 'appropriate' behaviour towards 'the terrorist'.

Contemplating the previously absurd

A third potential research direction terrorism research could pursue has to do more with political possibilities so far not considered. As we have seen in this book the construction of terrorism in a particular way influences the policy options we believe to be appropriate against it. Therefore constructivist terrorism research highlights issues previously ignored and makes it possible to ask questions which materialist understandings of terrorism would consider absurd. In other words, a constructivist approach to terrorism does not only offer alternative means of investigating traditional questions, but in addition opens up new areas of research which were previously considered taboo. For example, as indicated in the beginning and the end of this book, if 'new terrorists' are constituted as religiously motivated fanatics which use extreme, indiscriminate violence to achieve absurd goals and if they are discursively constructed as an 'uncivilised evil' and as a 'disease', dialogue and contact with such 'terrorists' becomes problematic and dangerous. Therefore, policies which would require engagement such as negotiations, concessions and reconciliation fall outside of the options considered as appropriate.

In this regard, the notion of reconciliation with 'new terrorists' is particularly interesting (Renner and Spencer 2009). While such suggestions may appear naïve, utopian or simply absurd in the case of sub-state terror groups such as al-Qaeda, the notion of reconciliation in a conflict involving state terror is generally considered a good idea. And it is widely accepted not only in academia but in international politics as a whole that reconciliation can positively contribute to peaceful coexistence and a functioning society after violent conflict and repression. After state terrorism reconciliation can facilitate the restoration of ruptured relationships and the overcoming of traumas derived from past experiences through the initiation of a far-reaching transformation of societal beliefs, attitudes, identities and emotions about the own group and the other (Humphrey 2002; Rigby 2001; Lerche 2000). And scholars within Transitional Justice and Conflict Resolution agree that reconciliation can be fostered by political means. While some stress the importance of problem-solving workshops and track-two-diplomacy, others emphasise the value of public apologies or the joint writing of a historical narrative of the past conflict. The most common suggestion however is the establishment of a commission which is tasked with balancing amnesty with accountability through the process of truth telling. While the amnesty of offenders allows them to regain membership and reintegrate into society, truth telling is assumed to contribute to reconciliation by establishing acknowledgement and responsibility for past crimes and thereby healing the individual and societal psyche and restoring moral order (Hayner 2001; Minow 1998).

Yet while reconciliation is considered appropriate to overcome societal rifts in the case of state terror, the notion of reconciliation is not generally applied to sub-state terrorism even though it is widely acknowledged, even by traditional terrorism researchers such as Walter Laqueur (1999) that state terrorism is far more violent, excessive and deadly than the sub-state variety. So maybe the absence of reconciliatory policies against terrorism are not so much due to the physical nature of the act but rather due to the words, labels and metaphors used to predicate the 'terrorist' as something unengageable.

By considering terrorism as a social construction and reflecting on the idea that there are no objective facts about 'terrorism' one can start questioning the established absurdity of 'unthinkable' policies. It would therefore be highly interesting to investigate further the policy options which have fallen outside of the measures considered appropriate against terrorism. Such research would not only further elaborate a constructivist understanding of terrorism research but indicate that not only 'terrorism' but also 'counter-terrorism' is what one makes of it.

Notes

Introduction

1 See for example Terrorism and Political Violence; Studies in Conflict and Terrorism or Critical Studies on Terrorism.
2 See for example degree courses at St. Andrews University in the UK, Pennsylvania State University in the US or Murdoch University in Australia.
3 See for example the Centre for the Study of Terrorism and Political Violence or the International Center of the Study of Terrorism.
4 For more on information on the leading academics and experts on terrorism see Reid (1993) and Raphael (2009).
5 Recently Lee Jarvis has noted the importance of interpretivist perspectives on terrorism which in his opinion are 'capable of addressing the discipline's continuing analytical limitations' (Jarvis 2009a: 7).

Chapter 1

1 For a more detailed analysis of the early history of terrorism see: Sinclair (2003) Anderson, and Sloan (2003) or Carr (2002).
2 For a more detailed look at terrorism and WMDs see Falkenrath et al. (1998) or Gurr and Cole (2000).
3 For more on the connection of anarchism and 'new terrorism' in the form of al-Qaeda see Gelvin (2008).
4 On this point see also Zimmermann (2004).
5 For a detailed history of suicide terrorism see Reuter (2004).

Chapter 2

1 For a very good summary of counter-terrorism classifications see: Crelinsten and Schmid (1992).
2 Even in the German literature on terrorism one can encounter a number of different ways of classifying counter-terror policies (Daase 2002). For example Peter Waldman (1998) distinguishes between *marco, meso* and *micro* levels of counter-terrorism while Ulrich Schneckener (2004) notes the difference between *operative* and *structural* anti-terror measures and differentiates between military and diplomatic as well as measures which guard against and prevent terrorist attacks.
3 The inability to deter terrorists is questioned by authors such as Bowen (2004) or Zagare (2006).
4 For more on the spiral of violence and revenge see Waldmann (2001).
5 One has to note that many different laws are considered to play an indirect role in the struggle against terrorism. Even if they do not directly focus on

terrorism, laws regulating the possession of guns and explosives, racketeering or law regarding drug-trafficking or pirate DVD sales have an influence on a state's ability to deal with terrorism.

6 On this problem of inter agency cooperation see the 9/11 Commission Report: Final Report of the National Commission on Terrorist Attacks Upon the United States, Official Government Edition, available at: http://www.gpoaccess.gov/911/ [accessed on 11.03.2008].

7 See for example The International Convention for the Suppression of the Financing of Terrorism, available at http://untreaty.un.org/English/Terrorism/Conv12.pdf [accessed 10.10.2007] or partly the United Nations Security Council Resolution 1373 & 1566, available at http://www.undemocracy.com/S-RES-1373(2001).pdf [accessed 10.10.2007] or http://www.undemocracy.com/S-RES-1566(2004).pdf [accessed 10.10.2007].

8 For more detail see: Financial Action Task Force on Money Laundering (2004) *Special Recommendations on Terrorist Financing*, Available at: http://www.fatf-gafi.org/dataoecd/8/17/34849466.pdf [accessed 05.11.06].

9 For more information on terrorist financing see: Napoleoni (2004); Schott (2006); Ehrenfeld (2003); Biersteker et al. (2007).

10 For more information on how the hawala system works see: Jost and Sandhu (2000).

11 US Customs and Border Protection 'Money and other Monetary Instruments', available at: http://www.cbp.gov/xp/cgov/travel/vacation/kbyg/money.xml [accessed 09.07.09].

12 Bundesministerium der Finanzen 'Barmittel- und Bargeldkontrollen im Verkehr mit Drittländern und innerhalb der Europäischen Union', available at: http://www.zoll.de/c0_reise_und_post/a0_reiseverkehr/f0_bargeldverkehr/index.html [accessed 10.07.09].

13 HM Revenue & Customs 'Carrying cash in and out of the United Kingdom', available at: http://customs.hmrc.gov.uk/channelsPortalWebApp/downloadFile?contentID=HMCE_PROD1_027380 [accessed on 09.07.09].

Chapter 3

1 For more information on the counter-terrorism measures implemented by different governments see: Buckley and Fawn (2003); von Hippel (2005) or Alexander (2002).

2 Government Accountability Office: *Combating Terrorism – Determining and Reporting Federal Funding Data*, Report to Congressional Requesters, GAO-06-161, (2006), pp. 1–2, available at: www.gao.gov/new.items/d06161.pdf [accessed 15.06.09].

3 The Government Performance Results Act of 1993, Office of Management and Budget, available at: http://www.whitehouse.gov/omb/mgmt-gpra/gplaw2m.html [accessed 15.06.09].

4 Progress Report in the Global War on Terrorism, Washington: The White House, available at: http://www.whitehouse.gov/homeland/progress/ [accessed 15.06.09].

5 See: Three Years of Progress in the War on Terrorism, Fact Sheet, The White House, Office of the Press Secretary, Washington DC, September 11, 2004,

available at: http://merln.ndu.edu/archivepdf/hls/WH/20040911.pdf [accessed 15.06.09].
6 On the effectiveness of assassinations also see: Hafez and Hatfield (2006).
7 For other examples where statistical models are being applied to evaluate the effectiveness of counter-terrorism see: Enders and Sandler (2005); Wilson et al. (2006); Enders and Sandler (1995); Sandler and Arce (2003).
8 United States Department of State: *Patterns of Global Terrorism 2003*, available at: http://www.state.gov/s/ct/rls/crt/2003/ [accessed 13.07.09].
9 Some of the databases available include *'International Terrorism: Attributes of Terrorist Events'* (ITERATE) or *'Terrorism in Western Europe: Event Data'* (TWEED) as well as the *RAND-MIPT Terrorism Incident database.*
10 The MIPT Terrorism Knowledge Base was available at: http://www.tkb.org/Home.jsp but has now been removed from public access.
11 For a number of explanations for this phenomenon see: Slovic (2000); Lerner et al. (2003); Loewenstein et al. (2001); Sunstein (2003).
12 Booth (2008: 74) criticised this attitude and points out that most historians have never met their subjects they study such as roman emperors or Tudor kings.
13 *The Sunday Times* (London) cited on the back cover of Gunaratna (2003a).
14 For more information on the issue of scientific fieldwork in a violent conflict see Nordstrom and Robben (1995).
15 For more information on the Critical Studies on Terrorism Working Group see: http://www.bisa.ac.uk/groups/7/index.asp [accessed on the 06.02.2008].
16 On the issue of interdisciplinarity in terrorism studies especially in Germany see Spencer and Biazza (2008).
17 For a serious engagement by traditional terrorism scholars with critical terrorism studies see for example Horgan and Boyle (2008) or Weinberg and Eubank (2008) and for a more vulgar response see Jones and Smith (2009).
18 For further criticism of Critical Terrorism Studies see Egerton (2009); Joseph (2009) or Stokes (2009).

Chapter 4

1 This is not to mean that constructivism should be considered the cutting edge of IR.
2 Booth (2008: 74) also questions the vital importance of primary engagement with one's subject as he points out that historian rarely ever meet the protagonists of their research such as Tudor Kings or Holy Roman emperors.
3 This section is only a very brief introduction to the central ideas of what can be broadly described as constructivist thought. For more information on Constructivism in IR see for example: Adler (1997), Checkel (1998), Fierke and Jørgensen (2001), Wiener (2003); Guzzini and Leander (2006).
4 The contrast to rationalism has been questioned to some extend as the logic of consequence can also be a logic of appropriateness. For more on the problems of contrasting rationalism with constructivism see Fearon and Wendt (2002) or Hurd (2008).
5 For translations of al-Qaeda's own discourse, see Lawrence (2005) and Mansfield (2006).

6 See for example the Researching and Applying Metaphor (RaAM) Association conferences, http://www.raam.org.uk/.

7 See for example Metaphor and Symbol which is its 22 year of publication and was previously called Metaphor and Symbolic Activity.

8 One of the very few exceptions which analyse the role of metaphors in terrorism and counter-terrorism is Kruglanski et al. (2007).

9 Exceptions here include Mongoven (2006), Zhang (2007) and most famously Lakoff (2001).

10 These types of metaphors are also sometimes referred to a 'major' and 'mini' metaphors, see for example Kitis and Milapides (1997).

11 On the issue of causality of ideas and discourse on policy see for example Yee (1996) or Wendt (1999: 77–88).

12 One has to note that the decision of what is metaphorical and what is not is also down to interpretations. On this point see in particular Low (1999: 49): 'There is always going to be a measure of subjectivity or randomness in identifying expressions'.

Chapter 5

1 For an exception see Thornborrow (1993) and Winfield et al. (2002).

2 See Media Tenor http://www.medientenor.com/newsletters.php?id_news= 239 [accessed on 2.2.2008].

3 Please note that, all subsequent footnotes provide only one example of each metaphorical expression found in the *Bild* or *The Sun* together with the title of the article and the page number and author were possible (All translations are my own).

4 Kai Diekmann, *Bild*, 'Kriegserklärung an die Menschheit', 12.9.2001, p. 1.

5 'Kamikaze-Angriff', Peter Scholl-Latour, *Bild*, 'Gibt es jetzt Krieg, Herr Scholl-Latour?', 12.9.2001, p. 5.

6 'Kamikaze-Flieger', *Bild*, 'Fünf Minuten Stille für Amerika', 13.9.2001, p. 14.

7 'Kamikaze-Piloten', *Bild*, 'Der Flugplan des Terrors', 14.9.2001, p. 4.

8 'Kamikaze Attentäter', Gordon Thomas, *Bild*, 'Warum haben FBI und CIA so grausam versagt?', 13.9.2001, p. 4.

9 'Kamikaze-Waffen', *Bild*, 'Großer Gott steh uns bei!', 12.9.2001, p. 1.

10 'Kamikaze Flüge', *Bild*, 'Zehntausende verlieren Job', 20.9.2001, p. 1.

11 'Kriegserklärung', *Bild*, 'Das ist bin Ladens Kriegserklärung', 25.9.2001, p. 1.

12 'Kriegsgebiet', *Bild*, 'Großer Gott steh uns bei!', 12.9.2001, p. 2.

13 'Terror-Krieg', *Bild*, 'Sensationelle Fernsehbilder zeigen bin Laden mit seinem Terror-Strategen', 6.10.2001, p. 2.

14 'Befehl', *Bild*, 'Osama bin Laden gratuliert den Attentätern', 13.9.2001, p. 4.

15 'Privat-Armee', *Bild*, 'Wo steckt bin Laden?', 19.9.2001, p. 4.

16 'Soldaten', *Bild*, 'Nach 26 Tagen schlagen die US-Streitkräfte zu', 8.10.2001, p. 3.

17 'Terroristen Armee', Gordon Thomas, *Bild*, 'Das FBI jagt bin Laden mit 180 Spionage-Satelliten', 14.9.2001, pp. 2–3.

18 'Todestruppe', 'Daniel Böcking, Stefan Schneider and Marco Schwartz', *Bild*, 'Das Netz des Bösen in Deutschland', 20.9.2001, p. 4.

19 'Terror-Truppen', *Bild*, 'Das sind die Pass-Fälscher von Terror-Chef bin Laden', 28.9.2001, p. 2.

20 Definition of 'troop' found in the *Dictionary of English* (2005): Second Edition, Revised, Oxford: Oxford University Press, p. 1889.

21 'Veteranen', Gordon Thomas, *Bild*, 'Das FBI jagt bin Laden mit 180 Spionage-Satelliten', 14.9.2001, pp. 2–3.

22 *Oxford Dictionary of English* (2005): Second Edition, Revised, Oxford: Oxford University Press, p. 1962.

23 *Collins English Dictionary* (1998), Millennium Edition, Glasgow: Harper Collins Publishers, p. 1695.

24 'kampferfahren', *Bild*, 'Der Bergbunker von Osama bin Laden', 15.9.2001, p. 5.

25 'Gottes-, Glaubens- und Heilige-Krieger', *Bild*, 'Wer sind die Selbstmord Piloten?', 12.9.2001, p. 4; Peter Scholl-Latour, *Bild*, 'Gibt es jetzt Krieg, Herr Scholl-Latour?', 12.9.2001, p. 5; *Bild*, 'Das Massaker von New York wurde in Hamburg geplant', 14.9.2001, p. 2.

26 'Terror-Kommandos', *Bild*, 'Neue Terror-Kommandos unterwegs?', 15.9.2001, p. 1.

27 'Selbstmordkommando', Gordon Thomas, *Bild*, 'Das FBI jagt bin Laden mit 180 Spionage-Satelliten', 14.9.2001, pp. 2–3.

28 *Oxford Dictionary of English* (2005): Second Edition, Revised, Oxford: Oxford University Press, p. 346.

29 *Collins English Dictionary* (1998): Millennium Edition, Glasgow: Harper Collins Publishers, p. 322.

30 'Terror-Strategen', *Bild*, 'Sensationelle Fernsehbilder zeigen bin Laden mit seinem Terror-Strategen', 6.10.2001, p. 2.

31 'Terror-Logistiker', *Bild*, 'Das Gesicht der Schleierfrau', 21.9.2001, p. 2.

32 Merriam-Webster Online dictionary available at: www.m-w.com.

33 'Arsenal', Martin S. Lambeck, *Bild*, 'CIA befürchtet neue Attentate', 19.9.2001, p. 2.

34 *Bild*, 'Der Bergbunker von Osama bin Laden', 15.9.2001, p. 5.

35 'Kommandozentral', *Bild*, 'Der Angriff', 8.10.2001, p. 1.

36 'Stützpunkte', *Bild*, 'US-Regierung weist Taliban-Vorschlag zurück', 21.9.2001, p. 2.

37 'Tarnung', Daniel Böcking, Stefan Schneider and Marco Schwartz, *Bild*, 'Das Netz des Bösen in Deutschland', 20.9.2001, p. 4.

38 *Oxford Dictionary of English* (2005): Second Edition, Revised, Oxford: Oxford University Press, p. 249.

39 'Befehl', *Bild*, 'Osama bin Laden gratuliert den Attentätern', 13.9.2001, p. 4.

40 'Top-Terrorist', *Bild*, 'Osama bin Laden gratuliert den Attentätern', 13.9.2001, p. 4.

41 'Terror-Chef', *Bild*, 'Wer ist der Terror-Chef', 12.9.2001, p. 4.

42 'Terroristenführer', *Bild*, 'So jagt US-Präsident Bush den schlimmsten Terroristen der Welt', 18.9.2001, p. 2.

43 'Terror-Boss', *Bild*, 'Wo steckt bin Laden?', 19.9.2001, p. 4.

44 'Oberterrorist', *Bild*, 'Wo steckt bin Laden?', 19.9.2001, p. 4.

45 'Stratege des Terrors', Gordon Thomas, *Bild*, 'Das FBI jagt bin Laden mit 180 Spionage-Satelliten', 14.9.2001, p. 3.

46 'Terror-Fürst', *Bild*, 'Hier versteckt sich der Terror-Fürst', 15.9.2001, p. 5.

47 'Terror-Scheich', Gordon Thomas, *Bild*, 'Das FBI jagt bin Laden mit 180 Spionage-Satelliten', 14.9.2001, pp. 2–3.

48 'Pate des Terrors', *Bild*, 'Haben die Terroristen einen im Weißen Haus?', 15.9.2001, p. 5.

49 'dirigiert', *Bild*, 'Osama bin Laden. Sein böses Leben', 15.9.2001, p. 5.

50 'befielt', *Bild*, 'Osama bin Laden. Sein böses Leben', 15.9.2001, p. 5.

51 'kriminelle', Jürgen Todenhöfer, *Bild*, 'Mr. President, treffen Sie die Schuldigen, nicht die Unschuldigen', 17.9.2001, p. 4.

52 'Täter', Kai Diekmann, *Bild*, 'Kriegserklärung an die Menschheit', 12.9.2001, p. 1.

53 'Mörder', *Bild*, 'Es gibt keine Einteilung in gute Völker und böse', 15.9.2001, p. 4.

54 'Sturm', *Bild*, 'Bin Laden droht mit Todes-Piloten', 11.10.2001, p. 1.

55 'Attentats-Welle', *Bild*, 'Bin Laden spurlos verschwunden', 24.9.2001, p. 1.

56 'Terror-Welle', *Bild*, 'Angst von Anschlägen in Deutschland', 21.9.2001, p. 4.

57 'Katastrophe', *Bild*, 'Um 8.48 Uhr explodierte der 1. Jet im World Trade Center', 12.9.2001, p. 2.

58 Merriam-Webster Online dictionary available at: www.m-w.com.

59 *Oxford Dictionary of English* (2005): Second Edition, Revised, Oxford: Oxford University Press, p. 271.

60 'Terrorkatastrophe', *Bild*, 'Mami, gibt es Krieg? Wie man Kindern die Angst nimmt', 13.9.2001, p. 10.

61 'Das Böse', *Bild*, 'Besiegen sie das Böse?', 19.9.2001, p. 5.

62 'barbarisch', *Bild*, 'Jetzt sind wir alle Amerikaner weil ...', 13.9.2001, p. 6.

63 'monströs', *Bild*, 'Putin versetzt Luftabwehr in Gefechtsbereitschaft', 12.9.2001, p. 6.

64 'Terror-Monster', *Bild*, 'Ist bin Laden schon aus Afghanistan geflohen?', 22.9.2001, p. 2.

65 'teuflischer Terror', *Bild*, 'Fünf Minuten Stille für Amerika', 13.9.2001, p. 14.

66 'Inferno', *Bild*, 'So erlebte BILD-Reporter Michael Remke das Inferno in New York', 12.9.2001, p. 4.

67 *Collins English Dictionary* (1998): Millennium Edition, Glasgow: Harper Collins Publishers, p. 832.

68 'Hölle', *Bild*, 'Die seltsamen Legenden von New York', 24.9.2001, p. 3.

69 'Flammenhölle', *Bild*, 'Über 190 verbrannten im Pentagon', 17.9.2001, p. 3.

70 'Apokalypse', *Bild*, 'Die Woche der Apokalypse', 17.9.2001, p. 4.

71 'Teufel', C. Schniedermann and E. Koch, *Bild*, 'In New York erlebten wir die Handlanger des Teufels', 21.9.2001, p. 4.

72 'teuflischer Angriff', Gordon Thomas, *Bild*, 'Warum haben FBI und CIA so grausam versagt?', 13.9.2001, p. 4.

73 'apokalyptisch', Peter Scholl-Latour, *Bild*, 'Gibt es jetzt Krieg, Herr Scholl-Latour?', 12.9.2001, p. 5.

74 'Reiter der Apokalypse', *Bild*, 'Post von Wagner', 12.9.2001, p. 2.

75 'terroristische Barbarei', *Bild*, 'Jetzt sind wir alle Amerikaner weil ...', 13.9.2001, p. 2.

76 'unmenschlich', *Bild*, 'Jetzt sind wir alle Amerikaner weil ...', 13.9.2001, p. 6.

77 'Terror-Bestie', *Bild*, 'Terror-Bestie lebte acht Jahre in Deutschland', 14.9.2001, p. 1.

78 'wahnsinnig', *Bild*, 'Putin versetzt Luftabwehr in Gefechtsbereitschaft', 12.9.2001, p. 6.

79 'krank', *Bild*, 'Deutschland weint mit Amerika', 12.9.2001, p. 12.

80 'Schlachtfeld', *Bild*, 'Mitternacht stand das Paradies in Flammen', 14.10.2002, p. 8.

81 'Trupp', Manfred Quiring, *Bild*, 'Wir sprengen alle in die Luft', 24.10.2002, p. 2.

82 'Kampftruppe', *Bild*, 'Wir sind bereit zu sterben', 25.10.2002, p. 2.

83 'Kommando', M. Quiring and J. Hartmann, *Bild*, 'Die Todgeweihten', 25.10.2002, p. 2.

84 'Allianz gegen den Terror', Rolf Kleine, *Bild*, 'Ein abscheuliches Verbrechen', 25.10.2002, p. 2.

85 'Krieg', Paul C. Martin, *Bild*, 'Sicherheit ist Menschenrecht!', 28.10.2002, p. 2.

86 'Terrorismus-Krieg', Herbert Kremp, *Bild*, 'Bitte die Wahrheit', 29.10.2002, p. 2.

87 'Anti-Terror Krieg', Jürgen Todenhöfer, *Bild*, 'Härte und Gerechtigkeit', 26.10.2002, p. 2.

88 'Krieger', *Bild*, 'Der brutale Terror der Tschetschenen-Krieger', 26.10.2002, p. 2.

89 'Tatort', *Bild*, 'Ich sah, wie Trümmer eine Frau enthauptet haben', 14.10.2002, p. 9.

90 'Täter', Ute Brüssel and Einar Koch, *Bild*, 'Terror-Bomben gegen Urlauber auf der ganzen Welt?', 15.10.2002, p. 4.

91 'Mord', *Bild*, 'Das ist Deutschlands gefährlichster Häftling', 23.10.2002, p. 7.

92 'Mörder', Andreas Englisch, Julia Fischer, Volker Koop and Tobias Lobe, *Bild*, 'Wie viele Menschen darf man opfern, um andere zu retten', 29.10.2002, p. 2.

93 'überfallen', *Bild*, 'Terroristen überfallen Theater', 24.10.2002, p. 1.

94 'Indiz', Einar Koch, *Bild*, 'Gleich müssen die Eltern in die Leichenhalle', 17.10.2002, p. 12.

95 'Verbrechen', Rolf Kleine, *Bild*, 'Ein abscheuliches Verbrechen', 25.10.2002, p. 2.

96 'Katastrophe', *Bild*, 'Bomben-Terror gegen Urlauber. 200 Tote!', 14.10.2002, p. 1.

97 'Terrorwelle', R. Kleine and D. Schülter, *Bild*, 'War es Osama bin Laden', 14.10.2002, p. 8.

98 'Barbarei', Paul C. Martin, *Bild*, 'Sicherheit ist ein Menschenrecht!', 28.10.2002, p. 2.

99 'teuflische Anschläge', R. Kleine and D. Schülter, *Bild*, 'War es Osama bin Laden', 14.10.2002, p. 8.

100 'Inferno', *Bild*, 'Mitternacht stand das Paradies in Flammen', 14.10.2002, p. 8.

152 Notes

101 'Hölle', *Bild*, 'Papa, ich bin schrecklich verbrannt. Aber ich lebe', 15.10.2002, p. 4.
102 'Flammenhölle', *Bild*, 'Bomben-Terror gegen Urlauber. 200 Tote!', 14.10.2002, p. 1.
103 'Feuerhölle', Andrea Brösel and Frank Rolle, *Bild*, 'Ohnmächtig lag die Deutsche in der Flammen-Hölle', 16.10.2002, p. 8.
104 'Terror-Hölle', Andrea Brösel, *Bild*, 'Ich überlebte die Terror-Hölle', 15.10.2002, p. 1.
105 'irre Terroristen', Jens Hartmann, *Bild*, 'So quälen sie die Geiseln von Moskau', 26.10.2002, p. 2.
106 One should however note that the first attack was carried out on a Saturday and therefore did not find a mention in the *Bild* until Monday. By this time the news was fairly old and as a result one can argue that the story did not warrant the dedication of extensive page space.
107 'Krieg', *Bild*, 'Steuert bin Laden aus seiner Höhle den Terror?', 22.11.2003, p. 2.
108 'Kriegsgebiet', *Bild*, 'Steuert bin Laden aus seiner Höhle den Terror?', 22.11.2003, p. 2.
109 'getarnt', R. Eichinger, T. Lobe and H. J. Vehlewald, *Bild*, 'Überall blutüberströmte, weinende Menschen', 21.11.2003, p. 10.
110 'Befohlen', *Bild*, 'Istanbul-Attentäter hatten eine Tonne Sprengstoff', 17.11.2003, p. 2.
111 'Kommandiert', *Bild*, 'Steuert bin Laden aus seiner Höhle den Terror?', 22.11.2003, p. 2.
112 'Tatort', *Bild*, 'Istanbul-Attentäter hatten eine Tonne Sprengstoff', 17.11.2003, p. 2.
113 'Verdächtige', *Bild*, 'Legten diese Männer die Bomben von Istanbul', 25.11.2003, p. 1.
114 'Tatverdacht', *Bild*, 'Istanbul-Attentäter hatten eine Tonne Sprengstoff', 17.11.2003, p. 2.
115 'verbrecherische Anschläge', *Bild*, 'Müssen Deutsche jetzt auch den Terror-Notfall üben?', 22.11.2003, p. 2.
116 'Schurkenstück', *Bild*, 'Steuert bin Laden aus seiner Höhle den Terror?', 22.11.2003, p. 2.
117 'Hydra', *Bild*, 'Steuert bin Laden aus seiner Höhle den Terror?', 22.11.2003, p. 2.
118 'Terror Inferno', *Bild*, 'Terror-Inferno! Die Welt in neuer Angst', 21.11.2003, p. 1.
119 'teuflische Absicht', *Bild*, 'Wir werden diese Terroristen ausrotten', 21.11.2003, p. 10.
120 This may be due to the limited number of overall articles.
121 'Krieg', Georg Gafron, *Bild*, 'Krieg gegen die Zivilisation', 15.3.2004, p. 2.
122 'Militärsprecher der Al Qaida', *Bild*, 'Das unheimliche Bekenner-Video', 15.3.2004, p. 3.
123 'Terror-Truppe', *Bild*, 'Wer war der Terror-Scheich?', 23.3.2004, p. 12
124 'Al Qaida-Krieger', A. Klinger, C. Martin, K. Feldhaus, J. Fischer and J. Reichelt, *Bild* 'Die Spur führt zu Al Qaida', 15.3.2004, p. 3.
125 'Terror-Befehl', *Bild*, 'Gab er den Terror-Befehl von Madrid?', 16.3.2004, p. 1.

126 'kommandiert', A. Klinger, *Bild*, 'Wir werden Madrid mit Leichen spicken', 17.3.2004, p. 2.

127 'drillen', Andreas Klinger, *Bild*, 'Der Bomber von Madrid', 18.3.2004, p. 2.

128 'Al Qaida Boss', Andreas Klinger, *Bild*, 'Der Bomber von Madrid', 18.3.2004, p. 2.

129 'Al Qaida Führung', *Bild*, 'Marines jagen bin Laden', 1.4.2004, p. 1.

130 'Mörder', Malte Biss and Andreas Klinger, *Bild*, 'So feige! So sinnlos! Ihr Mörder!', 12.3.2004, p. 1.

131 'Terrormord', *Bild*, 'Verdammte 11. Angst vor Attentaten am Ostersonntag', 7.4.2004, p. 1.

132 'Massenmord', Malte Biss and Andreas Klinger, *Bild*, 'Um 7.35 Uhr explodierte die erste Bombe', 12.3.2004, p. 7.

133 'mörderische Strategie', Frank A. Meyer, *Bild*, 'Darf bin Laden getötet werden?', 1.4.2004, p. 2.

134 'verbrecherischer Anschlag', Rolf Kleine, *Bild*, 'Schily fordert Raster-Fahndung in ganz Europa', 27.3.2004, p. 2.

135 'Täter', Bild, 'Neue Festnahmen in Madrid', 23.3.2004, p. 2.

136 'Verdächtige', *Bild*, 'Madrid-Terror in Deutschland geplant?', 26.3.2004, p. 1.

137 'Komplizen', *Bild*, 'Hier explodieren die Attentäter', 5.4.2004, p. 12.

138 'Terror-Spur', *Bild*, 'Terror-Spur führt nach Marokko', 16.3.2004, p. 2.

139 'aufklären', *Bild*, 'Terror-Spur führt nach Marokko', 16.3.2004, p. 2.

140 'Katastrophe', *Bild*, 'Kommt der Terror zu uns?', 15.3.2004, p. 2.

141 'barbarische', A. Klinger, C. Martin, K. Feldhaus, J. Fischer and J. Reichelt, *Bild*, 'Die Spur führt zu Al Qaida', 15.3.2004, p. 3.

142 'teuflische', Herbert Kremp, *Bild*, 'Mitten ins stolze Herz Spaniens', 12.3.2004, p. 2.

143 'Hydra', Herbert Kremp, *Bild*, 'Mitten ins stolze Herz Spaniens', 12.3.2004, p. 2.

144 'Inferno', *Bild*, 'Islamisten erklären Spanien den Krieg', 6.4.2004, p. 1.

145 'kranker Kopf', *Bild*, 'Wird heute bin Ladens Gehirn verhaftet?', 20.3.2004, p. 12.

146 'Pest', Peter Boenisch, *Bild*, 'Was uns die Spanier lehren', 16.3.2004, p. 2.

147 'Verrückte', *Bild*, '911, verdammte Zahl der Angst', 13.3.2004, p. 12.

148 'Terror-Irrsinn', *Bild*, 'Terror-Irrsinn!', 26.3.2004, p. 22.

149 'Verbrecher', *Bild*, 'Wer steckt hinter dem Anschlag', 8.7.2005, p. 3.

150 'mörderisch', Peter Michalski, Peter Moufarrege, Kristina Rommel, Michael Gärtner, Kai Feldhaus, Einar Koch and Dittmar Jurko, *Bild*, 'Um 8.51 Uhr zerfetzte es die erste U-Bahn', 8.7.2005, p. 2.

151 'Täter', *Bild*, 'In den Taschen der Opfer klingeln noch die Handys', 11.7.2005, p. 8.

152 'Verdächtiger', *Bild*, 'Waren es 4 Selbstmord-Attentäter?', 13.7.2005, p. 6.

153 'Mörder', Georg Gaffron, *Bild*, 'Die, netten' Terroristen', 14.7.2005, p. 2.

154 'ermorden', *Bild*, 'Terroristen ermorden ägyptischen Botschafter', 8.7.2005, p. 4.

155 'terroristisches Verbrechen', Einar Koch, *Bild*, 'BILD-Interview mit Bundesinnenminister Otto Schily', 25.7.2005, p. 11.

156 'Killer', Peter Michalski, *Bild*, 'Er war's!', 14.7.2005, p. 8.

157 'Terrorbande', *Bild*, 'Terroristen ermorden ägyptischen Botschafter', 8.7.2005, p. 4.

158 'Komplizen', Peter Michalski, *Bild*, 'Was passiert mit den Leichen der zerfetzten Attentäter?', 19.7.2005, p. 6.

159 *Oxford Dictionary of English* (2005): Second Edition, Revised, Oxford: Oxford University Press, p. 10.

160 'Al Qaida-Terrorwelle', *Bild*, 'Wieder Bomben in London', 22.7.2005, p. 1.

161 'Katastrophenzone', Peter Michalski, Peter Moufarrege, Kristina Rommel, Michael Gärtner, Kai Feldhaus, Einar Koch and Dittmar Jurko, *Bild*, 'Um 8.51 Uhr zerfetzte es die erste U-Bahn', 8.7.2005, p. 2.

162 'barbarische Terroranschläge', Peter Michalski, Peter Moufarrege, Kristina Rommel, Michael Gärtner, Kai Feldhaus, Einar Koch and Dittmar Jurko, *Bild*, 'Um 8.51 Uhr zerfetzte es die erste U-Bahn', 8.7.2005, p. 2.

163 'Bomben-Barbaren', Peter Michalski, Christina Mänz, Monika Kennedy, Peter Moufarrege, Julian Reichelt, Andreas Thielen, Michael Gärtner, Kristina Rommel and Dittmar Jurko, *Bild*, 'Jagt auf die Bomben-Barbaren', 9.7.2005, p. 4.

164 'teuflischer Terrorplan', Peter Michalski, *Bild*, 'Wollten die Attentäter gar nicht sterben?', 18.7.2005, p. 8.

165 'Inferno', Peter Michalski, Peter Moufarrege, Kristina Rommel, Michael Gärtner, Kai Feldhaus, Einar Koch and Dittmar Jurko, *Bild*, 'Um 8.51 Uhr zerfetzte es die erste U-Bahn', 8.7.2005, p. 2.

166 'Hölle', *Bild*, 'Ich sah abgerissene Beine auf den Gleisen', 9.7.2005, p. 5.

167 'Wahnidee', Einar Koch, *Bild*, 'BILD-Interview mit Bundesinnenminister Otto Schily', 25.7.2005, p. 11.

168 See Newspaper Marketing Agency at http://www.nmauk.co.uk/nma/do/ live/factsAndFigures?newspaperID=17 [accessed 4.3.2009].

169 See http://www.newspapers24.com/largest-newspapers.html [accessed 4.3.2009].

170 For more on the role of tabloids in Britain see McLachlan and Golding (2000) or Conboy (2006).

171 Trevor Kavanagh and David Wooding, *The Sun*, 'Are we at war? Absolutely', 17.9.2001, p. 2.

172 Richard Littlejohn, *The Sun*, 'War to the Death', 18.9.2001, p. 13.

173 Trevor Kavanagh, *The Sun*, 'Bush orders 100 combat jets to the Gulf', 20.9.2001, p. 1.

174 Paul Thompson and Brian Flynn, *The Sun*, 'A terrible tragedy has just befallen my nation', 12.9.2001, p. 4.

175 George Pascoe-Watson, *The Sun*, 'I won. Smithy takes crown and makes Howard Shadow Chancellor', 14.9.2001, p. 22.

176 *The Sun*, 'America in terror', 12.9.2001, p. 13.

177 Brian Flynn, *The Sun*, 'Spirit of the Blitz', 14.9.2001, pp. 8–9.

178 *The Sun*, 'All the world must unite to defeat these evil cowards', 12.9.2001, p. 10.

179 Neil Syson, *The Sun*, 'Moment the plane hit', 12.9.2001, p. 8.

180 Mike Sullivan, *The Sun*, 'Bin Laden's Terror HQ ... a London semi', 20.9.2001, p. 9.

181 George Pascoe-Watson, *The Sun*, 'World on a knife-edge', 19.9.2001, p. 4.

182 Paul Thompson and Trevor Kavanagh, *The Sun*, 'Operation Infinite Justice', 20.9.2001, p. 4.
183 John Kay, *The Sun*, 'MI5: There is no need for panic', 28.9.2001, p. 6.
184 Oliver Harvey, *The Sun*, 'Fairytales of New York', 25.9.2001, p. 8.
185 Neil Syson, *The Sun*, 'Would you believe it', 19.9.2001, p. 1.
186 Brian Flynn, *The Sun*, '43 dead Brits named', 20.9.2001, p. 6.
187 Paul Thompson, *The Sun*, 'FBI charge 1st suspect on hijacks', 26.9.2001, p. 11.
188 Richard Littlejohn, *The Sun*, 'War to the death', 18.9.2001, p. 13.
189 Neil Syson and Nick Parker, *The Sun*, 'No 1 Suspect', 12.9.2001, p. 18.
190 Paul Thompson and Nick Parker, *The Sun*, 'Bush hits Bin where it'll hurt', 25.9.2001, p. 49.
191 Nick Parker, Paul Thompson and Stewart Whittingham, *The Sun*, 'Nest of Killers', 26.9.2001, p. 11.
192 George Pascoe-Watson, *The Sun*, 'Forces are ready to go', 28.9.2001, p. 6.
193 Paul Thompson and Brian Flynn, *The Sun*, 'They Must Have Killed Thousands – Fanatics trigger global alert', 12.9.2001, p. 2.
194 Merriam-Webster Online dictionary available at: www.m-w.com.
195 Nick Parker, *The Sun*, 'How Could it Happen – Nowhere is safe from terrorists', 12.9.2001, p. 24.
196 Andrew Parker, *The Sun*, 'We have no choice, says hero's mum', 9.10.2001, p. 9.
197 David Wooding, *The Sun*, 'Notting Hill bank link to murders', 20.9.2001, p. 9.
198 Simon Hughes and Sara Nathan, *The Sun*, 'Partners in Evil', 6.10.2001, p. 9.
199 Simon Hughes, *The Sun*, 'Clues that nail warlord', 24.9.2001, p. 5.
200 Tim Spanton and Emma Shrimsley, *The Sun*, 'How we could hit back', 14.9.2001, p. 19.
201 Jamie Pyatt, *The Sun*, 'Race to escape', 20.9.2001, p. 5.
202 Nick Parker, *The Sun*, 'Blitz is coming...', 17.9.2001, p. 4.
203 Oliver Harvey, *The Sun*, 'So why do they hate us?', 13.9.2001, pp. 18–19.
204 Merriam-Webster Online dictionary available at: www.m-w.com.
205 'a military attack usually involving direct combat with enemy forces', see Merriam-Webster Online dictionary available at: www.m-w.com, Trevor Kavanagh, *The Sun*, 'Time to Stand and Fight Evil', 17.9.2001, p. 8.
206 Nick Parker and Paul Thompson, *The Sun*, 'Hijackers: Paradise awaits us', 29.9.2001, p. 7.
207 Merriam-Webster Online dictionary.
208 Henry Kissinger, *The Sun*, 'There can be no half measures. We must win a decisive victory over terrorism', 17.9.2001, p. 9.
209 Nick Parker, *The Sun*, 'How could it happen?', 12.9.2001, p. 24.
210 Definition of 'enemy' in Merriam-Webster Online dictionary.
211 George Pascoe-Watson, *The Sun*, 'Brave PM flies into Pakistan war zone', 3.10.2001, p. 6.
212 Richard Littlejohn, *The Sun*, 'War to the death', 18.9.2001, p. 13.
213 Irwin Stelzer, *The Sun*, 'A Britain free from Europe is essential in war on terrorism', 9.10.2001, p. 8.

214 Paul Thompson and Brian Flynn, *The Sun*, 'They must have killed thousands', 12.9.2001, p. 2.
215 Paul Thompson, *The Sun*, 'Now go get 'em George', 14.9.2001, p. 2.
216 *The Sun*, 'Day that changed the world', 12.9.2001, p. 1.
217 Paul Thompson and Brian Flynn, *The Sun*, 'A terrible tragedy has just befallen my nation', 12.9.2001, p. 4.
218 Brian Flynn, *The Sun*, 'The largest target in US', 12.9.2001, p. 20.
219 Sara Nathan, *The Sun*, 'Mast that once stood at 1,368 ft', 15.9.2001, p. 32.
220 Charles Rae, *The Sun*, 'Queen cries along with us all', 15.9.2001, p. 6.
221 Paul Thompson and Brian Flynn, *The Sun*, 'A terrible tragedy has just befallen my nation', 12.9.2001, p. 4.
222 *The Sun*, 'All the world must unite to defeat these evil cowards', 12.9.2001, p. 10.
223 Trevor Kavanagh, *The Sun*, 'Time to stand and fight evil', 17.9.2001, p. 8.
224 *The Sun*, 'Together we will bring peace to the world', 18.9.2001, p. 12.
225 Richard Littlejohn, *The Sun*, 'We're all American now', 14.9.2001, p. 13.
226 Paul Thompson, *The Sun*, 'World unites against terror', 13.9.2001, p. 2.
227 Trevor Kavanagh, *The Sun*, 'Time to stand and fight evil', 17.9.2001, p. 8.
228 Nick Parker, *The Sun*, 'Riddle of ,fifth hijack, foiled by cancellation', 19.9.2001, p. 4.
229 *The Sun*, 'All the world must united to defeat these evil cowards', 12.9.2001, p. 10.
230 Tom Worden, Sara Nathan and Martin Wallace, *The Sun*, 'War zone .. It's Armageddon', 12.9.2001, p. 14.
231 Nick Parker and Paul Thompson, *The Sun*, 'Hijackers: Paradise awaits us', 29.9.2001, p. 7.
232 Tim Spanton, *The Sun*, 'Did they learn on pounds 50 CD Rom?', 13.9.2001, p. 17.
233 Trevor Kavanagh, *The Sun*, 'Blair. We have incontrovertible evidence bin Laden did it. We will get him, stop him', 1.10.2001, p. 5.
234 Richard Littlejohn, *The Sun*, 'We're all American now', 14.9.2001, p. 13.
235 Richard Littlejohn, *The Sun*, 'We're all American now', 14.9.2001, p. 13.
236 Paul Thompson, *The Sun*, 'Maniac's passport is found in rubble', 17.9.2001, p. 6.
237 Richard Littlejohn, *The Sun*, 'We're all American now', 14.9.2001, p. 13.
238 Paul Thompson, *The Sun*, 'We'll never be defeated', 18.9.2001, p. 4.
239 Paul Thompson and Mel Hunter, *The Sun*, 'America thought Pentagon was safe. Nobody counted on a jet dropping from the sky', 12.9.2001, p. 16.
240 Graham Diggines, *The Sun*, '5-Year Blitz kills 4,000 Innocents', 14.10.2002.
241 Senan Hogan, *The Sun*, 'We lived through two blasts', 14.10.2002.
242 George Pascoe-Watson, *The Sun*, 'Blair: war on terror is as important as World War 2', 16.10.2002.
243 Simon Hughes and George Pascoe-Watson, *The Sun*, 'Terror men have changed tactics since 9/11 ... they've moved on to soft targets', 15.10.2002.
244 *The Sun*, 'Bin Laden' alive and plotting', 9.11.2002.
245 Simon Hughes and George Pascoe-Watson, *The Sun*, 'Terror men have changed tactics since 9/11 ... they've moved on to soft targets', 15.10.2002.
246 Definition of 'campaign' in Merriam-Webster Online dictionary.
247 Grant Rollings, *The Sun*, 'Oz will still back US', 15.10.2002.

248 Duncan Larcombe, *The Sun*, 'Get Abu', 14.10.2002.
249 *The Sun*, 'Why the world mustn't sleep', 14.10.2002.
250 *The Sun*, 'Siege ended in Tragedy but Putin had no choice', 29.10.2002.
251 George Pascoe-Watson, *The Sun*, 'Blair: war on terror is as important as World War 2', 16.10.2002.
252 *The Sun*, 'Bali outrage shows we must win war on terror', 15.10.2002.
253 *The Sun*, 'Siege ended in Tragedy but Putin had no choice', 29.10.2002.
254 *The Sun*, 'Four seized in Swoop by Bomb Police', 17.10.2002.
255 Grant Rollings, *The Sun*, 'Oz will still back US', 15.10.2002.
256 Trevor Kavanagh, *The Sun*, 'Another wake-up call for the civilised world', 14.10.2002.
257 *The Sun*, 'Why the world mustn't sleep', 14.10.2002.
258 Trevor Kavanagh, *The Sun*, 'Saddam is not a separate problem', 15.10.2002.
259 John Coles, *The Sun*, 'I'd shoot them for killing my son', 15.10.2002.
260 Frank Thorne, *The Sun*, 'Heavenly Island turned into Hell', 16.10.2002.
261 Trevor Kavanagh, *The Sun*, 'Another wake-up call for the civilised world', 14.10.2002.
262 Trevor Kavanagh, *The Sun*, 'Another wake-up call for the civilised world', 14.10.2002.
263 Philip Cardy, *The Sun*, 'I searched the morgue but I can't find my wife', 14.10.2002.
264 Trevor Kavanagh, *The Sun*, 'Another wake-up call for the civilised world', 14.10.2002.
265 *The Sun*, 'Why the world mustn't sleep', 14.10.2002.
266 *The Sun*, 'Why the world mustn't sleep', 14.10.2002.
267 *The Sun*, 'Depths of evil', 15.10.2002.
268 John Coles, *The Sun*, 'I'd shoot them for killing my son', 15.10.2002.
269 Brian Flynn, *The Sun*, 'Bush: Al-Qa'ida did it', 15.10.2002.
270 *The Sun*, 'Bali outrage shows we must win war on terror', 15.10.2002.
271 *The Sun*, 'Depths of evil', 15.10.2002.
272 Simon Hughes and Jamie Pyatt, *The Sun*, 'A rugby tour to hell', 15.10.2002.
273 Frank Thorne, *The Sun*, 'Heavenly Island turned into Hell', 16.10.2002.
274 Simon Hughes and George Pascoe-Watson, *The Sun*, 'Terror men have changed tactics since 9/11 ... they've moved on to soft targets', 15.10.2002.
275 *The Sun*, 'Siege ended in Tragedy but Putin had no choice', 29.10.2002.
276 *The Sun*, 'The real threat to world peace', 21.11.2003.
277 Neil Syson, *The Sun*, 'Alive. Brit's blown-up lover found in a hospital bed', 22.11.2003.
278 Andy Wilks, *The Sun*, 'Osama Car Bombs threat to Britain', 18.11.2003,
279 Trevor Kavanagh, *The Sun*, 'Tough new laws to protect us from terrorism', 24.11.2003.
280 Trevor Kavanagh, *The Sun*, 'Tough new laws to protect us from terrorism', 24.11.2003.
281 Trevor Kavanagh, *The Sun*, 'Tough new laws to protect us from terrorism', 24.11.2003.
282 *The Sun*, 'Bush protest was sick after Istanbul attack', 24.11.2003.
283 Trevor Kavanagh, *The Sun*, 'Operation Big Bang', 24.11.2003.
284 Neil Syson, Jamie Pyatt and Andrew Parker, *The Sun*, 'Saved by a shops trip', 22.11.2003.

285   John Kay, Neil Syson and Jamie Pyatt, *The Sun*, 'Time for Peace...? Tell it to Bin Laden', 21.11.2003.
286   John Kay, *The Sun*, 'Murder of a good guy', 21.11.2003.
287   *The Sun*, 'The real Threat to World Peace', 21.11.2003.
288   *The Sun*, 'Bush protest was sick after Istanbul attack', 24.11.2003.
289   Neil Syson, *The Sun*, 'My agony by bomb widow', 24.11.2003.
290   Neil Syson, *The Sun*, 'Alive. Brit's blown-up lover found in a hospital bed', 22.11.2003.
291   *The Sun*, 'Bush protest was sick after Istanbul attack', 24.11.2003.
292   David Wooding, *The Sun*, 'World on alert', 13.3.2004, p. 6.
293   Richard Littlejohn, *The Sun*, 'Being anti-war won't save you', 16.3.2004, p. 11.
294   Tom Warden and Neil Syson, *The Sun*, '9/11 link to rail horror 'bombers'', 15.3.2004, p. 6.
295   James Clench, *The Sun*, 'Battle for Osama No 2', 19.3.2004, p. 7.
296   Neil Syson and Mike Darvill, *The Sun*, 'Operation death trains', 12.3.2004, p. 2.
297   *The Sun*, 'War on world', 16.3.2004, p. 8.
298   Trevor Kavanagh, *The Sun*, 'Howard: Stand by America', 20.3.2004, p. 2.
299   Richard Littlejohn, *The Sun*, 'Being anti-war won't save you', 16.3.2004, p. 11.
300   Trevor Kavanagh, *The Sun*, 'Frontline Europe', 12.3.2004, p. 6.
301   James Clench, *The Sun*, 'Battle for Osama No 2', 19.3.2004, p. 7.
302   Trevor Kavanagh, *The Sun*, 'On the loose ... 4 Brits trained to fight our men with an AK-47', 18.3.2004, p. 4.
303   Neil Syson and Mike Darvill, *The Sun*, 'Operation death trains', 12.3.2004, p. 2.
304   Trevor Kavanagh, *The Sun*, 'Enemy on our streets', 18.3.2004, p. 1.
305   *The Sun*, 'Madrid Warlord in Britain', 18.3.2004, p. 5.
306   Neil Syson and Mike Darvill, *The Sun*, 'The Train was cut open like a can of tuna', 12.3.2004, p. 4.
307   Neil Syson and Mike Darvill, *The Sun*, 'The Train was cut open like a can of tuna', 12.3.2004, p. 5.
308   *The Sun*, 'Murderers damned by the world', 12.3.2004, p. 4.
309   Michael Lea, *The Sun*, 'Hook's web of evil', 17.3.2004, p. 6.
310   Neil Syson and Tom Worden, *The Sun*, 'Two million unit to defy terrorists', 13.3.2004, p. 6.
311   Trevor Kavanagh, *The Sun*, 'Frontline Europe', 12.3.2004, p. 6.
312   Neil Syson and Mike Darvill, *The Sun*, 'The train was cut open like a can of tune', 12.3.2004, p. 5.
313   *The Sun*, 'Murderers damned by the world', 12.3.2004, p. 4.
314   Simon Hughes, *The Sun*, 'UK...You will pay...Bin Laden's on way', 3.4.2004, p. 11.
315   Simon Hughes, *The Sun*, 'UK...You will pay...Bin Laden's on way', 3.4.2004, p. 11.
316   *The Sun*, 'Warlord in UK link', 5.4.2004, p. 13.
317   Michael Lea, *The Sun*, 'Hook's Web of Evil', 17.3.2004, p. 6.
318   Michael Lea, *The Sun*, 'Hook's Web of Evil', 17.3.2004, p. 6.
319   Michael Lea, *The Sun*, 'Hook's Web of Evil', 17.3.2004, p. 6.

320 Richard Littlejohn, *The Sun*, 'Being Anti-War won't save you', 16.3.2004, p. 11.
321 *The Sun*, 'Slaughter of the innocent', 12.3.2004, p. 8.
322 Richard Littlejohn, *The Sun*, 'Being Anti-War won't save you', 16.3.2004, p. 11.
323 Michael Lea, *The Sun*, 'Hook's Web of Evil', 17.3.2004, p. 6.
324 *The Sun*, 'Don't grass rant', 2.4.2004, p. 2.
325 *The Sun*, 'Hook's Web of Evil', 17.3.2004, p. 6.
326 John Kay and Grant Rollings, *The Sun*, 'Worst since Blitz', 8.7.2005, p. 20.
327 Richard Littlejohn, *The Sun*, 'I thought Ian Blair was recruiting Muslims for the police – not al-Qaeda', 12.7.2005, p. 11.
328 Richard Littlejohn, *The Sun*, 'Hello bombers ... and welcome to Londonistan', 9.7.2005, p. 8.
329 *The Sun*, 'Gang's mystery man', 14.7.2005, p. 4.
330 Mike Sullivan and George Pascoe-Watson, *The Sun*, '7/7: Suicide squad on CCTV at King's Cross', 13.7.2005, pp. 2–3.
331 Simon Hughes, *The Sun*, 'Bombers at airport on visit to al-Qaeda', 19.7.2005, p. 9.
332 Simon Hughes, *The Sun*, 'Get back in your cave', 5.8.2005, p. 8.
333 John Kay and Mike Sullivan, *The Sun*, 'More cells out there', 1.8.2005, p. 8.
334 Definition of 'quartermaster' in Merriam-Webster Online dictionary.
335 Trevor Kavanagh, *The Sun*, 'Let's hope the bombers are on holiday too', 3.8.2005, p. 8.
336 Ian Hepburn, *The Sun*, '56 minutes of Hell', 8.7.2005, p. 2.
337 *The Sun*, 'True Brit grit', 9.7.2005, p. 10.
338 Andy McNab, *The Sun*, 'Enemy would rather die than be caught', 22.7.2005, p. 8.
339 Brian Flynn and John Kay, *The Sun*, 'Disciples of Osama', 8.7.2005, p. 16.
340 Simon Hughes and John Kay, *The Sun*, 'Hate Britain', 9.7.2005, p. 8.
341 Andy McNab, *The Sun*, 'A tragic casualty of war', 25.7.2005, p. 6.
342 *The Sun*, 'Deadly times, deadly action', 23.7.2005, p. 8.
343 Anthony France, *The Sun*, 'Why here? Why now?', 12.7.2005, p. 9.
344 Richard Littlejohn, *The Sun*, 'Hello bombers ... and welcome to Londonistan', 9.7.2005, p. 8.
345 Andy McNab, *The Sun*, 'A tragic casualty of war', 25.7.2005, p. 6.
346 Brian Flynn, Kathryn Lister, Steve Kennedy and Emma Cox, *The Sun*, 'Tunnel of Blood', 8.7.2005, p. 6.
347 Trevor Kavanagh, *The Sun*, 'We shall prevail .. terrorists shall not', 8.7.2005, p. 18.
348 Mike Sullivan and Anthony France, *The Sun*, 'Gang 'return' to flat to get more explosives', 27.7.2005, pp. 4–5.
349 Mike Sullivan and George Pascoe-Watson, *The Sun*, 'Backpack butchers. Terror mob had bombs in rucksacks', 13.7.2005, p. 2.
350 *The Sun*, 'Keep calm', 13.7.2005, p. 8.
351 James Clench, *The Sun*, 'My outrage, by Brit Muslim', 8.7.2005, p. 9.
352 *The Sun*, 'Cop leads the way on tube', 12.7.2005, p. 7.
353 Deidre Sanders, *The Sun*, 'Awakened memories of tsunami', 8.7.2005, p. 6.
354 Brandon Malinsky, *The Sun*, 'Yesterday the French were all annoyed with you but today we are all Londoners', 8.7.2005, p. 23.

160   *Notes*

355   Deidre Sanders, *The Sun*, 'Awakened memories of tsunami', 8.7.2005, p. 6.
356   Andy McNab, *The Sun*, 'Cops had no choice', 23.7.2005, p. 6.
357   Ian Hepburn, *The Sun*, '56 minutes of hell', 8.7.2005, p. 2.
358   *The Sun*, 'Hewitt's 'bastard' rage', 9.7.2005, p. 6.
359   *The Sun*, 'Evil across our planet', 8.7.2005, p. 17.
360   *The Sun*, 'Geldorf's "discust"', 8.7.2005, p. 18.
361   Trevor Kavanagh, *The Sun*, 'We shall prevail .. terrorists shall not', 8.7.2005, p. 18.
362   *The Sun*, 'Out spirit will never be broken', 8.7.2005, p. 6.
363   *The Sun*, '56 minutes of hell', 8.7.2005, p. 2.
364   *The Sun*, 'Out spirit will not be broken', 22.7.2005, p. 6.
365   Lorraine Kelly, *The Sun*, 'I'm so angry our kids are growing up in world of terror', 9.7.2005, p. 23.
366   *The Sun*, 'Shocked at evil attack but proud and defiant', 11.7.2005, p. 36.
367   Charles Rae, Alex Peake and Elise Jenkins, *The Sun*, 'He mumbled a prayer, bag went bang .. 3 heroes piled in', 22.7.2005, p. 6.
368   *The Sun*, 'Abuse of Britain', 12.7.2005, p. 8.
369   Virginia Wheeler, *The Sun*, 'You don't expect your boy to turn into one of the 4 Horsemen of the Apocalypse', 18.7.2005, p. 8.
370   Ally Ross, *The Sun*, 'Horror in my street', 8.7.2005, p. 11.
371   Andrew Parker, John Askill and Brian Flynn, *The Sun*, 'We've got him', 28.7.2005, p. 5.
372   Richard Littlejohn, *The Sun*, 'I thought Ian Blair was recruiting Muslims for the police – not for al-Qaeda', 12.7.2005, p. 11.
373   Richard White, *The Sun*, 'Muslims' 21/7 plea', 25.7.2005, p. 7.
374   Richard Littlejohn, *The Sun*, 'If Blair used the laws we have, we wouldn't need a Stable Door Act', 22.7.2005, p. 9.
375   *The Sun*, 'Silence that said it all', 15.7.2005, p. 6.
376   Richard Littlejohn, *The Sun*, 'If Blair used the laws we have, we wouldn't need a Stable Door Act', 22.7.2005, p. 9.
377   Brian Flynn and John Kay, *The Sun*, 'Disciples of Osama', 8.7.2005, p. 16.
378   *The Sun*, 'Outrage as Ken justifies suicide nuts', 20.7.2005, p. 4.
379   Trevor Kavanagh, *The Sun*, 'Let's hope the bombers are on holiday too', 3.8.2005, p. 8.
380   *The Sun*, 'Show them we are not afraid', 14.7.2005, p. 8.
381   *The Sun*, 'Send him Bak', 20.7.2005, p. 1.
382   Simon Hughes and George Pascoe-Watson, *The Sun*, 'Terror men have changed tactics since 9/11 ... they've moved on to soft targets', 15.10.2002.
383   George Pascoe-Watson, *The Sun*, 'Brave PM flies into Pakistan war zone', 3.10.2001, p. 6.
384   'Al Qaida Kopf', *Bild*, 'Gab er den Terror-Befehl von Madrid?', 16.3.2004, p. 1.

Chapter 6

1   *Süddeutsche Zeitung*, 'Terror-Krieg gegen Amerika', 12.9.2001, p. 1.
2   *Rheinische Post*, 'Krieg gegen die Zivilisation', 12.9.2001, p. 1.
3   *Die Tageszeitung*, 'Krieg gegen die USA', 12.9.2001, p. 1.

4   *Neues Deutschland*, 'Terrorkrieg gegen die USA. Tausende Tote in New York', 12.9.2001, p. 1.
5   *The Mirror*, 'War on the World', 12.9.2001, p. 1.
6   *The Guardian*, 'A Declaration of War', 12.9.2001, p. 1.
7   'Regierungserklärung von Bundeskanzler Schröder vor dem Deutschen Bundestag zum Terrorakt in den USA', 12.9.2001, available at: http://archiv.bundesregierung.de/bpaexport/regierungserklaerung/57/55757/multi.htm [accessed on 26.10.2008], emphasis added.
8   Three hundred and thirty-six members of the Bundestag voted in favour and 326 voted against the notion of military action.
9   Similarly, however, one has to consider that the closed ranks of the SPD and the Green Party could also be partly attributed to the question of confidence rather than to the support of military action.
10 ARD DeutschlandTREND, October 2001, *Infratest dimap*, available at: http://www.infratest-dimap.de/uploads/media/dt0110.pdf [accessed 1.6.2009].
11 See for example 'Geringe Angst vor Terror', *n-tv.de Emnid-Umfrage*, 11.1.2002, available at: http://www.n-tv.de/461091.html [accessed 23.4.2009].
12 See for example 'Mehrheit befürwortet Bundeswehreinsatz', *Spiegel Online*, 7.11. 2001, available at: http://www.spiegel.de/politik/deutschland/0,1518,166516,00.html [accessed 23.4.2009] or 'Deutsche wollen Bundeswehr-Einsatz gegen Terrorismus', *Handelsblatt.com*, 22.9.2001, available at: http://www.handelsblatt.com/archiv/deutsche-wollen-bundeswehr-einsatz-gegen-terrorismus%3B462232 [accessed 23.4.2009].
13 For more on *Operation Active Endeavour* see the official NATO website at: http://www.nato.int/issues/active_endeavour/index.html [accessed 24.10.2008].
14 Here for see: 'Antrag der Bundesregierung auf Einsatz bewaffneter deutscher Streitkräfte bei der Unterstützung der gemeinsamen Reaktion auf terroristische Angriffe gegen die USA', Deutscher Bundestag, 7.11.2001, available at: http://www.documentArchiv.de/brd/2001/bundesregierung-antrag-bundeswehr.html [accessed 25.10.2008].
15 Also see: 'KSK Bundeswehr-Elitetruppe in Afghanistan unterfordert', *Die Welt*, 18.9.2008, available at: http://www.welt.de/politik/article2461710/Bundeswehr-Elitetruppe-in-Afghanistan-unterfordert.html [accessed 25.10.2008].
16 'Britain "at war with terrorism"', *BBC*, 16.9.2001, available at: http://news.bbc.co.uk/2/hi/uk_news/politics/1545411.stm [accessed 29.6.2009].
17 'The Guardian Poll October 2001', *ICM Research*, 10–11.10.2001, available at: http://www.icmresearch.co.uk/pdfs/2001_october_guardian_afghanistan_poll_1.pdf, [accessed 14.4.2009] or 'Evening Standard London Poll October 2001/War in Afghanistan', *ICM Research*, 10–11.10.2001, available at: http://www.icmresearch.co.uk/pdfs/2001_october_evening_standard_war_in_afghanistan.pdf [accessed 14.4.2009].
18 'The Guardian Afghan Poll – October 2001', *ICM Research*, 26–28.10.2001, available at: http://www.icmresearch.co.uk/pdfs/2001_october_guardian_afghanistan_poll_2.pdf [accessed 14.4.2009].
19 'UK troops land in Afghanistan, *BBC*, 16.11.2001, available at http://news.bbc.co.uk/2/hi/uk_news/politics/1658816.stm [accessed 13.4.2009].
20 'Operations in Afghanistan: Background Briefing 1', *Ministry of Defence*, available at: http://www.mod.uk/DefenceInternet/FactSheets/Operations Factsheets/OperationsInAfghanistanBackgroundBriefing1.htm [accessed 14.4.2009].

162 *Notes*

21 'Operations in Afghanistan: British Forces', *Ministry of Defence*, available at: http://www.mod.uk/DefenceInternet/FactSheets/OperationsFactsheets/Oper ationsInAfghanistanBritishForces.htm [accessed 14.4.2009].

22 'Operations in Afghanistan: Background Briefing 2', *Ministry of Defence*, available at: http://www.mod.uk/DefenceInternet/FactSheets/Operations Factsheets/ OperationsInAfghanistanBackgroundBriefing2.htm [accessed 14.4.2009].

23 *The Sun*, 'He's Bang to Rights', 6.2.2003.

24 'The War on Iraq. Prepared for ITN', *YouGov*, 10–12.1.2003, available at: http://www.yougov.co.uk/extranets/ygarchives/content/pdf/ITN030101001.pdf [accessed 17.4.2009].

25 'The Propaganda War – Part II. Prepared for Blakeway Productions and Channel 4 News', *YouGov*, 7–10.2.2003, available at: http://www.yougov.co.uk/ extranets/ygarchives/content/pdf/YOU020101110.pdf [accessed: 17.4.2009].

26 'Iraq War Tracker. Prepared for Daily Telegraph and ITV News', *YouGov*, 11.4.2003, available at: http://www.yougov.co.uk/extranets/ygarchives/content/ pdf/tem030101007_1.pdf [accessed 17.4.2009].

27 'British Public Opinion Shifts to Support Iraq War', *Australian Broadcasting Corporation*, 3.4.2003, available at: http://www.abc.net.au/lateline/content/ 2003/s824112.htm [accessed 11.5.2009].

28 For this see Chapter 2.

29 Deutschland TREND November 2001, conducted by Infratest dimap for the ARD, available at: http://www.infratest-dimap.de/uploads/media/dt0111.pdf [accessed 1.6.2009].

30 For more information on the Terrorism Act of 2000 and counter-terrorism prior to 9/11 see Bonner (1992; 2000) or Taylor (2002).

31 For detailed information on the Anti-Terrorism, Crime and Security Act 2001 see Walker (2002).

32 The full text of the act is available at: http://www.opsi.gov.uk/acts/acts2005/ ukpga_20050002_en_1 [accessed 25.6.2009].

33 The full text of the act is available at: http://www.opsi.gov.uk/acts/acts2006/ ukpga_20060011_en_1 [accessed 25.6.2009].

34 'BBC Daily Politics Show Poll', *Populus*, 6–7.6.2007, available at: http://populus limited.com/uploads/download_pdf-040707-The-Daily-Politics-Fighting-Terrosrism.pdf [accessed 25.6.2009].

35 'Times Poll', *Populus*, 4–6.11.2005, available at: http://populuslimited.com/ uploads/download_pdf-061105-The-Times-Political-Attitudes.pdf [accessed 25.6.2009].

36 'Sky News/YouGov Survey Results', *YouGov*, 4–5.11.2005, available at: http:// www.yougov.co.uk/extranets/ygarchives/content/pdf/DBD050101009_1.pdf [accessed 25.6.2009].

37 See the official BBK website at: http://www.bbk.bund.de/nn_402322/DE/ 01__BBK/BBK__node.html__nnn=true [accessed 23.3.2009].

38 See for example http://www.denis.bund.de/infobaum.html?585 [accessed 23.3.2009].

39 See for example the Academy for Crisis Management, Emergency Planning and Civil Protection (AKNZ): http://www.bbk.bund.de/cln_007/nn_398724/ SharedDocs/Publikationen/Brosch_C3_BCren__und__Faltbl_C3_A4tter_20D ownload/Flyer__AKNZ,templateId=raw,property=publicationFile.pdf/Flyer_ AKNZ.pdf [accessed 17.3.2009].

40 See for example the THW document 3300: 'Einsatzoptionen des THW bei Terrorismus, Anschlägen, Attentate, Sabotage', available at: http://www.thw. bund.de/SharedDocs/publikationen/Einsatzoptionen/Dokumente__EOPt/ EOpt__3300__Terrorismus__Anschl_C3_A4gen__Attentate__Sabotage,template Id=raw,property=publicationFile.pdf/EOpt_3300_Terrorismus_Anschl%C3%A4 gen_Attentate_Sabotage.pdf [accessed 17.3.2009].
41 See: http://www.johanniter.de/org/juh/org/land/nds/presse/archiv07/de386844. htm [accessed 7.5.2009].
42 Civil Contingencies Act 2004, available at: http://www.opsi.gov.uk/acts/ acts2004/pdf/ukpga_20040036_en.pdf [accessed 11.5.2009].
43 See: http://www.cabinetoffice.gov.uk/ukresilience/ccs.aspx [accessed 16.5.2009].
44 For more information on UK Resistance see: http://www.cabinetoffice. gov.uk/ ukresilience.aspx [accessed 14.5.2009].
45 The booklet is available at: http://www.direct.gov.uk/en/Government citizens-andrights/Dealingwithemergencies/Preparingforemergencies/DG_176035 [accessed 11.5.2009].
46 'UK Terror Attack exercise planned', *BBC*, 3.3.2003, available at: http://news. bbc.co.uk/2/hi/uk_news/politics/2814087.stm [accessed 11.5.2009].
47 For more on the notion of monsters in international relations see Devetak (2005).
48 See, 'Bush vows to rid the world of "evil-doers"', CNN, available at: http:// archives.cnn.com/2001/US/09/16/gen.bush.terrorism/ [accessed 7.5.2009].
49 Merriam Webster Online, available at: http://www.merriam-webster.com/ dictionary/barbarian [accessed 7.5.2009].
50 *Oxford Dictionary of English* (2005): Second Edition, Revised, Oxford: Oxford University Press, p. 129.
51 *Oxford Dictionary of English* (2005): Second Edition, Revised, Oxford: Oxford University Press, p. 129.
52 Deutschland Trends April 2004, Infratest dimap conducted for the ARD, available at: http://www.infratest-dimap.de/uploads/media/dt0404.pdf [accessed 1.6.2009].
53 'Terrorism Poll conducted for the BBC', *ICM Research*, 5–6.2.2003, available at: http://www.icmresearch.co.uk/pdfs/2003_february_bbc_Radio_five_live_ terrorism_poll.pdf [accessed 22.5.2009].
54 'Terrorist Bombings & The Olympics Survey', *Populus*, 8–10.7.2005, available at: http://www.populuslimited.com/uploads/download_pdf-100705-The-Times-Terrorism.pdf [accessed 30.6.2009].
55 'Terrorism Survey conducted for the BBC', *ICM Research*, 23–24.4.2004, available at: http://www.icmresearch.co.uk/pdfs/2004_may_bbc_terrorism_poll.pdf [accessed 22.5.2009].
56 'Terrorism Poll conducted for the BBC', *ICM Research*, 5–6.2.2003, available at: http://www.icmresearch.co.uk/pdfs/2003_february_bbc_Radio_five_live_ terrorism_poll.pdf [accessed 22.5.2009].
57 For the full text see: http://news.bbc.co.uk/2/hi/middle_east/3628069.stm [accessed 22.5.2009].
58 For the full text see: http://news.bbc.co.uk/2/hi/middle_east/4628932.stm [accessed 22.5.2009].
59 *Agence France Press*, 'Germany rejects Bin Laden "truce" offer', 15.4.2004 or *Spiegel Online* 'Europa steht zusammen', 15.4.2004; *Frankfurter Rundschau*, 'Bin Laden bietet Frieden; Europäer weisen Angebot ab', 16.4.2004.

60 Translated from 'Keine Verhandlungen mit Terroristen', Available at: http://archiv.bundesregierung.de/bpaexport/artikel/30/637330/multi.htm [accessed 15.5.2009].

61 *Agence France Press*, 'USA will mit bin Laden nicht verhandeln', 20.1.2006 or *Associated Press Worldstream*, 'USA schließen Verhandlungen mit Al Kaida kategorisch aus; Washington reagiert gelassen auf Bin-Laden-Drohung – Auch Berlin sieht keine geänderte Gefahrenlage', 20.1.2006.

62 *Associated Press Worldstream*, 'European nations reject purported truce offer from bin Laden', 16.4.2004.

63 'größenwahnsinniger Bastard', *Bild*, 'Post von Wagner', 16.4.2004, p. 2.

64 *Bild*, 'Post von Wagner', 16.4.2004, p. 2.

65 *Bild*, 'Post von Wagner', 16.4.2004, p. 2.

66 'verhöhnen', *Bild*, 'Bin Laden will mit Europa Frieden schließen', 16.4.2004, p. 2.

67 *Frankfurter Rundschau*, 'Bin Laden bietet Frieden; Europäer weisen Angebot ab', 16.4.2004.

68 *The Daily Telegraph*, 'Bin Laden's truce offer rejected as "absurd". Taped message from al-Qa'eda chief calls on Europe to abandon America', 16.4.2004, p. 1.

69 *The Evening Standard*, 'Europe is offered a truce in "new Bin Laden message"', 15.4.2004, p. 1.

70 *The Sun*, 'Peace off bin Laden', 16.4.2004.

71 *Die Welt*, '"Wenn ihr unser Blut vergießt, vergießen wir eures"; Osama bin Laden meldet sich nach langer Zeit wieder zu Wort und bietet den Europäern einen Waffenstillstand an', 16.4.2004.

72 *Agence France Press*, 'Alleged bin Laden truce offer merits "contempt": British FM', 15.4.2004.

73 *The Sun*, 'Peace off bin Laden', 16.4.2004.

74 *The Observer*, 'Blair has lost his grip', 18.4.2004, p. 25.

75 Peter Bergen interviewed by CNN Live Today, 'Bin Laden truce turned down by European Leaders; Japanese Hostages Released in Iraq', 15.4.2004.

76 *The Express*, 'Keep terror front united', 16.4.2004, p. 12.

77 *Sunday Telegraph*, 'Bin Laden makes an offer that he cannot deliver', 18.4.2004, p. 24.

78 *The Sun*, 'Peace off bin Laden', 16.4.2004.

79 *The Sun*, 'We'll Never agree to Terror chief's "Truce"', 19.4.2004.

80 *The Mirror*, 'The War on Terror: Binsane', 16.4.2004. p. 5.

81 *The Express*, 'Why we can never make peace with evil Osama', 16.4.2004, p. 12.

82 *The Daily Telegraph*, 'Force can crack Islamist terror', 21.4.2004, p. 22.

83 *Daily Star*, 'I'm a political wannabe', 16.4.2004, p. 2.

84 *Sunday Telegraph*, 'Bin Laden makes an offer that he cannot deliver', 18.4.2004, p. 24.

85 *The Express*, 'We will pay dearly if we give in to this madman', 16.4.2004, p. 12.

Conclusion

1 There are a vast number of other discourses which may also be of interest for Terrorism Studies in the future such as the 'terrorists' own discourse about themselves. And although a number of scholars have called for more direct

contact with terrorists and emphasised the importance of interviews, the existence of websites, videos and even already compiled volumes of statement and
press releases (Lawrence 2005; Mansfield 2006) means that analysis of the
terrorist's own discourse is not as difficult and hazardous as it may seem.
2 For more detail see http://www.americasarmy.com/
3 For more detail see http://web.archive.org/web/20050105091655/www.special-
force.net/english/indexeng.htm
4 See http://edition.cnn.com/2007/WORLD/meast/08/16/hezbollah.game.reut/
index.html

References

Abdel-Nour, F. (2004) 'An International Ethics of Evil?', in *International Relations* 18(4): 425–439.

Adler, E. (1997) 'Seizing the Middle Ground: Constructivism in World Politics', in *European Journal of International Relations* 3(3): 319–363.

Adler, E. (2002) 'Constructivism and International Relations', in W. Carlsnaes, T. Risse and B. A. Simmons (eds) *Handbook of International Relations*. Thousands Oaks: Sage, pp. 95–118.

Alberts, J. (1972) *Massenpresse als Ideologiefabrik. Am Beispiel "Bild"*. Frankfurt am Main: Athenäum Verlag.

Aldrich, R. J. (2004) 'Transatlantic Intelligence and Security Cooperation', in *International Affairs* 80(4): 731–753.

Altheide, D. L. (2006) *Terrorism and the Politics of Fear*. Lanham: AltaMira Press.

Alexander, Y. (ed.) (2002) *Combating Terrorism – Strategies of Ten Countries*. Ann Arbor: University of Michigan Press.

Alexander, Y. and Hoenig, M. M. (eds) (2001) *Super Terrorism: Biological, Chemical and Nuclear*. Ardsley: Transnational Publishers.

Anderson, R. D. (2004) 'The Causal Power of Metaphor. Cueing Democratic Identities in Russia and Beyond', in F. A. Beer and C. De Landtsheer (eds) *Metaphorical World Politics*. East Lansing: Michigan State University Press, pp. 91–108.

Anderson, R. N. and Smith, B. L. (2005) 'Death: Leading Causes for 2002', in *National Vital Statistics Reports* 53(17). Available at: http://www.cdc.gov/nchs/data/nvsr/nvsr53/nvsr53_17.pdf Accessed 7.4.2009.

Anderson, S. and Sloan, S. (1995) *Historical Dictionary of Terrorism*. New Jersey: The Scarecrow Press.

Anderson, S. and Sloan, S. (2003) *Terrorism: Assassins to Zealots*. Lanham: Scarecrow Press.

Aristotle (1982) *Poetics*. Oxford: Clarendon Press.

Arquilla, J., Ronfeldt, D. and Zanini, M. (1999) 'Networks, Netwar, and Information-Age Terrorism', in I. O. Lesser, B. Hoffman, J. Arquilla, D. Ronfeldt, M. Zanini and B. M. Jenkins (eds) *Countering the New Terrorism*. Santa Monica: RAND, pp. 39–84.

Atkinson, S. E., Sandler, T. and Tschirhart, J. (1987) 'Terrorism in a Bargaining Framework', in *Journal of Law and Economics* 30(1): 1–21.

Attwood, R. (2007) 'Study of Terrorism Steps up to New Level', *The Times*, 22.6.2007. Available at: http://www.timeshighereducation.co.uk/story.asp?storyCode=209437&sectioncode=26 Accessed 11.03.2009.

Aubrey, S. M. (2004) *The New Dimension of International Terrorism*. Zurich: Vdf Hochschulverlag.

Bamford, B. W. C. (2004) 'The United Kingdom's "War Against Terrorism"', in *Terrorism and Political Violence* 16(4): 737–756.

Bapat, N. A. (2006) 'State Bargaining with Transnational Terrorist Groups', in *International Studies Quarterly* 50(1): 213–229.

Barker, J. (2003) *The No-Nonsense Guide to Terrorism*. Oxford: New Internationalist Publications.

Barnaby, W. (2002) *Biowaffen – Die unsichtbare Gefahr*. München: Wilhelm GoldmannVerlag.

Basile, M. (2004) 'Going to the Source: Why Al Qaeda's Financial Network is Likely to Withstand the Current War on Terrorist Financing', in *Studies in Conflict and Terrorism* 27(3): 169–185.

Bates, B. R. (2004) 'Audiences, Metaphors, and the Persian Gulf War', in *Communication Studies* 55(3): 447–463.

Beckmann, J. (2007) *Comparative Legal Approaches to Homeland Security and Anti-Terrorism*. Aldershot: Ashgate.

Beer, F. A. and De Landtsheer, C. (eds) (2004a) *Metaphorical World Politics*. East Lansing: Michigan State University Press.

Beer F. A. and De Landtsheer, C. (2004b) 'Metaphors, Politics, and World Politics', in F. A. Beer and C. De Landtsheer (eds) *Metaphorical World Politics*. East Lansing: Michigan State University Press, pp. 5–52.

Benjamin, D. and Simon, S. (2002) *The Age of Sacred Terror*. New York: Random House.

Bennett, R. M. (2003) *Elite Forces. The World's Most Formidable Secret Armies*. London: Virgin Books.

Bensahel, N. (2006) 'A Coalition of Coalitions: International Cooperation Against Terrorism', in *Studies in Conflict and Terrorism* 29(1): 35–49.

Bergen, P. L. (2001) *Holy War Inc.: Inside the Secret World of Osama bin Laden*. New York: The Free Press.

Bergesen, A. J. and Lizardo, O. (2004) 'International Terrorism and the World-System', in *Sociological Theory* 22(1): 38–52.

Bergensen, A. J. and Han, Y. (2005) 'New Directions for Terrorism Research', in *International Journal of Comparative Sociology* 46(1–2): 133–151.

Berkowitz, B. (2002) 'Intelligence and the War on Terrorism', in *Orbis* 46(2): 289–300.

Bernstein, R. J. (2005) *The Abuse of Evil. The Corruption of Politics and Religion since 9/11*. Cambridge: Polity.

Bhatia, A. (2009) 'The Discourse of Terrorism', in *Journal of Pragmatics* 41(2): 279–289.

Biersteker, T. J. (2002) 'Targeting Terrorist Finances: The New Challenges of Financial Market Globalization', in K. Booth and T. Dunne (eds) *Worlds in Collision: Terror and the Future of Global Order*. Basingstoke: Palgrave, pp. 74–84.

Biersteker, T. J., Eckert, S. and Passas, N. (2007) *Financing Global Terrorism*. London: Routledge.

Bigo, D. (2002a) *To Reassure, and Protect, After September 11*. New York: Social Science Research Council, Available at: http://www.ssrc.org/sept11/essays/bigo. htm Accessed 23.06.2009.

Bigo, D. (2002b) 'Security and Immigration: Toward a Critique of the Governmentality of Unease', in *Alternatives: Global, Local, Political* 27(Special Issue): 63–92.

Black, M. (1979) 'How Metaphors Work: A Reply to Donald Davidson', in *Critical Inquiry* 6(1): 131–143.

Blakeley, R. (2007) 'Bringing the State back into Terrorism Studies', in *European Political Science* 6(3): 228–235.

Boggs, C. and Pollard, T. (2006) 'Hollywood and the Spectacle of Terrorism', in *New Political Science* 28(3): 335–351.

Bogost, I. (2007) *Persuasive Games: The Expressive Power of Videogames*. Cambridge: MIT Press.

Bonner, D. (1992) 'United Kingdom: The United Kingdom Responses to Terrorism', in *Terrorism and Political Violence* 4(4): 171–205.

Bonner, D. (2000) 'The United Kingdom's Response to Terrorism: The Impact of Decisions of European Judicial Institutions and of the Northern Ireland, Peace Process', in F. Reinares (ed.) *European Democracies Against Terrorism. Governmental Policies and Intergovernmental Cooperation*. Aldershot: Ashgate, pp. 31–71.

Booth, K. (2008) 'The Human Face of Terror: Reflections in a Cracked Looking-Glass', in *Critical Studies on Terrorism* 1(1): 65–79.

Booth, W. C. (1978) 'Metaphor as Rhetoric: The Problem of Evaluation', in *Critical Inquiry* 5(1): 49–72.

Border and Immigration Agency (2008) *Introducing Compulsory Identity Cards for Foreign Nationals*. London: Home Office. Available at: http://www.ukba.home office.gov.uk/sitecontent/documents/managingourborders/compulsory-idcards/IDcards/foreignnationalsforidcards.pdf?view=Binary Accessed 30.6.2009.

Bowen, W. Q. (2004) 'Deterrence and Asymmetry: Non-state Actors and Mass Casualty Terrorism', in *Contemporary Security Policy* 25(1): 54–70.

Bowyer-Bell, J. (1978) *A Time of Terror*. New York: Basic Books.

Bowyer-Bell, J. (2000) *The IRA 1968–2000: Analysis of a Secret Army*. London: Frank Cass.

Brannan, D. W., Esler, P. F. and Strindberg, N. T. A. (2001) 'Talking to 'Terrorists': Towards an Independent Analytical Framework for the Study of Violent Substate Activism', in *Studies in Conflict and Terrorism* 24(1): 3–24.

Breen Smyth, M. (2007) 'A Critical Research Agenda for the Study of Political Terror', in *European Political Science* 6(3): 260–267.

Breen Smyth, M. (2008) 'Lessons Learned in Counter-terrorism in Northern Ireland: An Interview with Peter Sheridan', in *Critical Studies on Terrorism* 1(1): 111–123.

Breen Smyth, M. (2009) 'Subjectivities, "Suspect Communities", Governments and the Ethics of Research on "Terrorism"', in R. Jackson, M. Breen Smyth and J. Gunning (eds) *Critical Terrorism Studies. A New Research Agenda*. London: Routledge, pp. 194–215.

Breen Smyth, M., Gunning, J., Jackson, R., Kassimeris, G. and Robinson, P. (2008) 'Critical Terrorism Studies – An Introduction', in *Critical Studies on Terrorism* 1(1): 1–4.

Broomby, R. (2002) 'Letter from Berlin – Rob Broomby on Germany's Emerging International Role', *BBC World Service*, 13.5.2002. Available at: http://www.bbc. co.uk/worldservice/europe/europetoday/letters/020513_rbroomby.shtml Accessed 25.10.2008.

Brophy-Baermann, B. and Conybeare, J. A. C. (1994) 'Retaliating Against Terrorism: Rational Expectations and the Optimality of Rules versus Discretion', in *American Journal of Political Science* 38(1): 196–210.

Buckley, M. and Fawn, R. (eds) (2003) *Global Responses to Terrorism – 9/11, Afghanistan and Beyond*. London: Routledge.

Bueno de Mesquita, E. (2007) 'Politics and the Suboptimal Provision of Counter-terror', in *International Organization* 61(1): 9–36.

Bueno de Mesquita, E. and Dickson, E. (2007) 'The Propaganda of the Deed': Terrorism, Counter-Terrorism, and Mobilization', in *American Journal of Political Science* 49(3): 515–530.

Bukow, S. (2005) 'Deutschland. Mit Sicherheit weniger Freiheit über den Umweg Europa', in G. J. Glaeßner and A. Lorenz (eds) *Europäisierung der Inneren Sicherheit*. Wiesbaden: VS Verlag, pp. 43–62.

Bundesamt für Bevölkerungsschutz und Katastrophenhilfe (2009) *Schutz und Hilfe für die Bevölkerung*. Available at: http://www.bbk.bund.de/cln_027/nn_398002/SharedDocs/Publikationen/Brosch_C3_BCren__und__Faltbl_C3_A4tter_20Download/Broschuere_Wir-ueberuns,templateId=raw,property=publicationFile.pdf/Broschuere_Wir-ueber-uns.pdf Accessed 23.3.2009.

Bundesministerium des Inneren (2005a) 'Zivil- und Katastrophenschutz in Deutschland', in Bundesministerium des Inneren (ed.) *Nach dem 11 September 2001. Maßnahmen gegen den Terror*. Berlin: BMI, pp. 144–152.

Bundesministerium des Inneren (2005b) 'Mehr Geld und Personal für die innere Sicherheit im Jahr 2002', in Bundesministerium des Inneren (ed.) *Nach dem 11 September 2001. Maßnahmen gegen den Terror*. Berlin: BMI, pp. 50–61.

Burke, J. (2003) *Al Qaeda. Casting a Shadow of Terror*. New York: I.B. Tauris.

Burke, K. (1945) *A Grammar of Motives*. Berkley: University of California Press.

Burnett, J. and Whyte, D. (2005) 'Embedded Expertise and the New Terrorism', in *Journal for Crime, Conflict and the Media* 1(4): 1–18.

Byman, D. (2003a) 'Measuring the War on Terrorism: A First Appraisal', in *Current History* 102(668): 411–416.

Byman, D. (2003b) 'Scoring the War on Terrorism', in *The National Interest*, (Summer): 75–84.

Byman, D. (2003c) 'Al Qaeda as an Adversary: Do We Understand Our Enemy?', in *World Politics* 56(1): 139–163.

Byman, D. (2006) 'The Decision to Begin Talks with Terrorists: Lessons for Policy-makers', in *Studies in Conflict and Terrorism* 29(5): 403–419.

Cameron, L. (1999) 'Operationalising 'Metaphor' for Applied Linguistic Research', in L. Cameron and G. Low (eds) *Researching and Applying Metaphor*. Cambridge: Cambridge University Press, pp. 3–38.

Cameron, G. (2004) 'Weapons of Mass Destruction Terrorism Research: Past and Future', in A. Silke (ed.) *Research on Terrorism-Trends, Achievement and Failures*. London: Frank Cass, pp. 72–90.

Campbell, D. (1998) *Writing Security: United States Foreign Policy and the Politics of Identity*. Minneapolis: University of Minnesota Press.

Campbell, D. and Shapiro, M. J. (2007) 'Guest Editors' Introduction', in *Security Dialogue* 38(2): 131–137.

Carr, C. (1996/1997) 'Terrorism and Warfare. The Lesson of Military History', in *World Policy Journal* 13(4): 1–12.

Carr, C. (2002) *The Lessons of Terror – A History of Warfare against Civilians*. New York: Random House.

Carter, A. B., Deutch, J. and Zelikow, P. (1999) 'Catastrophic Terrorism', in *Foreign Affairs* 77(6): 80–94.

Carver, T. and Pikalo, J. (eds) (2008) *Political Language and Metaphor. Interpreting and Changing the World*. London: Routledge.

Cauley, J. and Im, E. I. (1988) 'Intervention Policy Analysis of Skyjackings and Other Terrorist Incidences', in *American Economic Review* 78(2): 27–31.

Celmer, M. A. (1987) *Terrorism, U.S. Strategy, and Regan Policies*. New York: Greenwood Press.

Chaliand, G. and Blin, A. (2007) 'Zealots and Assassins', in G. Chaliand and A. Blin (eds) *The History of Terrorism. From Antiquity to Al Qaeda*. Berkeley: University of California Press, pp. 55–78.

Chalk, P. (1995) 'Liberal Democratic Response to Terrorism', in *Terrorism and Political Violence* 7(4): 10–44.

Chalk, P. (1996) *West European Terrorism and Counter-Terrorism – The Evolving Dynamic*. Basingstoke: Macmillan Press.

Charteris-Black, J. (2003) 'Speaking with Forked Tongue: A Comparative Study of Metaphor and Metonymy in English and Malay Phraseology', in *Metaphor and Symbol* 18(4): 289–310.

Charteris-Black, J. (2004) *Corpus Approaches to Critical Metaphor Analysis*. Basingstoke: Palgrave Macmillan.

Charteris-Black, J. (2005) *Politicians and Rhetoric. The Persuasive Power of Metaphor*. Basingstoke: Palgrave Macmillan.

Charteris-Black, J. (2006) 'Britain as a Container: Immigration Metaphors in the 2005 Election Campaign', in *Discourse and Society* 17(5): 563–581.

Checkel, J. T. (1998) 'The Constructivist Turn in International Relations Theory', in *World Politics* 50(2): 324–348.

Chilton, P. (1996a) *Security Metaphors: Cold War Discourse from Containment to Common House*. New York: Peter Lang.

Chilton, P. (1996b) 'The Meaning of Security', in F. A. Beer and R. Hariman (eds) *Post-Realism. The Rhetorical Turn in International Relations*. East Lansing: Michigan State University Press, pp. 193–216.

Chilton, P. and Ilyin, M. (1993) 'Metaphor in Political Discourse: The Case of the "Common European House"', in *Discourse and Society* 4(1): 7–31.

Chilton, P. and Lakoff, G. (1999) 'Foreign Policy by Metaphor', in C. Schäffner and A. L. Wenden (eds) *Language and Peace*. Amsterdam: Harwood Academic Publishers, pp. 37–59.

Cilluffo, F. J. and Tomarchio, J. T. (1998) 'Responding to New Terrorist Threats', in *Orbis* 42(3): 439–451.

Claridge, D. (1999) 'Exploding the Myths of Superterrorism', in *Terrorism and Political Violence* 11(4): 133–148.

Clark, E. (2002) 'German Military Reforms: Moving Towards Counter-Terrorism Capabilities'. Washington: Center for Defense Information. Available at: http://www.cdi.org/terrorism/germanreforms.cfm Accessed 24.09.2008.

Clifford, J. and George E. M. (eds) (1986) *Writing Culture: The Poetics and Politics of Ethnography*. Berkeley: University of California Press.

Clutterbuck, R. (1990) *Terrorism and Guerrilla Warfare*. London: Routledge.

Clutterbuck, R. (1992) 'Negotiating with Terrorists', in *Terrorism and Political Violence* 4(4): 263–287.

Cobban, H. (1981) *The Palestinian Liberation Organisation, People, Power and Politics*. Cambridge: Cambridge University Press.

Cole, D. (2003) 'The New McCarthyism: Repeating History in the War on Terrorism', in *Harvard Civil Rights-Civil Liberties Law Review* 38(1): 1–30.

Collins, J. and Glover, R. (eds) (2002) *Collateral Language: a User's Guide to America's New War*. New York: New York University Press.

Collins, S. (2004) 'Dissuading State Support of Terrorism: Strikes or Sanctions? (An Analysis of Dissuasion Measures Employed Against Libya)', in *Studies in Conflict and Terrorism* 27(1): 1–18.

Combs, C. C. (2000) *Terrorism in the Twenty-First Century*, (2nd Edn). London: Prentice-Hall.

Conboy, M. (2006) *Tabloid Britain. Constructing a Community through Language.* London: Routledge.

Congleton, R. D. (2002) 'Terrorism, Interest-Group Politics, and Public Policy. Curtailing Criminal Modes of Political Speech', in *The Independent Review*, VII(1): 47–67.

Connolly, K. (2001) 'German Troops to Join War Effort', *The Guardian*, 7.11.2001.

Coogan, T. P. (1995) *The IRA*. London: Harper Collins.

Copeland, T. (2001) 'Is the New Terrorism Really New? An Analysis of the New Paradigm for Terrorism', in *Journal of Conflict Studies* XXI(2): 91–105.

Cordesman, A. (2006) 'The Lesson of International: Co-operation in Counter-Terrorism', in *The RUSI Journal* 151(1): 48–53.

Cornish, P. (2005) 'The United Kingdom', in K. von Hippel (ed.) *Europe Confronts Terrorism*. Basingstoke: Palgrave, pp. 146–167.

Craft, S. and Wanta, W. (2004) 'U.S. Public Concerns in the Aftermath of 9/11: A Test of Second Level Agenda-Setting', in *International Journal of Public Opinion Research* 16(4): 456–463.

Crelinsten, R. (1989) 'Terrorism, Counter-Terrorism and Democracy: The Assessment of National Security Threats', in *Terrorism and Political Violence* 1(2): 242–269.

Crelinsten, R. (2000) 'Terrorism and Counter-Terrorism in a Multi-Centric World: Challenges and Opportunities', in M. Taylor and J. Horgan (eds) *The Future of Terrorism*. London: Frank Cass, pp. 170–196.

Crelinsten, R. and Schmid, A. (1992) 'Western Responses to Terrorism: A Twenty-Five Year Balance Sheet', in *Terrorism and Political Violence* 4(4): 307–340.

Crenshaw, M. (1981) 'The Causes of Terrorism', in *Comparative Politics* 13(4): 379–399.

Crenshaw, M. (1991) 'How Terrorism Declines', in *Terrorism and Political Violence* 3(1): 69–87.

Crenshaw, M. (1992) 'Current Research on Terrorism: The Academic Perspective', in *Studies in Conflict and Terrorism* 15(1): 1–11.

Crenshaw, M. (1995) 'Thoughts on Relating Terrorism to Historical Context', in M. Crenshaw (ed.) *Terrorism in Context*. University Park: Pennsylvania State University Press, pp. 3–24.

Crenshaw, M. (2000) 'The Psychology of Terrorism: An Agenda for the 21st Century', in *Political Psychology* 21(2): 405–420.

Crenshaw, M. (2001) 'Counterterrorism Policy and the Political Process', in *Studies in Conflict and Terrorism* 24(5): 329–337.

Crenshaw, M. (2003) '"New" versus "Old" Terrorism', in *Palestine-Israel Journal of Politics, Economics and Culture* 10(1). Available at: http://www.pij.org/details.php?id=80 Accessed 29.4.2009.

Crenshaw, M. (2007) 'The Debate over "New" vs. "Old" Terrorism'. Paper presented at the American Political Science Association Annual Meeting, Chicago, 30.8–2.09.2007.

Cronin, A. K. (2002/2003) 'Behind the Curve: Globalization and International Terrorism', in *International Security* 27(3): 30–58.

Daase, C. (2001) 'Terrorismus – Begriffe, Theorien und Gegenstrategien. Ergebnisse und Probleme sozialwissenschaftlicher Forschung', in *Die Friedens-Warte* 76(1): 55–79.

Daase, C. (2002) 'Terrorismus: Der Wandel von einer reaktiven zu einer proaktiven Sicherheitspolitik der USA nach dem 11. September 2001', in C. Daase, S. Feske and I. Peters (eds) *International Risikopolitik. Der Umgang mit neuen Herausforderungen in den internationalen Beziehungen.* Baden-Baden: Nomos, pp. 113–142.

Daase, C. (2008) 'Die RAF und der Internationale Terrorismus', in W. Kraushaar (ed.) *Die RAF. Entmythologisierung einer terroristischen Organisation.* Bonn: Bundeszentral für Politische Bildung, pp. 233–269.

Daase C. and Spencer, A. (2010) 'Terrorismus', in C. Masala, F. Sauer and A. Wilhelm (eds) *Handbuch der Internationalen Politik.* Wiesbaden: VS Verlag, pp. 403–425.

Davidson, D. (1978) 'What Metaphors Mean', in S. Sacks (ed.) *On Metaphor.* Chicago: Chicago University Press, pp. 29–45.

Deignan, A. (2003) 'Metaphoric Expressions and Culture: An Indirect Link', in *Metaphor and Symbol* 18(4): 255–271.

De Landtsheer, C. and De Vrij, I. (2004) 'Talking about Srebrenica: Dutch Elites and Dutchbat. How Metaphors Change during Crisis', in F. A. Beer and C. de Landtsheer (eds) *Metaphorical World Politics.* East Lansing: Michigan State University Press, pp. 163–189.

Della Porta, D. (1995a) 'Left-Wing Terrorism in Italy', in M. Crenshaw (ed.) *Terrorism in Context.* University Park: Pennsylvania State University Press, pp. 105–159.

Della Porta, D. (1995b) *Social Movements, Political Violence and the State.* Cambridge: Cambridge University Press.

Der Derian, J. (2001) *Virtuous War: Mapping the Military-Industrial-Media-Entertainment Network.* Boulder: Westview.

Der Derian, J. (2005) 'Imaging Terror: Logos, Pathos and Ethos', in *Third World Quarterly* 26(1): 23–37.

Devetak, R. (2005) 'The Gothic Scene of International Relations: Ghosts, Monsters, Terror and the Sublime After September 11', in *Review of international Studies* 31(4): 621–643.

Diez, T. and Squire, V. (2008) 'Traditions of Citizenship and the Securitisation of Migration in Germany and Britain', in *Citizenship Studies* 12(6): 565–581.

Donohue, L. K. (2007) 'Britain's Counterterrorism Policy', in D. Zimmermann and A. Wenger (eds) *How States Fight Terrorism. Policy Dynamics in the West.* London: Lynne Rienner, pp. 17–58.

Dorman, A. (2003) 'Loyal Ally. The United Kingdom', in M. Buckley and R. Fawn (eds) *Global Responses to Terrorism. 9/11, Afghanistan and Beyond.* London: Routledge, pp. 66–78.

Doty, R. L. (1993) 'Foreign Policy as Social Construction: A Post-Positivist Analysis of U.S. Counterinsurgency Policy in the Philippines', in *International Studies Quarterly* 37(3): 297–320.

Doty, R. L. (1998) 'Immigration and the Politics of Security', in *Security Studies* 8(2–3): 71–93.

Drulák, P. (2005) 'Metaphors and Creativity in International Politics', in *Discourse Politics Identity Working Paper Series* 3.

Drulák, P. (2006) 'Motion, Container and Equilibrium: Metaphors in the Discourse about European Integration', in *European Journal of International Relations* 12(4): 499–531.

Drulák, P. (2008) 'Identifying and Assessing Metaphors. Discourse on EU Reform', in T. Carver and J. Pikalo (2008) *Political Language and Metaphor. Interpreting and Changing the World.* London: Routledge, pp. 105–118.

Drulák, P. and Königove, L. (2007) 'Figuring Out Europe: EU Metaphors in the Minds of Czech Civil Servants', in *Perspectives* 15(1): 5–23.

Duyvesteyn, I. (2004) 'How New is the New Terrorism?', in *Studies in Conflict & Terrorism* 27(5): 439–454.

Duyvesteyn, I. (2007) 'The Role of History and Continuity in Terrorism Research', in M. Ranstorp (ed.) *Mapping Terrorism Research: State of the Art, Gaps and Future Directions.* London: Routledge, pp. 51–75.

Eco, U. (1994) *The Limits of Interpretation.* Bloomington: Indiana University Press.

Edelman, M. (1971) *Politics as Symbolic Action.* Chicago: Markham Publishing Company.

Egerton, F. (2009) 'A Case for a Critical Approach to Terrorism', in *European Political Science* 8(1): 57–67.

Ehrenfeld, R. (2003) *Funding Evil: How Terrorism Is Financed and How to Stop It.* Chicago: Bonus Books.

Eland, I. (1998) 'Does U.S. Intervention Overseas Breed Terrorism? The Historical Record', in *Foreign Policy Briefing Paper* 50. Washington, Cato Institute.

Ellis, J. O. (2008) 'Countering Terrorism with Knowledge', in H. Chen, E. Reid, J. Sinai, A. Silke and B. Ganor (eds) *Terrorism Informatics. Knowledge Management and Data Mining for Homeland Security.* New York: Springer, pp. 141–155.

El-Qorchi, M. (2002) 'Hawala', in *Finance and Development* 39(4): 31–33.

Enders, W., Sandler, T. and Cauley, J. (1990) 'UN Conventions, Technology and Retaliation in the Fight Against Terrorism: An Econometric Evaluation', in *Terrorism and Political Violence* 2(1): 83–105.

Enders, W. and Sandler, T. (1993) 'The Effectiveness of Antiterrorism Policies: A Vector-Autoregression-Intervention Analysis', in *American Political Science Review* 87(4): 829–844.

Enders, W. and Sandler, T. (1995) 'Terrorism: Theory and applications', in K. Hartley and T. Sandler (eds) *Handbook of Defense Economics*, Vol. 1. Amsterdam: North-Holland, pp. 213–249.

Enders, W. and Sandler, T. (2000) 'Is Transnational Terrorism Becoming More Threatening? A Time-Series Investigation', in *The Journal of Conflict Resolution* 44(3): 307–332.

Enders, W. and Sandler, T. (2005) *The Political Economy of Terrorism.* Cambridge: Cambridge University Press.

Eppright, C. T. (1997) '"Counterterrorism" and Conventional Military Force: The Relationship Between Political Effect and Utility', in *Studies in Conflict and Terrorism* 20(4): 333–344.

Erickson, C. W. (2008) 'Thematics of Counter-Terrorism: Comparing 24 and MI-5/Spook', in *Critical Studies on Terrorism* 1(3): 343–358.

Fairclough, N. (1992) *Discourse and Social Change.* Cambridge: Polity Press.

Falkenrath, R. (2001) 'Analytic Models and Policy Prescriptions: Understanding Recent Innovations in U.S. Counterterrorism', in *Studies in Conflict and Terrorism* 24(3): 159–181.

Falkenrath, R., Newman, R. D. and Thayer, B. A. (1998) *America's Achilles' Heel: Nuclear, Biological, and Chemical Terrorism and Covert Attack*. Cambridge: MIT.

Faria, J. R. (2006) 'Terrorist Innovation and Anti-Terrorist Policies', in *Terrorism and Political Violence* 18(1): 47–56.

Fearon, J. D. and Wendt, A. (2002) 'Rationalism and Constructivism in International Relations Theory', in W. Carlsnaes, T. Risse and B. A. Simmons (eds) *Handbook of International Relations*. London: Sage, pp. 52–72.

Ferguson, N. (2001) 'Clashing Civilizations or Mad Mullahs: The United States between Formal and Informal Empire', in S. Talbott and N. Chanda (eds) *The Age of Terror: America and the World after September 11*. New York: Basic Books, pp. 115–141.

Ferguson, C. D. and Potter, W. C. (2005) *The Four Faces of Nuclear Terrorism*. London: Routledge.

Ferrari, F. (2007) 'Metaphor at Work in the Analysis of Political Discourse: Investigating a 'Preventive War' Persuasion Strategy', in *Discourse and Society* 18(5): 603–625.

Fiebig-von Hase, R. and Lehmkuhl, U. (eds) (1997) *Enemy Images in American History*. Oxford: Berghahn Books.

Field, A. (2009) 'The "New Terrorism": Revolution or Evolution', in *Political Studies Review* 7(2): 195–207.

Fielding, N. and Fouda, Y. (2003) *Masterminds of Terror. The Truth Behind the Most Devastating Terrorist Attack the World has Ever Seen*. Edinburgh: Mainstream Publishing.

Fierke, K. (2007) 'Constructivism', in T. Dunne, M. Kurki and S. Smith (eds) *International Relations Theory: Discipline and Diversity*. Oxford: Oxford University Press, pp. 166–184.

Fierke, K. and Jørgensen, K. E. (eds) (2001) *Constructing International Relations. The Next Generation*. London: M.E. Sharpe.

Flowerdew, J. and Leong, S. (2007) 'Metaphors in the Discursive Construction of Patriotism: the Case of Hong Kong's Constitutional Reform Debate', in *Discourse and Society* 18(3): 273–294.

Foss, S. (1996) *Rhetorical Criticism: Exploration and Practice*, (2nd Edn). Prospect Heights: Waveland.

Freedman, L. (2002) 'A New Type of War', in K. Booth and T. Dunne (eds) *World in Collision: Terror and the Future of Global Order*. Basingstoke: Palgrave, pp. 37–47.

Frey, B. S. and Luechinger, S. (2003) 'Measuring Terrorism', Institute of Empirical Research in Economics University of Zurich, in *Working Paper* 171. Institute for Empirical Research in Economics University of Zurich.

Frey, B. S., Luechinger, S. and Stutzer, A. (2004) 'Calculating Tragedy: Assessing the Cost of Terrorism', in *Working Paper* 205. Institute for Empirical Research in Economics University of Zurich.

Friedman, B. (2004) 'Leap Before You Look: The Failure of Homeland Security', in *Breakthroughs* XIII(1): 29–40.

Fussey, P. and Richards, A. (2008) 'Researching and Understanding Terrorism: A Role for Criminology?', in *Criminal Justice Matters* 74(1): 37–39.

Gabrys, E. (2008) *Kriegsberichterstattung der BILD-Zeitung: Inhalts- und Strukturanalyse zum Kosovo- und Irakkrieg*. Saarbrücken: VDM Verlag.

Gallie, W. B. (1956) 'Essentially Contested Concepts', in *Proceedings of the Aristotelian Society* 56: 167–198.

Ganor, B. (2002) 'Defining Terrorism: Is One Man's Terrorist Another Man's Freedom Fighter?', in *Police Practice and Research* 3(4): 287–304.

Ganor, B. (2005) *The Counter-Terrorism Puzzle: A Guide for Decision Makers.* Brunswick: Transaction Publishers.

Gearson, J. (2002) 'The Nature of Modern Terrorism', in L. Freedman (ed.) *Super-terrorism – Policy Responses.* Oxford: Blackwell Publishing, pp. 7–24.

Gearty, C. (1997) *The Future of Terrorism.* London: Phoenix.

Geis, A. (2006) 'Spotting the "Enemy"? Democracies and the Challenge of the "Other"', in A. Geis, L. Brock and H. Müller (eds) *Democratic Wars, Looking at the Dark Side of Democratic Peace.* Houndsmills: Palgrave, pp. 142–169.

Gelvin, J. L. (2008) 'Al-Qaeda and Anarchism: A Historian's Reply to Terrorology', in *Terrorism and Political Violence* 20(4): 563–581.

George, A. (1991) 'The Discipline of Terrorology', in A. George (ed.) *Western State Terrorism.* Cambridge: Polity, pp. 76–101.

Gibbs, R. (1999) 'Researching Metaphor', in L. Cameron and G. Low (eds) *Researching and Applying Metaphor.* Cambridge: Cambridge University Press, pp. 29–47.

Gilbert, P. (1994) *Terrorism, Security and Nationality: An Introductory Study in Applied Political Philosophy.* London: Routledge.

Glover, R. (2002) 'The War on ____', in J. Collins and R. Glover (eds) *Collateral Language. A Users Guide to America's New War.* New York: New York University Press, pp. 207–222.

Glucksberg, S. (2001) *Understanding Figurative Language. From Metaphor to Idiom.* Oxford: Oxford University Press.

Gozzi, R. (1999) *The Power of Metaphor in the Age of Electronic Media.* New Jersey: Hampton Press.

Gray, J. (2002) 'Why Terrorism is Unbeatable', in *New Statesman* 131(4575): 50–54.

Grayson, K., Davies, M. and Philpott, S. (2009) 'Pop goes IR? Researching the Popular Culture – World Politics Continuum', in *Politics* 29(3): 155–163.

Greiber, S. (2007) 'Oldenburger Johanniter für Verdienste ausgezeichnet', *Die Johanniter.* Available at: http://www.johanniter.de/org/juh/org/land/nds/org/weser/wir/aktuell/meldungen/2007/de448788.htm Accessed 15.04.2009.

Grob-Fitzgibbon, B. (2004) 'From the Dagger to the Bomb: Karl Heinzen and the Evolution of Political Terror', in *Terrorism and Political Violence* 16(1): 97–115.

Guelke, A. (1998) *The Age of Terrorism and the International Political System.* London: I. B. Tauris.

Guelke, A. (2006) *Terrorism and Global Disorder.* London: I.B. Tauris.

Gunaratna, R. (2003a) *Inside Al Qaeda: Global Network of Terror.* New York: Berkley Books.

Gunaratna, R. (2003b) 'Al Qaeda, Organisation and Operations', in M. Buckley and R. Fawn (eds) *Global Responses to Terrorism. 9/11, Afghanistan and Beyond.* London: Routledge, pp. 37–51.

Gunaratna, R. (2006) 'The Post-Madrid Face of Al Qaeda', in *The Washington Quarterly* 27(3): 91–100.

Gunning, J. (2007a) 'A Case for Critical Terrorism Studies', in *Government and Opposition* 43(3): 363–393.

Gunning, J. (2007b) 'Babies and Bathwaters: Reflecting on the Pitfalls of Critical Terrorism Studies', in *European Political Science* 6(3): 236–243.

Gurr, N. and Cole, B. (2000) *The New Face of Terrorism: Threats from Weapons of Mass Destruction*. London: I.B. Tauris.

Gurr, T. R. (1988) 'Empirical Research on Political Terrorism: The State of the Art and How it Might be Improved', in R. Slater and M. Stohl (eds) *Current Perspectives on International Terrorism*. New York: St Martin's Press, pp. 115–154.

Gurr, T. R. (2003) 'Terrorism in Democracies: When It Occurs, Why It Fails', in C. Kegley (ed.) *The New Global Terrorism: Characteristics, Causes, Controls*. Upper Saddle River: Prentice Hall, pp. 202–215.

Guzzini, S. (2000) 'A Reconstruction of Constructivism in International Relations', in *European Journal of International Relations* 6(2): 147–182.

Guzzini, S. and Leander, A. (eds) (2006) *Constructivism and International Relations: Alexander Wendt and his Critics*. London: Routledge.

Haes, J. W. H. (2002) 'Catching the Wave: German Media on September 11', in *Prometheus* 20(3): 277–280.

Hafez, M. M. and Hatfield, J. M. (2006) 'Do Targeted Assassinations Work? A Multivariant Analysis of Israel's Controversial Tactic during Al-Aqsa Uprising', in *Studies in Conflict and Terrorism* 29(4): 359–382.

Halter, E. (2006) *From Sun Tsu to Xbox: War and Video Games*. New York: Thunder's Mouth Press.

Haneda, Y. (2004) 'Wie gut ist Deutschland auf den Ernstfall vorbereitet?'. *Deutsches Rotes Kreuz*. Available at: http://www.drk.de/a-internettagebuch/041209_tagX/bericht.htm Accessed 23.03.2009.

Hansen, L. (2006) *Security as Practice: Discourse Analysis and the Bosnian War*. London: Routledge.

Hardin, R. (2004) 'Civil Liberties in the Era of Mass Terrorism', in *Journal of Ethics* 8(1): 77–95.

Harré, R. (2004) 'The Social Construction of Terrorism', in M. Fathali and A. J. Marsella (eds) *Understanding Terrorism: Psychosocial Roots, Consequences, and Interventions*. Washington, DC: American Psychological Association, pp. 91–102.

Hartmann-Mahmud, L. (2002) 'War as Metaphor', in *Peace Review* 14(4): 427–432.

Haubrich, D. (2006) 'Modern Politics in an Age of Global Terrorism: New Challenges for Domestic Public Policy', in *Political Studies* 54(2): 399–423.

Hayner, P. B. (2001) *Unspeakable Truths: Confronting State Terror and Atrocity*. London: Routledge.

Hein, K. (2004) 'Die Anti-Terrorpolitik der rot-grünen Bundesregierung', in S. Harnisch, C. Katsioulis and M. Overhaus (eds) *Deutsche Sicherheitspolitik. Eine Bilanz der Regierung Schröder*. Baden-Baden: Nomos, pp. 145–171.

Henderson, H. (2001) *Global Terrorism – The Complete Reference Guide*. New York: Checkmark Books.

Heradstveit, D. and Bonham, G. M. (2007) 'What the Axis of Evil Metaphor Did to Iran', in *Middle East Journal* 61(3): 421–440.

Herman, E. and O'Sullivan, G. (1989) *The 'Terrorism' Industry: The Experts and Institutions that Shape Our View of Terror*. New York: Pantheon Books.

Herron, K. G. and Jenkins-Smith, H. C. (2006) *Critical Masses and Critical Choices. Evolving Public Opinion on Nuclear Weapons, Terrorism and Security*. Pittsburgh: University of Pittsburgh Press.

Hewitt, C. (1984) *The Effectiveness of Anti-Terrorist Policies*. London: University Press of America.

Hewitt, S. (2008) *The British War on Terror*. London: Continuum.

Heymann, P. B. (2000) *Terrorism and America – A Commonsense Strategy for a Democratic Society*. Cambridge: MIT Press.

Heymann, P. B. (2001/2002) 'Dealing with Terrorism – An Overview', in *International Security* 26(3): 24–38.

Hirschmann, K. (2002) 'Internationaler Terrorismus gestern und heute: Entwicklung, Ausrichtung, Ziele', in H. Frank and K. Hirschmann (eds) *Die weltweite Gefahr – Terrorismus als internationale Herausforderung*. Berlin: Berliner Wissenschafts-Verlag, pp. 27–66.

Hitzler, R. (1993) 'Verstehen: Alltagspraxis und wissenschaftliches Programm', in T. Jung and S. Müller-Doohm (eds) *"Wirklichkeit" im Deutungsprozeß: Verstehen und Methoden in den Kultur- und Sozialwissenschaften*. Suhrkamp: Frankfurt am Main, pp. 223–240.

HM Government (2009) *Pursue, Prevent, Protect, Prepare. The United Kingdom's Strategy for Countering International Terrorism*. Norwich: TSO.

Hobijn, B. (2002) 'What Will Homeland Security Cost?', in *Economic Policy Review* 8(2): 21–33.

Hoffman, B. (1995) '"Holy Terror": The Implications of Terrorism Motivated by a Religious Imperative', in *Studies in Conflict and Terrorism* 18(4): 271–284.

Hoffman, B. (1997a) 'The Confluence of International and Domestic Trends in Terrorism', in *Terrorism and Political Violence* 9(2): 1–15.

Hoffman, B. (1997b) 'The Modern Terrorist Mindset: Tactics, Targets and Technologies', in *Columbia International Affairs Online Working Paper*. Available at: http://www.ciaonet.org/wps/hob03/ Accessed 16.09.2009.

Hoffman, B. (1998) *Inside Terrorism*. London: Indigo.

Hoffman, B. (1998/1999) 'Old Madness New Methods – Revival of Religious Terrorism Begs for Broader U. S. Policy', in *RAND Review* 22(2): 12–17.

Hoffman, B. (1999) 'Terrorism, Trends and Prospects', I. O. Lesser, B. Hoffman, J. Arquilla, D. F. Ronfeldt, M. Zanini and B. M. Jenkins (eds) *Countering the New Terrorism*. Santa Monica: RAND, pp. 7–38.

Hoffman, B. (2001) 'Change and Continuity in Terrorism', in *Studies in Conflict and Terrorism* 24(5): 417–428.

Hoffman, B. (2003) 'Al Qaeda, Trends in Terrorism, and Future Potentialities: An Assessment', in *Studies in Conflict and Terrorism* 26(6): 429–442.

Hoffman, B. (2004) 'Foreword', in A. Silke (ed.) *Research on Terrorism: Trends Achievements and Failures*. London: Frank Cass, pp. xvii–xix.

Hoffman, B. (2006) *Inside Terrorism*, (2nd Edn). New York: Columbia University Press.

Hoffman, B. and Morrison-Taw, J. (2000) 'A Strategic Framework for Countering Terrorism', in F. Reinares (ed.) *European Democracies Against Terrorism: Governmental Policies and Intergovernmental Cooperation*. Aldershot: Ashgate, pp. 3–29.

Holden, G. (2006) 'Cinematic IR, the Sublime, and the Indistinctness of Art', in *Millennium: Journal of International Studies* 34(3): 793–818.

Horchem, H. J. (1986) 'West Germany's Red Army Anarchists', in W. Gutteridge (ed.) *The New Terrorism*. London: Mansell Publishing, pp. 199–217.

Horgan, J. (1997) 'Issues in Terrorism Research', in *The Police Journal* 70(3): 193–202.

Horgan, J. (2004) 'The Case for Firsthand Research', in A. Silke (ed.) *Research on Terrorism: Trends Achievements and Failures*. London: Frank Cass, pp. 30–56.

Horgan, J. (2005) *The Psychology of Terrorism*. London: Routledge.

Horgan, J. (2008) 'Interviewing Terrorists: A Case for Primary Research', in H. Chen, E. Reid, J. Sinai, A. Silke and B. Ganor (eds) *Terrorism Informatics. Knowledge Management and Data Mining for Homeland Security*. New York: Springer, pp. 73–99.

Horgan, J. and Boyle, M. J. (2008) 'A Case Against "Critical Terrorism Studies"', in *Critical Studies on Terrorism* 1(1): 51–64.

Hoyt, T. D. (2004) 'Military Force', in A. K. Cronin and J. M. Ludes (eds) *Attacking Terrorism: Elements of a Grand Strategy*. Washington: Georgetown University Press, pp. 162–185.

Hülsse, R. (2003a) *Metaphern der EU-Erweiterung als Konstruktionen europäischer Identität*. Baden-Baden: Nomos.

Hülsse, R. (2003b) 'Sprache ist mehr als Argumentation. Zur wirklichkeitskonstituierenden Rolle von Metaphern', in *Zeitschrift für Internationale Beziehungen* 10(2): 211–246.

Hülsse, R. (2006) 'Imagine the EU: The Metaphorical Construction of a Supra-Nationalist Identity', in *Journal of International Relations and Development* 9(4): 396–421.

Humphrey, M. (2002) *The Politics of Atrocity and Reconciliation. From Terror to Trauma*. London: Routledge.

Hurd, I. (2008) 'Constructivism' in C. Reus-Smit and D. Snidal (eds) *The Oxford Handbook of International Relations*. Oxford: Oxford University Press, pp. 298–316.

Huysmans, J. (2005) *Nexus terrorism-immigration/asylum/refuge in parliamentary debates in the UK: Commons debates since 11 September 2001*. Report for ESRC project MIDAS (Migration, Democracy and Security) in the Security Challenges programme. Available at: http://www.midas.bham.ac.uk/ Content%20analysis %20of%20Commons%20Debates.pdf, Accessed 30.06.2009.

Huysmans, J. (2006) *The Politics of Insecurity: Fear, Migration and Asylum in the EU*. London: Routledge.

Hyde-Price, A. (2003) 'Redefining its Security Role. Germany', in M. Buckley and R. Fawn (eds) *Global Responses to Terrorism. 9/11, Afghanistan and Beyond*. London: Routledge, pp. 101–112.

Ivie, R. L. (2004) 'Democracy, War, and Decivilizing Metaphors of American Insecurity', in F. A. Beer and C. de Landtsheer (eds) *Metaphorical World Politics*. East Lansing: Michigan State University Press, pp. 75–90.

Jackson, B. (2006) 'Groups, Networks, or Movements: A Command-and-Control-Driven Approach to Classifying Terrorist Organizations and Its Application to Al Qaeda', in *Studies in Conflict and Terrorism* 29(3): 241–262.

Jackson, R. (2005) *Writing the War on Terror*. Manchester: Manchester University Press.

Jackson, R. (2007a) 'The Case for Critical Terrorism Studies: A Symposium', in *European Political Science* 6(3): 225–227.

Jackson, R. (2007b) 'The Core Commitments of Critical Terrorism Studies', in *European Political Science* 6(3): 244–251.

Jackson, R. (2007c) 'Constructing Enemies: 'Islamic Terrorism' in Political and Academic Discourse', in *Government and Opposition* 42(3): 394–426.

Jackson, R. (2008a) 'The Ghost of State Terror: Knowledge, Politics and Terrorism Studies', in *Critical Studies on Terrorism* 1(3): 377–392.

Jackson, R. (2008b) 'Counter-Terrorism and Communities: An Interview with Robert Lambert', in *Critical Studies on Terrorism* 1(2): 293–308.

Jackson, R. (2009) 'Knowledge, Power and Politics in the Study of Political Terrorism', in R. Jackson, M. Breen Smyth and J. Gunning (eds) *Critical Terrorism Studies. A New Research Agenda*. London: Routledge, pp. 66–83.

Jackson, R., Breen Smyth, M. and Gunning, J. (eds) (2009) *Critical Terrorism Studies: A New Research Agenda*. London: Routledge.

Jackson, R. and Sørensen, G. (2007) *Introduction to International Relations. Theories and Approaches*, (3rd Edn). Oxford: Oxford University Press.

Jacquard, R. (2001) *Au Nom d'Oussama Ben Laden. Dossier Secret sur le Terroriste le Plus Recherché du Monde*. Paris: Jean Picollec.

Jamieson, A. (1990) 'Identity and Morality in the Italian Red Brigades', in *Terrorism and Political Violence* 2(4): 508–520.

Jarvis, L. (2009a) 'The Spaces and Faces of Critical Terrorism Studies', in *Security Dialogue* 40(1): 5–27.

Jarvis, L. (2009b) *Times of Terror. Discourse, Temporality and the War on Terror*. Basingstoke: Palgrave.

Jenkins, B. (1975) 'International Terrorism: A New Mode of Conflict', in D. Carlton and C. Schaerf (eds) *International Terrorism and World Security*. London: Croom Helm, pp. 13–49.

Jenkins, B. (2001) 'Terrorism and Beyond: A 21st Century Perspective', in *Studies in Conflict and Terrorism* 24(5): 321–327.

Jones, D. M. and Smith, M. L. R. (2009) 'We're All Terrorists Now: Critical – or Hypocritical – Studies 'on' Terrorism?', in *Studies in Conflict and Terrorism* 32(4): 292–302.

Jordan, W. (1974) 'Aristotle's Concept of Metaphor in Rhetoric', in K. V. Erickson (ed.) *Aristotle: The Classical Heritage of Rhetoric*. Metuchen: Scarecrow, pp. 244–246.

Joseph, J. (2009) 'Critical of What? Terrorism and its Study', in *International Relations* 23(1): 93–98.

Jost, P. M. and Sandhu, H. S. (2000) *The Hawala Alternative Remittance System and Its Role in Money Laundering*. Lyon: Interpol General Secretariat. Available at: http://www.interpol.int/Public/FinancialCrime/MoneyLaundering/Hawala/ default.asp Accessed 23.06.2009.

Juergensmeyer, M. (2000) *Terror in the Mind of God: The Global Rise of Religious Violence*. Berkeley: University of California Press.

Juthe, A. (2005) 'Argument by Analogy', in *Argumentation* 19(1): 1–27.

Kamp, K. H. (2002) 'Sechs Thesen zu den Folgen des 11. September', in H. Frank and K. Hirschmann (eds) *Die weltweite Gefahr: Terrorismus als internationale Herausforderung*. Berlin: Berliner Wissenschafts-Verlag, pp. 417–431.

Kappeler, V. E. and Kappeler, A. E. (2004) 'Speaking of Evil and Terrorism: The Political and Ideological Construction of a Moral Panic', in Deflem, M. (ed.) *Terrorism and Counter-Terrorism: Criminological Perspectives*. Amsterdam: Elsevier, pp. 175–197.

Karmon, E. (1999) 'Deutsche Terroristen – haben sie sich mit den palästinensischen Terrororganisationen verbündet?', in *Politische Studien* 368: 71–94.

Katzenstein, P. J. (2002a) 'Same War, Different Views: Germany, Japan, and the War on Terrorism', in *Current History* 101(659): 427–435.

Katzenstein, P. J. (2002b) 'Sonderbare Sonderwege: Germany and 9/11', in *AICGS/ German-American Dialogue Working Paper Series*, American Institute for Contemporary German Studies. Available at: http://www.aicgs.org/documents/katzenstein.pdf Accessed 01.06.2009.

Kegley, C. (2003) 'The Characteristics, Causes, and Controls of the New Global Terrorism: an Introduction', in C. Kegley (ed.) *The New Global Terrorism: Characteristics, Causes, Controls*. Upper Saddle River: Prentice Hall, pp. 1–26.

Kehaulani Goo, S. (2005) 'List of Foiled Plots Puzzling to Some', *Washington Post*, 23 October.

Kennedy, P. (2001) 'Maintaining American Power: From Injury to Recovery', in S. Talbott and N. Chanda (eds) *The Age of Terror: America and the World after September 11*. New York: Basic Books, pp. 53–80.

Kepel, G. and Milelli, J. P. (2006) *Al-Qaida: Texte des Terrors*. München: Piper.

Kidder, R. M. (1986) 'Unmasking State-Sponsored Terrorism', in *Christian Science Monitor*, May 14.

Kim, Y. (2008) 'Negotiating with Terrorists: The Iterated Game of the Taliban Korean Hostage Case', in *Public Relations Review* 34(3): 263–268.

Kimhi, S. and Even, S. (2004) 'Who are the Palestinian Suicide Bombers', in *Terrorism and Political Violence* 16(4): 815–840.

King, G. and Tanya, K. (2006) *Tomb Raiders and Space Invaders: Videogame Forms and Contexts*. London: I.B. Tauris.

Kitis, E. and Milapides, M. (1997) 'Read it and Believe it: How Metaphor Constructs Ideology in News Discourse. A Case Study', in *Journal of Pragmatics* 28(5): 557–590.

Klein, U. (2000) 'Tabloidized Political Coverage in the German Bild Zeitung', in C. Sparks and J. Tulloch (eds) *Tabloid Tales, Global Debates over Media Standards*. Lanham: Rowman & Littlefield, pp. 177–194.

Koch, E. R. (2005) *Atom Waffen für Al Qaida*. Berlin: Aufbau-Verlag.

Kornprobst, M., Pouliot, V., Shah, N. and Zaiotti, R. (2008) (eds) *Metaphors of Globalization. Mirrors, Magicians and Mutinies*. Basingstoke: Palgrave Macmillan.

Kosnik, M. E. (2000) 'The Military Response to Terrorism', in *Naval War College Review* 53(2): 13–39.

Kovats-Bernat, C. (2002) 'Negotiating Dangerous Fields: Pragmatic Strategies for Fieldwork amid Violence and Terror', in *American Anthropologies* 104(1): 208–222.

Kövecses, Z. (2002) *Metaphor. A Practical Introduction*. Oxford: Oxford University Press.

Kratochwil, F. (1989) *Rules, Norms and Decisions: On the Conditions of Practical and Legal Reasoning in International Relations and Domestic Affairs*. Cambridge: Cambridge University Press.

Kratochwil, F. (2000) 'Constructing a New Orthodoxy? Wendt's 'Social Theory of International Politics' and the Constructivist Challenge', in *Millennium: Journal of International Studies* 29(1): 73–101.

Kruglanski, A. W., Crenshaw, M., Post, J. M. and Victoroff, J. (2007) 'What Should This Fight Be Called? Metaphors of Counterterrorism and Their Implication', in *Psychological Science in the Public Interest* 8(3): 97–133.

Kruse, I., Orren, H. E. and Angenendt, S. (2003) 'The Failure of Immigration Reform in Germany', in *German Politics* 12(3): 129–145.

Kushner, H. W. (2003) *Encyclopedia of Terrorism*. London: Sage Publications.

LaFree, G. and Dugan, L. (2004) 'How Does Studying Terrorism Compare to Studying Crime?', in M. Deflem (ed.) *Terrorism and Counter-Terrorism: Criminological Perspectives*. Amsterdam: Elsevier, pp. 53–74.

LaFree, G. and Dugan, L. (2007) 'Introducing the Global Terrorism Database', in *Terrorism and Political Violence* 19(2): 181–204.

Lakoff, G. (1992) 'Metaphor and War: The Metaphor System Used to Justify War in the Gulf', in M. Pütz (ed.) *Thirty Years of Linguistic Evolution*. Amsterdam: John Benjamin, pp. 463–481.

Lakoff, G. (1993) 'The Contemporary Theory of Metaphor', in A. Ortony (ed.) *Metaphor and Thought*, (2nd Edn). Cambridge: Cambridge University Press, pp. 202–251.

Lakoff, G. (2001) 'Metaphors of Terror'. Available at: www.press.uchicago.edu/News/911lakoff.html Accessed 16.09.2009.

Lakoff, G. and Johnson, M. (1980) *Metaphors We Live By*. Chicago: University of Chicago Press.

Landau, M. (1961) 'On the Use of Metaphor in Political Science', in *Social Research* 28(Autumn): 331–352.

Landes, W. M. (1978) 'An Economic Study of US Aircraft Hijackings, 1961–1976', in *Journal of Law and Economics* 21(April): 1–31.

Laqueur, W. (1977) *Terrorism*. London: Weidenfeld and Nicolson.

Laqueur, W. (1987) *The Age of Terrorism*. Boston: Little Brown.

Laqueur, W. (1996) 'Postmodern Terrorism', in *Foreign Affairs* 75(5): 24–36.

Laqueur, W. (1998) *Dawn of Armageddon*. New York: Oxford University Press.

Laqueur, W. (1999) *The New Terrorism: Fanaticism and the Arms of Mass Destruction*. London: Oxford University Press.

Laqueur, W. (2001a) *A History of Terrorism*. New Brunswick: Transaction Publishers.

Laqueur, W. (2001b) 'Left, Right, and Beyond: The Changing Face of Terror', in J. F. Hoge and G. Rose (eds) *How Did This Happen? Terrorism and the New War*. New York: Public Affairs, pp. 71–82.

Laqueur, W. (2003) *No End to War: Terrorism in the Twenty-First Century*. New York: Continuum.

Lawrence, B. (ed.) (2005) *Message to the World: The Statements of Osama bin Laden*. London: Verso.

Lazar, A. and Lazar, M. (2004) 'The Discourse of the New World Order: "Out-Casting" the Double Face of Threat', in *Discourse & Society* 15(2–3): 223–242.

Leach, E. (1977) *Custom, Law, and Terrorist Violence*. Edinburgh: Edinburgh University Press.

Leeds, B. A. (1999) 'Domestic Political Institutions, Credible Commitments, and International Cooperation', in *American Journal of Political Science* 43(4): 979–1002.

Leggemann, C. (2003) 'Der Einsatz von Streitkräften zur Terrorismusbekämpfung – Die aktuelle Debatte in Deutschland', in K. Hirschmann and C. Leggemann (eds) *Der Kampf gegen den Terrorismus. Strategien und Handlungserfordernisse in Deutschland*. Berlin: Berliner Wissenschafts-Verlag, pp. 255–280.

Legro, J. (2005) *Rethinking the World: Great Power Strategies and International Order*. Ithaca: Cornell University Press.

Leheny, D. (2002) 'Symbols, Strategies, and Choices for International Relations Scholarship After September 11', in *Dialogue IO* 1(1): 57–70.

Lepsius, O. (2004) 'Liberty, Security, and Terrorism: The Legal Position in Germany', in *German Law Journal* 5(5): 435–460.

Lerche, C. (2000) 'Peace Building Through Reconciliation', in *The International Journal of Peace Studies* 5(2): 1–17.

Lerner, J. S., Gonzalez, R. M., Small, D. A. and Fischhoff, B. (2003) 'Effects of Fear and Anger on Perceived Risks of Terrorism: A National Field Experiment', in *Psychological Science* 14(2): 144–150.

Lesser, I. O. (1999) 'Countering the New Terrorism: Implications for Strategy', in I. O. Lesser, B. Hoffman, J. Arquilla, D. Ronfeldt, M. Zanini and B. M. Jenkins (eds) *Countering the New Terrorism*. Santa Monica: RAND, pp. 85–144.

Lesser, I. O. (2002) 'Coalition Dynamics in the War against Terrorism', in *The International Spectator* 2: 43–50.

Lesser, I. O., Hoffman, B., Arquilla, J., Ronfeldt, D. F., Zanini, M. and Jenkins, B. M. (eds) (1999) *Countering the New Terrorism*. Santa Monica: RAND.

Levitt, M. (2002) 'The Political Economy of Middle East Terrorism', in *Middle East Review of International Affairs* 6(4): 49–65.

Levitt, M. (2003) 'Stemming the Flow of Terrorist Financing: Practical and Conceptual Challenges', in *Fletcher Forum of World Affairs* 27(1): 59–70.

Light, M. (2002) 'The Response to 11.9 and the Lessons of History', in *International Relations* 16(2): 275–280.

Little, R. (2007) *The Balance of Power in International Relations: Metaphor, Myths and Models*. Cambridge: Cambridge University Press.

Littlemore, J. (2003) 'The Effect of Cultural Background on Metaphor Interpretation', in *Metaphor and Symbol* 18(4): 273–288.

Llorente, M. A. (2002) 'Civilization versus Barbarism', in J. Collins and R. Glover (eds) *Collateral Language. A User's Guide to America's New War*. New York: New York University Press, pp. 39–51.

Loewenstein, G. F., Weber, E. U., Hsee, C. K. and Welch, N. (2001) 'Risk as Feelings', in *Psychological Bulletin*, 127(2): 267–286.

Low, G. (1999) 'Validating Metaphor Research Projects', in L. Cameron and G. Low (eds) *Researching and Applying Metaphor*. Cambridge: Cambridge University Press, pp. 48–65.

Löwenstein, S. (2008) 'Geheimnisumwitterte Elitekämpfer', in *Frankfurter Allgemeine Zeitung*, 7. August. Available at: http://www.faz.net/s/ Rub594835B672714 A1DB1A121534F010EE1/Doc~E87B146CDF6B04C2C9619AF3025BA6A8C~ATpl ~Ecommon~Scontent.html Accessed 25.10.2008.

Lule, J. (2004) 'War and its Metaphors: News Language and the Prelude to War in Iraq, 2003', in *Journalism Studies* 5(2): 179–190.

Lum, C., Kennedy, L. W. and Sherley, A. J. (2006) 'The Effectiveness of Counter-Terrorism Strategies', in *A Campbell Systematic Review* 2.

Luoma-aho, M. (2004) '"Arm" versus "Pillar": The Politics of Metaphors of the Western European Union at the 1990–91 Intergovernmental Conference on Political Union', in *Journal of European Public Policy* 11(1): 106–127.

Lupovici, A. (2009) 'Constructivist Methods: A Plea and Manifesto for Pluralism', in *Review of International Studies* 35(1): 195–218.

Lutz, J. M. and Lutz, B. J. (2004) *Global Terrorism*. London: Routledge.

Maaß, C. D. (2007) 'Die Afghanistan-Mission der Bundeswehr', in S. Mair (ed.) *Auslandseinsätze der Bundeswehr*. Berlin: SWP Studie, pp. 78–87.

Machin, D. and Van Leeuwen, T. (2005) 'Computer games as political discourse: The case of Blackhowk Down', in *Journal of Language and Politics* 4(1): 119–141.

Machin, D. and Suleiman, U. (2006) 'Arab and American Computer War Games. The Influence of a Global Technology on Discourse', in *Critical Discourse Studies* 3(1): 1–22.

Mahon, J. E. (1999) 'Getting Your Sources Right. What Aristotle Didn't Say', in L. Cameron and G. Low (eds) *Researching and Applying Metaphor*. Cambridge: Cambridge University Press.

Malik, O. (2001) *Enough of the Definition of Terrorism!*. London: Royal Institute of International Affairs.

Malinowski, B. (1959) *Crime and Custom in Savage Societies*. Paterson: Littlefield.

Malthaner, S. and Waldmann, P. (2003) 'Terrorism in Germany: Old and New Problems', in M. van Leeuwen (ed.) *Confronting Terrorism: European Experiences, Threat Perceptions and Policies*. The Hague: Kluwer Law International, pp. 111–128.

Malvesti, M. L. (2002) 'Bombing bin Laden: Assessing the Effectiveness of Air Strikes as a Counter-Terrorism Strategy', in *The Fletcher Forum of World Affairs* 26(1): 17–29.

Mansfield, L. (2006) *In His Own Words: A Translation of the Writing of Dr Ayman Al Zawahiri*. Available at: http://www.lulu.com/content/366458 Accessed 7.8.2008.

March, J. and Olson, J. (1989) *Rediscovering Institutions: The Organizational Basis of Politics*. New York: Free Press.

Marchak, P. (1999) *God's Assassins – State Terrorism in Argentina in the 1970s*. Montreal & Kingston: McGill-Queen's University Press.

Mauer, V. (2007) 'Germany's Counterterrorism Policy', in D. Zimmermann and A. Wenger (eds) *How States Fight Terrorism. Policy Dynamics in the West*. London: Lynne Rienner, pp. 59–78.

Maull, H. W. (1999) 'Germany and the Use of Force: Still a Civilian Power?', in *Trierer Arbeitspapiere zur Internationalen Politik* 2. Universität Trier: Lehrstuhl für Außenpolitik und Internationale Beziehungen.

Maull, H. W. (2001) 'The Guns of November? Germany and the Use of Force in the Aftermath of 9/11', in *German Foreign Policy Dialogue* 2(5): 13–15.

Mayntz, R. (2004) 'Organizational Forms of Terrorism – Hierarchy, Network, or a Type sui generis?', in *MPIfG Discussion Paper* 04/04. Cologne: Max-Planck-Institute for the Study of Societies.

McCauley, C. (1991) 'Terrorism, Research and Public Policy: An Overview', in *Terrorism and Political Violence* 3(1): 126–144.

McLachlan, S. and Golding, P. (2000) 'Tabloidization in the British Press: A Quantitative Investigation into Changes in British Newspapers, 1952–1997', in C. Sparks and J. Tulloch (eds) *Tabloid Tales: Global Debates over Media Standards*. Lanham: Rowman & Littlefield, pp. 75–89.

Merari, A. (1991) 'Academic Research and Government Policy on Terrorism', in *Terrorism and Political Violence* 3(1): 88–102.

Merari, A. (1993) 'Terrorism as a Strategy of Insurgency', in *Terrorism and Political Violence* 5(4): 213–251.

Meyer, J. W., Boli, J. and Thomas, G. M. (1987) 'Ontology and Rationalization in the Western Cultural Account', in G. M. Thomas, J. W. Meyer, F. O. Ramirez and J. Boli (eds) *Institutional Structure: Constituting State, Society, and the Individual*. Newbury Park: Sage, pp. 12–37.

Miko, F. T and Froehlich, C. (2004) 'Germany's Role in Fighting Terrorism: Implications for U.S. Policy', in *CRS Report to Congress*, December 27th, RL32710.

Miller, E. (1979) 'Metaphor and Political Knowledge', in *American Political Science Review* 73(1): 155–170.

Miller, M. (1995) 'The Intellectual Origin of Modern Terrorism in Europe', in M. Crenshaw (ed.) *Terrorism in Context*. University Park: Pennsylvania State University Press, pp. 27–62.

Miller, R. R. (1993) 'Negotiating with Terrorists: A Comparative Analysis of Three Cases', in *Terrorism and Political Violence* 5(3): 78–105.

Milliken, J. L. (1996) 'Metaphors of Prestige and Reputation in American Foreign Policy and American Realism', in F. A. Beer and R. Hariman (eds) *Post-Realism. The Rhetorical Turn in International Relations*. East Lansing: Michigan State University Press, pp. 217–238.

Milliken, J. (1999) 'The Study of Discourse in International Relations: A Critique of Research and Methods', in *European Journal of International Relations* 5(2): 225–254.

Milne, J. (2005) 'Ten Attempted Terror Attacks in London Since 9/11 Says Mayor', *The Guardian*, December 27.

Minow, M. (1998) *Between Vengeance and Forgiveness. Facing History after Genocide and Mass Violence*. Boston: Beacon Press.

Mio, J. S. (1997) 'Metaphor and Politics', in *Metaphor and Symbol* 12(2): 113–133.

Mongoven, A. (2006) 'The War on Disease and the War on Terror: A Dangerous Metaphorical Nexus?', in *Cambridge Quarterly of Healthcare Ethics* 15(4): 403–416.

Morag, N. (2005) 'Measuring Success in Coping with Terrorism: The Israeli Case', in *Studies in Conflict and Terrorism* 28(4): 307–320.

Morgan, M. J. (2004) 'The Origin of the New Terrorism', in *Parameters* XXXIV(1): 29–43.

Moss, R. (1972) *Urban Guerrillas*. London: Temple Smith.

Motroshilova, N. (2009) 'Barbarity as the Reverse Side of Civilisation', in *Diogenes* 56(2–3): 72–83.

Mueller, J. (2005a) 'Six Rather Unusual Propositions about Terrorism', in *Terrorism and Political Violence* 17(4): 487–505.

Mueller, J. (2005b) 'Response', in *Terrorism and Political Violence* 17(4): 523–528.

Mueller, J. (2005c) 'Simplicity and Spook: Terrorism and the Dynamics of Threat Exaggeration', in *International Studies Perspectives* 6(2): 208–234.

Mueller, J. (2006) *Overblown: How Politicians and the Terrorism Industry Inflate National Security Threats, and Why We Believe Them*. New York: Free Press.

Mueller, J. (2007) 'The Terrorism Industry: The Profits of Doom', in G. Kassimeris (ed.) *Playing Politics with Terrorism. A User's Guide*. London: Hurst & Company, pp. 301–320.

Münkler, H. (2004) 'Ältere und Jüngere Formen des Terrorismus. Strategien und Organisationsstrukturen', in W. Weidenfeld (ed.) *Herausforderung Terrorismus. Die Zukunft der Sicherheit*. Wiesbaden: VS Verlag, pp. 29–43.

Munshi, S. (2004) 'Television in the United States from 9/11 and the US's continuing "War on Terror"', in P. van der Veer and S. Munshi (eds) *Media, War, and Terrorism*. London: Routledge, pp. 46–60.

Murtimer, D. (1994) 'Reimagining Security: The Metaphors of Proliferation', in *YCISS Occasional Paper* 25.

Musharbash, Y. (2006) *Die neue al-Qaida. Innenansichten eines lernenden Terrornetzwerks*. Bonn: Bundeszentral für Politische Bildung.

Musolff, A. (2000) *Mirror Images of Europe: Metaphors in the Public Debate about Europe in Britain and Germany*. München: Iudicium.

Mythen, G. and Walklate, S. (2006) 'Criminology and Terrorism – Which Thesis? Risk Society or Governmentality', in *British Journal of Criminology* 46(3): 379–398.

Nacos, B. (1994) *Terrorism and the Media*. New York: Columbia University Press.

Nacos, B. (2006) *Terrorism and Counter-Terrorism: Understanding Threats and Responses in the Post-9/11 World*. New York: Pearson, Longman.

Napoleoni, L. (2004) *Terror Inc. Tracing the Money Behind Global Terrorism*. London: Penguin Books.

Nasiri, O. (2008) *Inside the Jihad*. New York: Basic Books.

Navias, M. S. (2002) 'Finance Warfare as a Response to International Terrorism', in L. Freedman (ed.) *Superterrorism: Policy Responses*. Oxford: Blackwell Publishing, pp. 57–79.

Netanyahu, B. (1995) *Fighting Terrorism. How Democracies can Defeat Domestic and International Terrorism*. New York: Farrar Straus Giroux.

Neumann, P. (2007) 'Negotiating with Terrorists', in *Foreign Affairs* 86(1): 128–138.

Noelle-Neumann, E. (2002) 'Terror in America: Assessments of the Attacks and Their Impact in Germany', in *International Journal of Public Opinion Research* 14(1): 93–98.

Noelle-Neumann, E. and Köcher, R. (2003) *Allensbacher Jahrbuch der Demoskopie 1998–2002*. Munich: KG Saur.

Nordstrom, C. and Robben, A. (eds) (1995) *Fieldwork Under Fire: Contemporary Studies of Violence and Survival*. Berkeley: University of California Press.

Norris, P., Kern, M. and Just, M. (eds) (2003) *Framing Terrorism. The News Media, the Government and the Public*. London: Routledge.

Norton-Taylor, R. (2002) 'Scores Killed by SAS in Afghanistan', *The Guardian*, 05.07.2002. Available at: http://www.guardian.co.uk/world/2002/jul/05/september11.afghanistan Accessed 13.4.2009.

Norton-Taylor, R. (2005) 'London and Washington Used Plot to Strengthen Iraq War Push', *The Guardian*, 14.4.2005. Available at: http://www.guardian.co.uk/uk/2005/apr/14/iraq.iraq Accessed 11.05.2009.

O'Brian, G. V. (2003) 'Indigestible Food, Conquering Hordes, and Waste Material: Metaphors of Immigration and the Early Immigration Restriction Debate in the United States', in *Metaphor and Symbol* 18(1): 33–47.

O'Brien, K. A. (2003) 'Information Age, Terrorism and Warfare', in *Small Wars and Insurgencies* 14(1): 183–206.

O'Leary, B. and Silke, A. (2007) 'Conclusion. Understanding and Ending Persistent Conflict: Bridging Research and Policy', in M. Heiberg, B. O'Leary and J. Tirman (eds) *Terror, Insurgency and the State: Ending Protracted Conflicts*. Philadelphia: University of Pennsylvania Press, pp. 387–426.

Onuf, N. (1989) *World of Our Making. Rules and Rule in Social Theory and International Relations*. Columbia: University of South Carolina Press.

Onuf, N. (1998) 'Constructivism: A User's Manual', in V. Kubálková, N. Onuf and P. Kowert (eds) *International Relations in a Constructed World*. Armonk: M.E. Sharpe, pp. 58–78.

Onuf, N. (2009) 'Making Terror/ism', in *International Relations* 23(1): 53–60.

Ortony, A. (1979) 'Metaphor: A Multidimensional Problem', in A. Ortony (ed.) *Metaphor and Thought*. Cambridge: Cambridge University Press, pp. 1–16.

Oswald, F. (2004) 'German Security After 9/11', in P. Shearman and M. Sussex (eds) *European Security After 9/11*. Aldershot: Ashgate, pp. 90–106.

Oxford Dictionary of English (2005), Second Edition, Revised. Oxford: Oxford University Press.

Paivio, A. (1979) 'Psychological Processes in the Comprehension of Metaphor', in A. Ortony (ed.) *Metaphor and Thought*. Cambridge: Cambridge University Press, pp. 150–171.

Paletz, D. L. and Schmid, A. P. (eds) (1992) *Terrorism and the Media*. London: Sage Publications.

Pancake, A. S. (1993) 'Taken by Storm: The Exploitation of Metaphor in the Persian Gulf War', in *Metaphor and Symbol* 8(4): 281–295.

Papacharissi, Z. and de Fatima Oliveira, M. (2008) 'News Frames Terrorism: A Comparative Analysis of Frames Employed in Terrorism Coverage in U.S. and U.K. Newspapers', in *The International Journal of Press/Politics* 13(1): 52–74.

Pape, R. A. (2003) 'The Strategic Logic of Suicide Terrorism', in *American Political Science Review* 97(3): 343–361.

Parachini, J. (2003) 'Putting WMD Terrorism into Perspective', in *The Washington Quarterly* 26(4): 37–50.

Paris, R. (2002) 'Kosovo and the Metaphor War', in *Political Science Quarterly* 117(3): 423–450.

Payne, S. (2002) 'Britain's New Anti-Terrorist Legal Framework', in *RUSI Journal* 147(3): 44–52.

Pereira, A. W. (2005) *Political (In)Justice, Authoritarianism and the Rule of Law in Brazil, Chile, and Argentina*. Pittsburgh: University of Pittsburgh Press.

Perl, R. (2005) 'Combating Terrorism: The Challenge of Measuring Effectiveness', in *CRS Report for Congress*, RL33160, Congressional Research Service. Available at: http://opencrs.com/getfile.php?rid=44170 Accessed 13.7.2009.

Pestana Barros, C. (2003) 'An Intervention Analysis of Terrorism: The Spanish ETA Case', in *Defence and Peace Economics* 14(6): 401–412.

Pettiford, L. and Harding, D. (2003) *Terrorism – The New World War*. London: Arcturus Publishing.

Pillar, P. R. (2001a) *Terrorism and U.S. Foreign Policy*. Washington: Brookings Institution Press.

Pillar, P. R. (2001b) 'Terrorism Goes Global: Extremist Groups Extend Their Reach Worldwide', in *Brookings Review* 19(4): 34–37.

Pillar, P. R. (2004) 'Counterterrorism after Al Qaeda', in *The Washington Quarterly* 27(3): 101–113.

Pouliot, V. (2007) '"Subjectivism": Towards a Constructivist Methodology', in *International Studies Quarterly* 51(2): 359–384.

Posen, B. R. (2001/2002) 'The Struggle against Terrorism. Grand Strategy, Strategy, and Tactics', in *International Security* 26(3): 39–55.

Post, J. M. (2008) *The Mind of the Terrorist*. Basingstoke: Palgrave.

Powell, R. (2007) 'Defending against Terrorist Attacks with Limited Resources', in *American Political Sciences Review* 101(3): 527–541.

Power, M. (2007) 'Digitized Virtuosity: Video War Games and Post-9/11 Cyber-Deterrence', in *Security Dialogue* 38(2): 271–288.

Pragglejaz Group (2007) 'MIP: A Method for Identifying Metaphorically Used Words in Discourse', in *Metaphor and Symbol* 22(1): 1–39.

Price, R. and Reus-Smit, C. (1998) 'Dangerous Liaisons? Critical International Theory and Constructivism', in *European Journal of International Relations* 4(3): 259–294.

Probst, P. S. (2005) 'Measuring Success in Countering Terrorism: Problems and Pitfalls', in *Lecture Notes in Computer Science* 3495: 316–321.

Pronin, E., Kennedy, K. and Butsch, S. (2006) 'Bombing versus Negotiating: How Preferences for Combating Terrorism are Affected by Perceived Terrorist Rationality', in *Basic and Applied Social Psychology* 28(4): 385–392.

Prunckun, H. W. Jr. and Mohr, P. B. (1996) 'Military Deterrence of International Terrorism: An Evaluation of Operation El Dorado Canyon', in *Studies in Conflict and Terrorism* 20(3): 267–280.

Purcell, W. M. (1990) 'Tropes, Transsumptio, Assumptio, and the Redirection of Studies in Metaphor', in *Metaphor and Symbolic Activity* 5(1): 35–53.

Quillen, C. (2002) 'A Historical Analysis of Mass Casualty Bombers', in *Studies in Conflict and Terrorism* 25(5): 279–292.

Ramakrishna, K. and Tan, A. (2002) 'The New Terrorism: Diagnosis and Prescriptions' in A. Tan and K. Ramakrishna (eds) *The New Terrorism – Anatomy, Trends and Counter-Strategies*. Singapore: Eastern Universities Press, pp. 3–29.

Ranstorp, M. (1994) 'Hizbullah's Command Leadership: Its Structures, Decision-Making and Relationship with Iranian Clergy and Institutions', in *Terrorism and Political Violence* 6(3): 303–339.

Ranstorp, M. (1996) 'Terrorism in the Name of Religion', in *Journal of International Affairs* 50(1): 41–62.

Ranstorp, M. (ed.) (2007a) *Mapping Terrorism Research: State of the Art, Gaps and Future Direction*. London: Routledge.

Ranstorp, M. (2007b) 'Introduction: Mapping Terrorism Research', in M. Ranstorp (ed.) *Mapping Terrorism Research: State of the Art, Gaps and Future Direction*. London: Routledge, pp. 1–28.

Ranstorp, M. (2009) 'Mapping Terrorism Studies after 9/11', in R. Jackson, M. Breen Smyth and J. Gunning (eds) *Critical Terrorism Studies. A New Research Agenda*. London: Routledge, pp. 13–33.

Raphael, S. (2009) 'In the Service of Power. Terrorism Studies and US Interventions in the Global South', in R. Jackson, M. Breen Smyth and J. Gunning (eds) *Critical Terrorism Studies. A New Research Agenda*. London: Routledge, pp. 49–65.

Raphaeli, N. (2003) 'Financing of Terrorism: Sources, Methods, and Channels', in *Terrorism and Political Violence* 15(4): 59–82.

Rapoport, D. (1984) 'Fear and Trembling: Terrorism in Three Religious Traditions', in *American Political Science Review* 78(3): 658–677.

Raufer, X. (1999) 'New World Disorder, New Terrorisms: New Threats for Europe and the Western World', in *Terrorism and Political Violence* 11(4): 30–51.

Raymond, G. A. (2003) 'The Evolving Strategies of Political Terrorism', in C. W. Kegley (ed.) *The New Global Terrorism: Characteristics, Causes, Controls*. Upper Saddle River: Prentice Hall, pp. 71–83.

Rayner, J. (1984) 'Between Meaning and Event: A Historical Approach to Political Metaphor', in *Political Studies* 32(4): 537–550.

Rediehs, L. J. (2002) 'Evil', in J. Collins and R. Glover, Ross (eds) *Collateral Language. A Users Guide to America's New War*. New York: New York University Press, pp. 65–78.

Rees, W. and Aldrich, R. J. (2005) 'Contending Cultures of Counterterrorism: Transatlantic Divergence or Convergence?', in *International Affairs* 81(5): 905–923.

Reeve, S. (1999) *The New Jackals: Ramzi Yousef, Osama bin Laden and the Future of Terrorism*. London: André Deutsch.

Reid, E. (1993) 'Terrorism Research and the Diffusion of Ideas', in *Knowledge and Policy*, 6(1): 17–38.

Reinares, F. (1998) 'Democratic Regimes, Internal Security Policy and the Threat of Terrorism', in *Australian Journal of Politics and History* 44(3): 351–371.

Renner, J. and Spencer, A. (2009) 'The (Im)possibility of Reconciliation after Terrorism'. Paper presented at the 5 ECPR General Conference Potsdam, 10–12.9.

Reuter, C. (2004) *My Life is a Weapon: A Modern History of Suicide Bombing*. Princeton: Princeton University Press.

Richardson, L. (2006) *What Terrorists Want: Understanding the Enemy, Containing the Threat*. London: John Murray.

Ricoeur, P. (1978) *The Rule of Metaphor*. London: Routledge and Kegan Paul.

Ricoeur, P. (1981) 'Metaphor and the Central Problem of Hermeneutics', in J. Thompson (ed.) *Paul Riceur: Hermeneutics and the Human Sciences*. Cambridge: Cambridge University Press, pp. 165–181.

Rigby, A. (2001) *Justice and Reconciliation. After the Violence*. Boulder: Lynne Rienner Publishers.

Ritchie, D. (2003) '"ARGUMENT IS WAR" – Or is it a Game of Chess? Multiple Meanings in the Analysis of Implicit Metaphor', in *Metaphor and Symbol* 18(2): 125–146.

Roell, P. (2003) 'Deutschlands Beitrag zur internationalen Terrorismusbekämpfung', in K. Hirschmann and C. Leggemann (eds) *Der Kampf gegen den Terrorismus. Strategien und Handlungserfordernisse in Deutschland*. Berlin: Berliner Wissenschafts-Verlag, pp. 125–142.

Rogers, P. (2003) 'The War on Terrorism: Winning or Losing', in *Briefing Paper* (September). Oxford: Oxford Research Group.

Romero, V. C. (2003) 'Decoupling "Terrorist" from "Immigrant": An Enhanced Role for the Federal Courts Post 9/11', in *Journal of Gender, Race & Justice* 7: 101–111.

Rooney, D. (2000) 'Thirty Years of Competition in the British Tabloid Press', in C. Sparks and J. Tulloch (eds) *Tabloid Tales: Global Debates over Media Standards*. Lanham: Rowman & Littlefield, pp. 91–109.

Ross, J. I. (1993) 'Structural Causes of Oppositional Political Terrorism: Towards a Causal Model', in *Journal of Peace Research* 30(3): 317–329.

Ross, J. I. (2006) *Political Terrorism – An Interdisciplinary Approach*. New York: Peter Lang.

Rubenstein, R. E. (1987) *Alchemists of Revolution: Terrorism in the Modern World*. New York: Basic Books.

Ryan, W. (1976) *Blaming the Victim*. New York: Vintage Books.

Sageman, M. (2004) *Understanding Terror Networks*. Philadelphia: University of Pennsylvania Press.

Sageman, M. (2008) *Leaderless Jihad*. Philadelphia: University of Pennsylvania Press.

Sageman, M. and Hoffman, B. (2008) 'Does Osama Still Call the Shots?', in *Foreign Affairs* 87(4): 163–166.

Said, E. (1979) *Orientalism*. London: Routledge & Kegan Paul.

Salter, M. (2002) *Barbarians and Civilisation in International Relations*. London: Pluto.

Sandler, T. (2003) 'Collective Action and Transnational Terrorism', in *World Economy* 26(6): 779–802.

Sandler, T. and Scott, J. L. (1987) 'Terrorist Success in Hostage Taking Incidents: An Empirical Study', in *Journal of Conflict Resolution* 31(1): 35–53.

Sandler, T. and Arce, D. (2003) 'Terrorism and Game Theory', in *Simulations & Gaming* 34(3): 319–337.

Sandler, T. and Enders, W. (2004) 'An Economic Perspective on Transnational Terrorism', in *European Journal of Political Economy* 20(2): 310–316.

Sandler, T. and Enders, W. (2005) 'Transnational Terrorism: An Economic Analysis', in H. W. Richardson, P. Gordon and J. E. Moore II (eds) *The Economic Impact of Terrorist Attacks*. Northampton, Edward Elgar, pp. 11–34.

Sandler, T. and Enders, W. (2007) 'Applying Analytical Methods to Study Terrorism', in *International Studies Perspective* 8(3): 287–302.

Sanger, D. E. (2005) 'The Struggle for Iraq: President's Address; 10 Plots Foiled Since Sept. 11, Bush Declares', *The New York Times*, 7.10.2005.

Santa Ana, O. (1999) '"Like an Animal I was Treated": Anti-Immigration Metaphor in US Public Discourse', in *Discourse and Society* 10(2): 191–224.

Sarbin, T. R. (2003) 'The Metaphor-to-Myth Transformation With Special Reference to the "War on Terrorism"', in *Peace and Conflict: Journal of Peace Psychology* 9(2): 149–157.

Schmid, A. (1989) 'Terrorism and the Media: The Ethics of Publicity', in *Terrorism and Political Violence* 1(4): 539–565.

Schmid, A. (1992) 'The Response Problem as a Definitional Problem', in *Terrorism and Political Violence* 4(4): 7–13.

Schmid, A. (1999) 'Terrorism and the Use of Weapons of Mass Destruction: From Where the Risk?', in *Terrorism and Political Violence* 11(4): 106–132.

Schmid, A. (2004) 'Frameworks for Conceptualising Terrorism', in *Terrorism and Political Violence* 16(2): 197–221.

Schmid, A. and Jongman, A. (1988) *Political Terrorism: A New Guide to Actors, Authors, Concepts, Data Bases, Theories and Literature*. Amsterdam: Transaction Books.

Schmitt, R. (2005) 'Systematic Metaphor Analysis as a Method of Qualitative Research', in *The Qualitative Report* 10(2): 358–394.

Schneckener, U. (2004) 'Transnationaler Terrorismus', in M. A. Ferdowsi (ed.) *Sicherheit und Frieden zu Beginn des 21. Jahrhunderts. Konzeptionen – Akteure – Regionen* (3rd Edn). München: Landeszentrale für Politische Bildung, pp. 341–362.

Schneider, B. (2003) *Beyond Fear – Thinking Sensibly About Security in an Uncertain World*. New York: Copernicus Books.

Scholzen, R. (2004) *KSK – Das Kommando Spezialkräfte der Bundeswehr*. Stuttgart: Motorbuch Verlag.

Schott, P. A. (2006) *Reference Guide to Anti-Money Laundering and Combating the Financing of Terrorism*. Washington: World Bank & International Monetary Fund.

Schröm, O. (2005) *Al Qaida. Akteure, Strukturen, Attentate*. Berlin: Aufbau Taschenbuch Verlag.

Schulze, F. (2004) 'Breaking the Cycle: Empirical Research and Postgraduate Studies on Terrorism', in A. Silke (ed.) *Research on Terrorism: Trends Achievements and Failures*. London: Frank Cass, pp. 161–185.

Schweitzer, Y. (2000) 'Suicide Terrorism: Development and Characteristics', *International Policy Institute for Counter Terrorism*, 21.4.2000. Available at: http://www.ict.org.il/Articles/tabid/66/Articlsid/42/currentpage/27/Default.aspx Accessed 16.9.2009.

Sederberg, P. (1995) 'Conciliation as Counter-Terrorist Strategy', in *Journal of Peace Research* 32(3): 295–312.

Sederberg, P. (2003) 'Global Terrorism: Problems of Challenge and Response', in C. W. Kegley (ed.) *New Global Terrorism: The Characteristics, Causes and Controls*. Upper Saddle River: Prentice Hall, pp. 267–284.

Servicio Paz and Justica Uruguay (1992) *Uruguay Nunca Más: Human Rights Violations 1972–1985*. Philadelphia: Temple University Press.

Shepherd, J. (2007) 'The Rise and Rise of Terrorism Studies', *The Guardian*, 3.07.2007. Available at: http://www.guardian.co.uk/education/2007/jul/03/highereducation.research Accessed 11.5.2009.

Shimko, K. L. (1994) 'Metaphors and Foreign Policy Decision Making', in *Political Psychology* 15(4): 655–671.

Shimko, K. L. (1995) 'Foreign Policy Metaphors: Falling "Dominos" and Drug "Wars"', in L. Neack, J. A. K. Hey and P. J. Haney (eds) *Foreign Policy Analysis. Continuity and Change in its Second Generation*. Englewood Cliffs: Prentice Hall, pp. 71–84.

Shultz, R. H. and Vogt, A. (2003a) 'It's War! Fighting Post-11 September Global Terrorism through a Doctrine of Preemption', in *Terrorism and Political Violence* 15(1): 1–30.

Shultz, R. H. and Vogt, A. (2003b) 'The Real Intelligence Failure on 9/11 and the Case for a Doctrine of Striking First', in R. D. Howard and R. L. Sawyer (eds) *Terrorism and Counterterrorism – Understanding the New Security Environment*. Guildford: McGraw-Hill, pp. 367–390.

Sifaoui, M. (2004) *Inside Al Qaeda: How I Infiltrated the World's Deadliest Terrorist Organization*. London: Granta Books.

Silberstein, S. (2002) *War of Words: Language, Politics and 9/11*. London: Routledge.

Silke, A. (1996) 'Terrorism and the Blind Men's Elephant', in *Terrorism and Political Violence* 8(3): 12–28.

Silke, A. (2001) 'The Devil You Know: Continuing Problems with Research on Terrorism', in *Terrorism and Political Violence* 13(4): 1–14.

Silke, A. (ed.) (2004a) *Research on Terrorism: Trends, Achievements and Failures*. London: Frank Cass.

Silke, A. (2004b) 'The Road Less Travelled: Recent Trends in Terrorism Research', in A. Silke (ed.) *Research on Terrorism: Trends Achievements and Failures*. London: Frank Cass, pp. 186–213.

Silke, A. (2007) 'The Impact of 9/11 on Research on Terrorism', in M. Ranstorp (ed.) *Mapping Terrorism Research: State of the Art, Gaps and Future Direction*. London: Routledge, pp. 76–93.

Silke, A. (2008) 'Research on Terrorism', in H. Chen, E. Reid, J. Sinai, A. Silke and B. Ganor (eds) *Terrorism Informatics. Knowledge Management and Data Mining for Homeland Security*. New York: Springer, pp. 27–50.

Simon, J. (1987) 'Misperceiving the Terrorist Threat', in *RAND Publication Series*, R-3423-RC (June). Available at: http://www.rand.org/pubs/reports/2008/R3423.pdf Accessed 14.11.2008.

Simon, J. (1994) *The Terrorist Trap*. Bloomington: Indiana University Press.

Simon, S. and Benjamin, D. (2000) 'America and the New Terrorism', in *Survival* 42(1): 59–75.

Simon, S. and Benjamin, D. (2001–2002) 'The Terror', in *Survival* 43(4): 5–18.

Sinai, J. (2007) 'New Trends in Terrorism Studies: Strengths and Weaknesses', in M. Ranstorp (ed.) *Mapping Terrorism Research: State of the Art, Gaps and Future Directions*. London: Routledge, pp. 31–50.

Sinclair, A. (2003) *An Anatomy of Terror – A History of Terrorism*. London: Macmillan.

Sisler, V. (2008) 'Digital Arabs: Representation in Video Games', in *Journal of Cultural Studies* 11(2): 203–220.

Sivak, M. and Flannagan, M. J. (2003) 'Flying and Driving after the September 11 Attacks', in *American Scientist* 91 (Jan–Feb): 6–8.

Slovic, P. (2000) *The Perception of Risk*. London: Earthscan Publications.

Sluka, J. (1995) 'Reflections on Managing Danger in Fieldwork: Dangerous Anthropology in Belfast', in C. Nordstrom and Robben, A. (eds) *Fieldwork Under Fire: Contemporary Studies of Violence and Survival*. Berkeley: University of California Press, pp. 276–294.

Sluka, J. (2008) 'Terrorism and Taboo: An Anthropological Perspective on Political Violence against Civilians', in *Critical Studies on Terrorism* 1(2): 167–183.

Sluka, J. (2009) 'The Contribution of Anthropology to Critical Terrorism Studies', in R. Jackson, M. Breen Smyth and J. Gunning (eds) *Critical Terrorism Studies. A New Research Agenda*. London: Routledge, pp. 138–155.

Smith, M. B. (2002) 'The Metaphor (and Fact) of War', in *Peace and Conflict: Journal of Peace Psychology* 8(3): 249–258.

Sontag, S. (1989) *Illness as a Metaphor and AIDS and its Metaphors*. New York: Doubleday.

Spencer, A. and Biazza, J. (2008) 'Deutsche Terrorismusforschung: Interdisziplinarität in der Terrorismusforschung', in *WeltTrends* 63: 134–135.

Sterling, C. (1981) *The Terror Network*. New York: Holt, Rinehart and Winston.

Stern, J. (2003a) *Terror in the Name of God: Why Religious Militants Kill*. New York: Harper Collins.

Stern, J. (2003b) 'Getting and Using the Weapons' in R. D. Howard and R. L. Slayer (eds) *Terrorism and Counterterrorism – Understanding the New Security Environment*. Guildford: McGraw-Hill, pp. 158–174.

Steven, G. C. S. and Gunaratna, R. (2004) *Counterterrorism – A Reference Handbook*. Santa Barbara: ABCClio.

Stevenson, J. (2004) 'Counter-terrorism: Containment and Beyond', in *Adelphi Paper* 367.

Stohl, M. (2003) 'The Mystery of the New Global Terrorism: Old Myths, New Realities?' in C. W. Kegley (ed.) *The New Global Terrorism – Characteristics, Causes, Controls*. Upper Saddle River: Prentice Hall, pp. 84–91.

Stohl, M. (2008) 'Old Myths, New Fantasies and the Enduring Realities of Terrorism', in *Critical Studies on Terrorism* 1(1): 5–16.

Stokes, D. (2009) 'Ideas and Avocados: Ontologising Critical Terrorism Studies', in *International Relations* 23(1): 85–92.

Sunstein, C. R. (2003) 'Terrorism and Probability Neglect', in *Journal of Risk and Uncertainty* 26(2–3): 121–136.

Szyszkowitz, T. (2005) 'Germany', in K. von Hippel (ed.) *Europe Confronts Terrorism*. Basingstoke: Palgrave Macmillan, pp. 43–58.

Taber, R. (1969) *The War of the Flea*. London: Paladin.

Takeyh, R. (2001) 'Islamism: R.I.P.', in *The National Interest* 63: 97–102.

Takeyh, R. and Gvosdev, N. (2002) 'Do Terrorist Networks Need a Home', in *Washington Quarterly* 25(3): 97–108.

Taylor, T. (2002) 'United Kingdom', in Y. Alexander (ed.) *Combating Terrorism: Strategies of Ten Countries*. Ann Arbor: University of Michigan Press, pp. 187–224.

Thornborrow, J. (1993) 'Metaphors of Security: A Comparison of Representation in Defence Discourse in Post-Cold War France and Britain', in *Discourse & Society* 4(1): 99–119.

Tonkiss, F. (1998) 'Analysing Discourse', in C. Seale (ed.) *Researching Society and Culture*. London: Sage, pp. 245–260.

Toros, H. (2008a) '"We Don't Negotiate with Terrorists!"': Legitimacy and Complexity in Terrorist Conflicts', in *Security Dialogue* 39(4): 407–426.

Toros, H. (2008b) 'Terrorists, Scholars and Ordinary People: Confronting Terrorism Studies with Field Experience', in *Critical Studies on Terrorism*, 1(2): 279–292.

Townshend, C. (2002) *Terrorism – A Very Short Introduction*. Oxford: Oxford University Press.

Transatlantic Trends (2004) The German Marshall Fund of the United States and the Compagnia di San Paolo. Available at: http://www.transatlantictrends. org/trends/doc/2004_english_key.pdf Accessed 22.4.2009.

Tucker, D. (1997) *Skirmishes at the Edge of Empire: The United States and International Terrorism*. Westport: Praeger.

Tucker, D. (2001) 'What's New About the New Terrorism and How Dangerous Is It?', in *Terrorism and Political Violence* 13(3): 1–14.

Tucker, J. B. (2000) (ed.) *Toxic Terror: Assessing Terrorist Use of Chemical and Biological Weapons*. Monterey: MIT Press.

Tudge, C. (2004) 'When Men Have Lost Their Reason: Is the War on Terrorism Working?', in *New Statesman*, 12.4.2004.

Turk, A. T. (2004) 'Sociology of Terrorism', in *Annual Review of Sociology* 30: 271–286.

Tsfati, Y. and Weimann, G. (2002) 'www.terrorism.com: Terror on the Internet', in *Studies in Conflict and Terrorism* 25(5): 317–332.

von Hippel, K. (ed.) (2005) *Europe Confronts Terrorism*. Basingstoke: Palgrave Macmillan.

Vosniadou, S. and Ortony, A. (1989) 'Similarity and Analogical Reasoning: A Synthesis', in S. Vosniadou and A. Ortony (eds) *Similarity and Analogical Reasoning*. New York: Cambridge University Press, pp. 1–17.

Wæver, O. (2004) 'Discursive Approaches', in A. Wiener and T. Diez (eds) *European Integration Theory*. Oxford: Oxford University Press, pp. 197–215.

Wæver, O. (2005) 'European Integration and Security: Analysing French and German Discourses on State, Nation and Europe', in D. Howarth and J. Torfing (eds) *Discourse Theory in European Politics: Identity, Policy and Governance*. Houndsmills: Palgrave Macmillan, pp. 33–67.

Waldmann, P. (1998) *Terrorismus – Provokation der Macht*. Munich: Gerling Akademie Verlag.

Waldmann, P. (2001) 'Revenge Without Rules: On the Renaissance of an Archaic Motif of Violence', in *Studies in Conflict and Terrorism* 24(6): 435–450.

Walker, C. (2002) *Blackstone's Guide to the Anti-Terrorism Legislation*. Oxford: Oxford University Press.

Walker, C. (2003) 'Policy Options and Priorities: British Perspectives', in M. van Leeuwen (ed.) *Confronting Terrorism: European Experiences, Threat Perceptions and Policies*. The Hague: Kluwer Law International, pp. 11–35.

Wardlaw, G. (1989) *Political Terrorism – Theory, Tactics, and Counter-measures*, (2nd Edn). Cambridge: Cambridge University Press.

Weber, C. (2006) *Imagining America at War: Morality, Politics and Film*. London: Routledge.

Wechsler, W. F. (2001) 'Strangling The Hydra – Targeting Al Qaeda's Finances', in J. F. Hoge and G. Rose (eds) *How Did This Happen? Terrorism and The New War*. New York: Public Affairs, pp. 129–143.

Weimann, G. and Winn, C. (1994) *The Theater of Terror. Mass Media and International Terrorism.* New York: Longman.

Weinberg, L., Pedahzur, A. and Hirsch-Hoefler, S. (2004) 'The Challenges of Conceptualizing Terrorism', in *Terrorism and Political Violence* 16(4): 777–794.

Weinberg, L. and Eubank, W. (2008) 'Problems with the Critical Studies Approach to the Study of Terrorism', in *Critical Studies on Terrorism* 1(2): 185–195.

Weintraub, S. (2002) 'Disrupting the Financing of Terrorism', in *The Washington Quarterly* 25(1): 53–60.

Weldes, J. (2003) 'Popular Culture, Science Fiction and World Politics: Exploring Intertextual Relations' in J. Weldes (ed.) *To Seek out New Worlds: Science Fiction and World Politics.* New York: Palgrave Macmillan, pp. 1–27.

Weldes, J. (2006) 'High Politics and Low Data: Globalization Discourses and Popular Culture', in D. Yanow and P. Schwartz-Shea (eds) *Interpretation and Method: Empirical Research Methods and the Interpretive Turn.* Armonk, NY: M. E. Sharpe, pp. 176–186.

Weller, C. (2001) 'Feindbilder. Ansätze und Probleme ihrer Erforschung', *InIIS-Arbeitspapier* 22/01, Universität Bremen. Available at: http://www.iniis.uni-bremen.de/pages/download.php?ID=11&SPRACHE=DE&TABLE =AP&TYPE= PDF Accessed 1.6.2009.

Wendt, A. (1992) 'Anarchy is What States Make of It. The Social Construction of Power Politics', in *International Organization* 46(2): 391–425.

Wendt, A. (1995) 'Constructing International Politics', in *International Security* 20(1): 71–81.

Wendt, A. (1999) *Social Theory of International Politics.* Cambridge: Cambridge University Press.

Wheeler, E. L. (1991) 'Terrorism and Military Theory: An Historical Perspective', in *Terrorism and Political Violence* 3(1): 6–33.

Wheelwright, P. (1962) *Metaphor and Reality.* Bloomington: Indiana University Press.

Whine, M. (2002) 'The New Terrorism', *International Policy Institute for Counter Terrorism*, 20.1.2002. Available at: http://www.ict.org.il/articles/articledet. cfm?articleid=427 Accessed 13.6.2005.

White, R. (2000) 'Issues in the Study of Political Violence: Understanding the Motives of Participants in Small Group Political Violence', in *Terrorism and Political Violence* 12(1): 95–108.

Wiener, A. (2003) 'Constructivism: The Limits of Bridging Gaps', in *Journal of International Relations and Development* 6(3): 252–275.

Wieviorka, M. (1995) 'Terrorism in the Context of Academic Research', in M. Crenshaw (ed.) *Terrorism in Context.* University Park: Pennsylvania State University Press, pp. 597–606.

Wight, C. (2009) 'Theorising Terrorism: The State, Structure and History', in *International Relations* 23(1): 99–106.

Wilkins, K. and Downing, J. (2002) 'Mediating Terrorism: Text and Protest in Interpretations of *The Siege*', in *Critical Studies in Media Communication* 19(4): 419–437.

Wilkinson, P. (1992) 'International Terrorism: New Risks to World Order', in J. Baylis and N. J. Rengger (eds) *Dilemmas of World Politics.* Oxford: Clarendon Press, pp. 228–260.

Wilkinson, P. (1996) 'The Role of the Military in Combating Terrorism in a Democratic Society', in *Terrorism and Political Violence* 8(3): 1–11.

Wilkinson, P. (2000) *Terrorism versus Democracy: The Liberal State Response*. London: Frank Cass.

Wilkinson, P. (2003) 'Why Modern Terrorism? Differentiating Types and Distinguishing Ideological Motivations', in C. Kegley (ed.) *The New Global Terrorism: Causes and Consequences*. Upper Saddle River: Prentice Hall, pp. 106–138.

Williams, C. (2004) *Terrorism Explained – The Facts about Terrorism and Terrorist Groups*. London: New Holland Publishers.

Wilson, A., Wilson, G. D. and Olwell, D. H. (eds) (2006) *Statistical Methods in Counterterrorism. Game Theory, Modelling, Syndromic Surveillance and Biometric Authentication*. New York: Springer.

Winer, J. M. and Roule, T. J. (2002) 'Fighting Terrorist Finance', in *Survival* 44(2): 87–104.

Winfield, B. H., Friedman, B. and Trisnadi, V. (2002) 'History as the Metaphor through which the Current World is Viewed: British and American Newspapers' Uses of History following the 11 September Terrorist Attack', in *Journalism Studies* 3(2): 289–300.

Wolfendale, J. (2006) 'Terrorism, Security, and the Threat of Counterterrorism', in *Studies in Conflict and Terrorism* 29(7): 753–770.

Woods, J. (2007) 'What We Talk about When We Talk about Terrorism: Elite Press Coverage of Terrorism Risk from 1997–2005', in *The International Journal of Press/Politics* 12(3): 3–20.

World Health Organization (2004) *World Report on Road Traffic Injury Prevention*. Geneva: WHO Press.

Worldviews (2002) *European Public Opinion & Foreign Policy*, The Chicago Council on Foreign Relations and the German Marshall Fund of the United States. Available at: http://www.worldviews.org/ Accessed 21.4.2009.

Wright, T. (2007) *State Terrorism in Latin America: Chile, Argentina and International Human Rights*. Lanham: Rowman & Littlefield Publishers.

Yee, A. (1996) 'The Causal Effects of Ideas on Politics', in *International Organization* 50(1): 69–108.

Zagare, F. C. (2006) 'Deterrence is Dead. Long Live Deterrence', in *Conflict Management and Peace Science* 23(2): 115–120.

Zangl, B. and Zürn, M. (2003) *Frieden und Krieg*. Frankfurt a. M.: Suhrkamp.

Zartman, W. (1990) 'Negotiating Effectively with Terrorists, in B. Rubin (ed.) *The Politics of Counterterrorism: The Ordeal of Democratic States*. Washington: Foreign Policy Institute, pp. 163–188.

Zartman, W. (2003) 'Negotiating with Terrorists', in *International Negotiation* 8(3): 443–450.

Zashin, E. and Chapman, P. (1974) 'The Use of Metaphor and Analogy: Towards a Renewal of Political Language', in *Journal of Politics* 36(2): 290–326.

Zehfuß, M. (1998) 'Sprachlosigkeit schränkt ein. Zur Bedeutung von Sprache in konstruktivistischen Theorien', in *Zeitschrift für Internationale Beziehungen* 5(1): 109–137.

Zhang, J. (2007) 'Beyond Anti-Terrorism: Metaphors as Message Strategy of Post-September-11 U.S. Public Diplomacy', in *Public Relations Review* 33(1): 31–39.

Zimmermann, D. (2004) 'Terrorism Transformed: The 'New Terrorism', Impact Scalability, and the Dynamic of Reciprocal Threat Perception', in *The Quarterly Journal* 3(1): 19–39.

Zinken, J. (2003) 'Ideological Imagination: Intertextual and Correlational Metaphors in Political Discourse', in *Discourse and Society* 14(4): 507–523.

Zulaika, J. and Douglass, W. A. (1996) *Terror and Taboo. The Follies, Fables and Faces of Terrorism*. New York: Routledge.

Zulaika, J. and Douglass, W. A. (2008) 'The Terrorist Subject: Terrorism Studies and the Absent Subjectivity', in *Critical Studies on Terrorism* 1(1): 27–36.

Zussman, A. and Zussman, N. (2005) 'Targeted Killings: Evaluating the Effectiveness of a Counter-Terrorism Policy', in *Discussion Paper* 2005.02. Bank of Israel Research Department: Jerusalem.

Zycher, B. (2003) *A Preliminary Benefit/Cost Framework for Counter-terrorism Public Expenditures*. RAND: Santa Monica.

Index

Printed in Great Britain
by Amazon